The Colonial Economy of NSW

A retrospective between 1788 and 1835

GORDON BECKETT

For book orders, email orders@traffordpublishing.com.sg

Most Trafford Singapore titles are also available at major online book retailers.

Printed in Singapore.

ISBN: 978-1-4669-2738-4 (sc)
ISBN: 978-1-4669-2739-1 (hc)
ISBN: 978-1-4669-2740-7 (e)

Trafford rev. 07/18/2012

 www.traffordpublishing.com.sg

Singapore
toll-free: 800 101 2656 (Singapore)
Fax: 800 101 2656 (Singapore)

THE GOVERNMENT BUSINESS ENTERPRISES AND THE COLONIAL ECONOMY 1788-1830

CHAPTER CONTENTS

Outline

Government business enterprises commenced from close to day one of the settlement in 1788. We can define them as government operated, financially supported and for the direct benefit of the colony as opposed to an export facility. The very first public enterprise was that of farming to raise food, supervise the few head of livestock that had arrived alive in the colony. Public farming kept the colony alive for the first few years before private farming based on selective land grants commenced.

The role of the commissariat in government economic planning

The commissariat had two key roles. It was an important economic driver and acted as a quasi-treasury to the colony for the first 30 years, until the B of NSW opened in 1817.

Detailing the Enterprises

The main enterprises commenced with the need for food production but shortly after moved onto the need for construction work, building materials and an export staple.

Introducing the Colonial Economy

The colonial economy was destined to grow in response to increasing population, the development of an infrastructure to underpin the colonial growth and living standards and the need for import replacing activities, in addition to the goal of creating an export market

Convict management

With few free settlers to fill the role of supervisors, and the military abdicating their duties in this respect, the job of convict supervision was left to the best-behaved convicts. This was a generally unsatisfactory position. The most prominent principal convict managers were Majors Druitt and Ovens, who were the first the reform convict work practices and set goals and plan targets for the convict workers.

Manufacturing in the commissariat

From the public business enterprises and the necessity of finding export staples, a secondary industry grew in the colony. Invention really was the mother of necessity. A secondary industry commenced in export replacement areas and spread to those areas of continuing need, such as agricultural equipment as that primary industry got underway, then onto manufacturing on behalf of British industries wanting to have a presence in the colony.

Operating and managing the government farms and the public enterprises

There was continual growth in the public farming and manufacturing areas for two reasons. The number of convicts arriving in the colony increased each month, so there were more mouths to feed, and more men to put into productive work. So output increased naturally but then so did the public works program, that kept the business enterprises operating, and then diversity of manufacturing commenced which meant more technical production and output. Much of this flowed to the private sector having been first established in the Lumber Yard.

Accounting and Finance in the public enterprises

The commissariat system after 1822 attracted many convict clerical assistants, so the bookkeeping indulgences were endless. Sadly few of these records survive, but we know that orders from government departments for supplies and the public works department for materials were prepare, whilst the commissariat and lumber yard used issue dockets to account for supplies transferred. The main accounting was not the number of inventory items made or issued in the commissariat but the money it was spending. Bills drawn by the commissariat supposedly reflected the amount of value going through the commissariat as opposed to the raw materials used the convict output or the value of materials issued on account of public works.

Measuring the economic impact of the enterprises on the economy

This will be the most difficult chapter to prepare. We will have to assess the GDP annually for the colony from 1800, and try and indicate what part was generated by the business enterprises. This will have to be done on an industry by industry basis to estimate the items of output the number of convicts in use for each item of manufacture and compare it with the gross GDP. The problem with this methodology is that most items produced by the commissariat enterprises had no value due to the convicts having no value as labourers and raw materials have no assigned value, thus convict output had no value.

CHAPTER 1

INTRODUCTION and OUTLINE

Introduction to Chapter One

From its commencement in 1788, the aim of the Colony of New South Wales was self-sufficiency even though it had been set up to solve the problem of Britain's overcrowded prisons. By 1823, the British Government had decided that it would limit its direct expenditure to the transportation of the convicts and their supplies while in transit; the Colonial Administrators would be responsible for the convicts' security, food, clothing and accommodation in the Colony. Furthermore, proceeds from the sale of Crown land were to be the exclusive reserve of the British authorities rather than the colonists. The Governors were therefore forced to look for ways in which the Colony could help to support itself through working the convicts to create food, minerals (e.g. coal production), roads, housing and public buildings. Other convicts were assigned to landowners on a fully-maintained basis, thus saving the British Treasury a great deal of money.

This policy of maintenance of convicts by the Government created the need for an accounting by the Colony to the British Parliament. This led to the appointment in 1824 of a Financial Controller/Colonial Accountant to prepare monthly and annual despatches to the British Colonial Secretary. Following self-government in 1856, the procedures changed as the Colony became fully responsible for its own economic planning and fiscal management.

A Brief Overview of the Government Store

The first storekeeper arrived with Governor Phillip and the First Fleet. Andrew Miller had been appointed whilst the Fleet was preparing to sail, initially to take responsibility for the loading and recording of requisitioned stores. Upon arrival in Sydney Cove, Miller's first task was to erect a stores tent, secure it as far as possible, and commence unloading from the ships the stores that would be required during the first few weeks. These stores and provisions included such items as tents, pots and cooking utensils, blankets, hospital equipment and supplies and tools for clearing the land and erecting tents. Little was known about local conditions and Phillip's plan to have a wooden storehouse built within a few weeks could not be accomplished. He had tried to anticipate a wide range of obstacles and challenges, but encountering a difficult landscape and understanding characteristics of the local forestry proved the most difficult of all. In their various reports, Cook, Banks and Matra all praised the local timbers after only a cursory evaluation but, with no expertise amongst his crew or the convict population, Phillip's task of clearing timber and using it for construction was almost impossible.[1]

Upon their arrival, Phillip relied on Miller to operate the most basic of stores and without burdening him with limiting rations as he anticipated that the second Fleet store ships would be carrying provisions for the next full year. Miller's biggest task was the security of the provisions; the remaining items were then to be unloaded so that the ships could return to naval service. Phillip later prepared a rationing program for Miller so that the provisions would last six months, the time Phillip thought the Second Fleet was behind his own.

The stress of establishing the commissary for the new settlement and acting as private secretary to the governor eventually broke Miller's health and he wanted to return home. However, he was not to see his home again; he died during the sea voyage back to England.

Miller's successor, John Palmer, had sailed as purser aboard Phillip's flagship, *Sirius*. He had joined the Navy at the age of nine and participated in a series of voyages to many parts of the world, including North America where he married into a wealthy colonial family. After the founding of the colony, and with the expectation that he would soon return to England, Palmer sailed with the *Sirius* to the Cape Colony and Batavia on a mission to purchase food for the struggling, and hungry, colony of NSW. Whilst shipping provisions from Sydney to Norfolk Island, the ship struck an uncharted submerged rock just southeast of the Island and sunk. Palmer was saved, but the *Sirius* and its cargo was lost and Phillip found a new posting for Palmer in Sydney, replacing Miller as chief store-keeper. It was a further seven years before Palmer sailed for England, but he soon returned to the colony with his wife and sister, Sophia. The Palmer family became financially secure with a magnificent walled estate, carved from the rocky terrain of Woolloomooloo Bay, just east of Farm Cove. Sophia (Palmer's sister-in-law) was to shortly marry Robert Campbell thus forming a strategic alliance between the colony's first successful trading house (Campbell

---

[1]   Cook & Banks had written positively (and subsequently amended by Beaglehole) about the lush landscape to be found at Botany Bay, and James Matra (another Cook crewman) extended this interest in local timber to its use as a trade item between the colony & Britain, when Matra submitted his recommendation of the use of the new land as a penal settlement. Refer also Beckett: 'Reasons for the Colony' in *British Colonial Investment in the Colony 1788-1856*.

& Co, the chief supplier of stores to the colony) and the chief procurer of provisions for the colonial store (John Palmer).[2]

Governor Phillip was active in most facets of the initial colonial administration, especially the planning for the new settlement and the difficult challenge of feeding the people. He found the soil conditions around Sydney Cove were unsuitable for vegetables, grain and fruit. The vegetable patches located in the Governor's Domain failed to provide the produce desired, and Phillip was constantly looking for new, more fertile locations. Travelling up what was to become known as the Parramatta River; he located more fertile soil, and what appeared to be a suitable clay reserve, on the south bank of the River; he named the area Rose Hill. Phillip planned a new settlement at the head of the river which he named Parramatta. Phillip recorded that, 'the soil is more suitable for cultivation than the hungry sand covering the hills near Sydney'[3]. It was imperative to grow food as quickly as possible and Parramatta offered the additional advantages of a constant supply of fresh water and a means of transporting food by boat rather than having to build a road.

During the Palmer administration of the stores, new settlements had to be served in addition to Norfolk Island established in 1789. Settlements were developed and serviced by branch stores in areas such as Hobart (1802), Port Dalrymple (later Launceston, 1802), Liverpool (1803), Hawkesbury (Windsor, 1802) and Bathurst (1814). The role of the main store in Sydney was constantly changing as was its location. All the stores required personnel and organisation as well as a good supply of clerical assistance and many of these roles were set-aside for trusted convicts and ticket-of-leave men. The reason for the use of convicts in a sensitive and secure area of government was straightforward. As Butlin has established, the cost of convict labour was a charge against the English Treasury and not included in the appropriation to the colony, so the use of convicts as workers for the government kept government civil salaries understated and artificially low. It was Commissioner Bigge who reviewed the workforce and, observing the number of convicts employed within government and thus civil service ranks, became aware of the understatement of costs in the colony. Butlin adds, 'as public employees, a great deal of convict labour was engaged on farming and public infrastructure construction and thus avoided being charged as a direct cost to the colony. It was more convenient, however, to transfer them into the labour market.

---

[2] Refer: Margaret Steven 'Merchant Campbell 1769-1846' and Beckett 'John Palmer   Commissary'
[3] HRNSW Vol 1, Part 2 p469 (Despatch by Governor Phillip to Hon W. Grenville)

The use of convicts as public Servants, in the sense of filling positions in the normal operations of government, has a special interest!'[4]

A list of some of the main provisions and supplies that arrived with the First Fleet indicated the role and difficulties facing the storekeeper. In addition to foodstuffs, supposedly sufficient for the first six months, some of the provisions and supplies which were shipped with the First Fleet in 1787, were:

ABLE 2.1 Supplies sent with the First Fleet

700 steel spades	63 coal buckets	700 clasp knives
30 grindstones	100 pairs of hinges	60 butcher's knives
700 iron shovels	80 carpenter's axes	500 tin-plates
330 iron pots	10 sets cooper's tools	100 pairs –scissors
700 garden hoes	20 shipwright's adzes	60 padlocks
6 hand-carts	40 corn-mills	30 box rulers
700 West India hoes	175 claw hammers	50 hayforks
4 timber carriages	12 ploughs	30 pincers
700 grubbing hoes	175 handsaws	42 splitting wedges
14 chains	50 pickaxes	100 plain measures
700 felling axes	140 angers	8000 fishhooks
14 fishing nets	700 wooden bowls	12 brick moulds
700 hatchets	700 gimlets	48 dozen fishing lines
5448 squares of glass	700 wooden platters	6 harpoons
700 axe handles	504 saw files	10000 bricks
200 canvas beds	10 forges	12 lances
747,000 nail of various sizes	300 chisels	

The complete list[5] of articles sent with the First Fleet was much longer and represented a storeman's nightmare if records of issues and returns were to be maintained. For instance, the unloading of stores and provisions for immediate use commenced on 7 February but; since the settlement held over 1,000 people, there was obviously not sufficient bedding, blankets, cooking utensils, or eating utensils for everyone[6]. The allowance of clothing for a male convict for a year was equally inadequate; although raw cloth, needles and cotton had arrived with the Fleet and female convicts could be encouraged to hand sew clothing if necessary. The records show that the total costs of all male and female convict clothing was only £4,144.

---

[4]   Butlin, N.G., 'What a way to run an Empire, fiscally!' *Working Paper in Economic History*, No. 55 (Australian National University, 1985) p.32. Butlin (p34) also questions the judgement of McMartin *Public Servants & Patronage* on this same point and states, "Colonial Officials chose to use convicts (in the public service context) because they were cheap and their charge loaded on Britain. Had the offer price for clerks been raised, one might expect more free or freed persons to seek the positions. Virtually none of the convict appointees appears as a charge in the Colonial Fund; they were supported by the Commissariat'. Butlin could also have pointed out that a subsequent head of the public service, and its main supporter (William Lithgow) found that there were virtually no trained or skilled clerical assistants in the colony and Lithgow took the time and opportunity to 'train' young men with potential for these roles, but then had great difficulty in retaining their services

[5]   HRNSW Vol 1, Part 2 p.16

[6]   The list of 'stores' and 'provisions' is found in both the HRNSW and in John Cobley *'Sydney Cove 1788'* Vol 1

In *'Botany Bay Mirages'*, Alan Frost has raised the question of whether the inadequate quantity of tools and supplies was deliberate, or merely poor planning. A case can be made for improper planning rather than deliberate mismanagement. Phillip was left in sole charge of the voyage and received very little guidance, support or interest from the Secretary of State's office, the Naval Board or the commissariat division of the British Treasury.[7] It is unlikely that, after a fairly ordinary career as a naval officer, Phillip would suddenly have reverted to poor leadership. Indeed, he had commented to the Naval Board that the vessels allotted to the Fleet were not adequate in size or number. He also questioned the short amount of time allowed for the planning process, but received no worthwhile response. Clearly, this was not regarded as a voyage of high importance compared with British naval activities in other parts of the world. So, the fact that Phillip used a great deal of judgment and commonsense, speaks volumes for his quiet confidence and determination that he was the most suitable choice as the head of this mission.

For the first storekeeper, local circumstances were such that the supplies brought from England needed to be carefully protected against theft and loss. The tools, in particular, were to be issued daily and returned each evening; however according to Marjorie Barnard, within 14 days of arriving in the colony, over one-third of the tools loaned out for chopping trees and clearing land had been lost, stolen or deliberately concealed from the storekeeper.[8] The chief cause was the unwillingness of convicts to work; removing the tools meant they were unable to chop firewood or cut timber framing for the new camp. As a way of keeping the tools in repair, Miller had set up forges on the banks of Sydney Cove and used iron and steel pieces brought out as ballast to forge new tools and replace lost items. Watkin Tench in his *'Narrative of the Expedition to Botany Bay'* provides some useful insights into the conditions faced by Phillip and Miller. In November 1788 he noted: 'Temporary, wooden stores, covered with thatch or shingles into which the cargoes of all the ships have been lodged, are completed, and a hospital erected'.[9] However, the stores were not to remain as such for long as the end of one such building was converted into a temporary church for Sunday services. These frail structures were neither fire-proof nor rat-proof and the summer of 1789 saw the end to these temporary structures when Phillip designed a new, sturdier and more permanent store in a location closer to the settlement's

[7] Alan Frost raises this possibility in *'Botany Bay Mirages'* Chapter 8 'No Cheaper Mode...' as does Barnard in *'Phillip of Australia'*.
[8] Barnard *'A History of Australia'* Chapter 3 'Taking Shape' *p60*.
[9] Flannery quotes Tench in *'1788 Watkin Tench'* p81

military camp. Later in 1789, Tench recorded that 'the storehouse was finished at Rose Hill (by then renamed Parramatta). It was 100 feet by 24 feet and was built of local brick, deep red in colour, but not as durable as the Sydney product'.[10]

Displaying rare frustration, Phillip wrote to Assistant Secretary of State, Phillip Stephens, in August 1790 'Leather is needed for soles for men's shoes and materials for mending them. Shoes here last but a very short time, and the want of these materials and thread to mend the clothing will render it impossible to make them serve more than half the time for which they were intended'. The following month Phillip wrote to Nepean, the Under-Secretary of State for the Colonies, and made two observations: 'I cannot help repeating that most of the tools sent out were as bad as ever' and, 'the wooden ware sent out were too small; they are called bowls and platters, but are not larger than pint basins. There was not one that would hold a quart'.[11]

Tench also described the development of the new town of Rose Hill and the buildings adjacent to the store: 'the new stone barracks is within 150 yards of the wharf, where all boats from Sydney unload. In addition there is an excellent barn, a granary, an enclosed yard to rear livestock, a commodious blacksmith's shop and a most wretched hospital, totally destitute of every convenience'.[12]

In 1790 Phillip told Nepean that the colony badly needed 'honest and intelligent settlers, and free men to act as superintendents of convicts'. Phillip also requested a new, more appropriate style of clothing for the convicts, even suggesting a form of mark to protect them from being sold. He badly needed a windmill, and requested axes, saws, combs, iron pots and 'two or three hundred iron frying pans which will be a saving of the spades'.[13] Unlike Macquarie some twenty years later, Phillip was of two minds about free enterprise in the colony. He did approve an open market, but then reverted to government importing 'specialty' items into the colony. According to Barnard, "in April 1792, Phillip established a regular market in Parramatta". It was for fish, grain, livestock, clothing and anything else that might legitimately be bought or sold. It was open to convicts. In October 1790, Phillip reported to Secretary Dundas in London: "The commissary was

---

[10] Flannery *ibid* p127
[11] Governor Phillip to Under- Secretary Nepean HRNSW Vol 1, Part 2 p481. In terms of the departmental hierarchy, the Colonial Office had a Secretary, an Under-Secretary and then a number of Assistant-Secretaries
[12] Flannery *ibid* p 145
[13] Governor Phillip to the Rt. Hon Henry Dundas HRNSW Vol 1 Part 2 p595

obliged to purchase various articles brought out by the sailing officers of the *Pitt*, where the private property sold in this settlement amounted to upwards of £4,000, which may serve in some measure to point out what might be bought by a ship loaded wholly on account of government".[14]

During 1792, Phillip was faced with a minor mutiny. The military under the leadership of Major Grose advised Phillip that they (the military) had chartered *The Britannia* to sail to the Cape for supplies. In spite of strong protests from Phillip, the ship sailed on 24 October and thus was born the 'pernicious system of private trading by the military'.[15] Phillip wrote movingly to the Right Hon. Henry Dundas, the Secretary of State in London, of this continuous struggle to get necessities: 'The period at which the colony will supply its inhabitants with animal foods is nearly as distant at present as it was when I first landed'. He added:

> '*I beg leave to observe that all those wants which have been pointed out in my different letters still exist: for iron pots, we have been nearly as distressed as for provisions: cross cut saws, axes and the various tools for husbandry are also much wanted; many of the articles are now made here, but the demand is greater than can be supplied because of the shortage of materials; many bales of clothing have been received, but arrive rotten and so injured from the damp that they have scarcely borne washing a second time'.*[16]

Butlin described the functions of the Commissariat in the following terms.

> '*The (British) Treasury described the commissary as one that 'keeps in the stores and issues provisions, fuel and light for the use of the service abroad'. Such a formal description fails to capture many of the crucial features of the Australian Commissariats and their subsidiaries. In addition the commissary in NSW became a source of foreign exchange and of local instruments of exchange. They were, at once, banks and credit agencies, and a springboard for banking enterprises. They were also the instruments for encouraging and reallocating productive activity for regulating staple prices and subsidies to such an extent that they have been perceived as 'staple markets'. The commissary also became the means for making supplementary allowances to officials, for compensating persons for performing public services for which no British appropriation existed or for totally funding some other public services. Through rations distribution, they effectively paid workers engaged in convict gangs on public infrastructure.*'[17]

That the commissariat operations reflected the changing needs within the colony is evidenced by its regular reorganisation. Until Macquarie's arrival, there had been stability in the organisation structure and only two commissaries had been appointed: the basic

---

[14]   Governor Phillip to the Rt. Hon Henry Dundas HRNSW Vol 1 Part 2 p.613
[15]   Barnard, *Phillip of Australia*, p. 126
[16]   Governor Phillip to the Rt. Hon Henry Dundas HRNSW Vol 1 Part 2 p.643
[17]   Butlin, N.G.' *What a way to run an Empire, Fiscally'* p52

operations of victualling convicts and selected settlers had remained constant, as had the provision of tools and equipment to convict work parties. Under Macquarie, the expansion of services provided by the commissariat had grown disproportionately and into relatively uncharted areas. He recognised the need for banking and financial services in the colony but, when his proposal for a chartered bank was rejected, he imposed that role on the commissariat. Likewise, the growing intake of convicts into the colony led to vast organisational strictures on government, and these imposts were assigned to the commissariat.

The demand on the commissariat was always significant and varied according to the number of convicts arriving in the colony, which in turn depended on the military and economic circumstances prevailing in Britain and Europe. On 1 February 1793, only five years after the First Fleet arrived in Botany Bay, Britain was at war with France, the Napoleonic Wars that dragged on until 1815. There were several important consequences: the attention of the British Government was distracted [18] away from the affairs of an insignificant and distant colony (Botany Bay); transportation of convicts became more difficult and less necessary; the flow of free immigrants to the colony was reduced even further; and it enabled a small group of elite military officers stationed in the colony to create a monopoly position. In spite of the *Navigation Acts,* the war in Europe provided an excuse to develop trade between the British colony and the American colonies, although it was one-sided in favour of the American shippers.

Heavy economic commitments to the war in Europe and a downturn in the British economy from 1810-1815 led to constant pressure from the British Government to reduce expenditure in the colony. The Colonial Office in London thought this could be partly accomplished by moving people 'off the store' and reducing expenditures on public works. Both of these alternatives affected commissary operations. Apart from foodstuffs, the commissary mainly bought timber for building, leather for boots and shoes, wool (hair) for blankets and supplies such as barley for brewing beer.

The commissariat received supplies from four general sources: imports, government farms and workshops, civil and military officers and private individuals. In some matters, the commissary strongly supported private enterprise - for instance the area under grain on government farms never rose above 10% of the total farmed land in the settlement and by

1808 this was insignificant[19].   Similarly, government cattle numbers, notwithstanding the lost herd later found in the Cow Pastures at Camden, represented a decreasing proportion of total cattle numbers in the colony, falling from 70% in 1800 to 12% in 1814, whilst government sheep numbers fell from 10% to 2% of those in the colony in the same period. The third Bigge Report provides an important insight into Commissariat activities. Commissioner John Thomas Bigge, a former Chief Justice of the West Indies colony of Jamaica, was appointed by Lord Bathurst to visit the Colony and assess progress and to evaluate the growing expenditures of Governor Macquarie.   The instruction to Commissioner Bigge read in part: 'you will inquire into the courts of justice, the judicial establishments and the police regulations of the colony[5]. You will also turn your attention to the question of education and religious instruction. The agricultural and commercial interests of the colony will further require your attentive consideration. With respect to them you will report to me their actual state and the means by which they can be promoted.' Bathurst added:

> I would more particularly refer to the authority, which the governor has hitherto exercised, of fixing the prices of staple commodities in the market, and of selecting the individuals, which shall be permitted to supply meat to the government stores. With respect to these regulations, you will investigate how far their repeal is likely to lead to any general inconvenience, or to any public loss. I am aware that when the colony was first established the necessity of husbanding the scanty means of supply and of regulating its issue, might justify an interference on behalf of the government; but now that the quantity of land in cultivation is so much increased, and the number of cultivators enlarged, I confess I have great reason to doubt the expediency of these regulations; at the same time I feel unwilling to recommend so material an alteration without some examination on the spot as to its probable effects.

A second letter of the same date and also from Earl Bathurst directed J.T. Bigge to consider the suitability of Sydney town as the main recipient of convicts and the opportunity of:

> ' forming on other parts of the coasts, or in the interior of the country, distinct establishments exclusively for the reception and proper employment of the convicts, who may hereafter be sent out. From such a measure, it is obvious that many advantages must result. It would effectively separate the convict from the free population, and the labour of forming a new settlement would afford constant means of employment, including that of a severe description.   By forming more than one of such separate establishments, the means of classifying the offenders, according to the degree of crime, could be facilitated. But on the other hand, you will have to consider, what would in the first instance, be the expense of the measures, and what may be the probable annual charge which may result from their adoption.'

---

[5] The first two paragraphs of Earl Bathurst's letter of 6th January 1819 to J.T. Bigge have been summarised for purposes of expediency

[6]The full instructions from Bathurst to Bigge and the correspondence from Bathurst to Sidmouth are printed

Earl Bathurst, in a separate note[6] to Viscount Sidmouth dated April 1817, set out his concerns of the mixing of convicts with free settlers and the problems resulting from ever increasing numbers of convicts being transported[7]. He wrote:

> *'Another evil resulting from the increased number (of convicts transported), is the great difficulty of subjecting any of the convicts to constant superintendence, either during the hours of work or relaxation; and the necessity of leaving a large proportion of them to the care of providing their own lodgings during the night, from the inadequacy of public buildings allotted to their reception, forms one of the most formidable objections to the current system. I intend to place the settlement on a footing that shall render it possible to enforce strict discipline, regular labour and constant superintendence, or the system of unlimited transportation to New South Wales must be abandoned. I propose the appointment of commissioners with full powers to investigate all the complaints which have been made, both with respect to the treatment of the convicts and the general administration of the government'.*

In his instructions to Commissioner Bigge, Bathurst had recognised the impact of over-regulation and enforced pricing of goods sold to the government stores. However, the commissariat (or Government store) relied on imports for its grain and meat supplies and, until 1800, to a lesser extent on the private sector. From 1804, grain was in reasonable supply, except in periods of drought, floods and disease, and was grown mainly by the small settlers. Cattle and sheep raising tended to be in the hands of the military and civil officers and other settlers with larger holdings. The government set basic prices for commodity purchases by the Stores, but these were often exceeded because of the general shortage of labour[7]. The governor set fixed prices for the commissariat for grain but the settlers found they had to sell at lower rates to influential middlemen, who then obtained the fixed price. This group had influence over what supplies the stores would buy and from whom. According to Linge[9, a similar clique] 'was able to buy up ships' cargoes and resell them at ten times the price and more' After 1800 Governor King tried to break the monopoly position of these groups (mainly officers) but his efforts brought only temporary relief to small settlers, many of whom were in debt.

The difficulty of changing the role and activities of small farmers was that the vast majority was ex-convicts with little literacy and certainly neither the knowledge nor capital to improve their farming techniques or buy stock and equipment. In Van Diemen's Land, Lt-Governor Sorrell lent small operators a bull or ram from the government herds and

---

with the third report by Bigge to Westminster, as presented to the House of Commons in February 1823

[7] Ritchie, John *Punishment and Profit*

[8] Fletcher, B.H 'The Development of Small-scale farming in NSW under Governor Hunter' JPRAHS, 50 pp 1-8

[9] G. J .R. Linge ' Industrial Awakening'

flocks for breeding purposes in an endeavour to improve the herd and provide some small assistance so these operators could acquire breeding livestock. Such arrangements was not extended to or followed in the colony of NSW although Samuel Marsden, a leading practitioner of flock improvement in the colony, did loan some special rams to neighbours and parishioners around Parramatta. The record shows Governor Darling loaned 'cows' to small farmers although this was a strange way of increasing the private herds rather than the public herds.

Commissioner Bigge[10] reported:

> 'Clerks in the Commissariat department generally consist of persons who have been convicts, and also of persons who are still in that position, but who have received tickets of leave. They receive pay, differing in amounts from 1s 6d to 5s per day, and 'lodging' money; they likewise receive the full ration, and a weekly allowance of spirits. A system must be installed that reduces the perpetual temptation to plunder from the necessary exposure of public property. It is for this reason recommended that public rations of bread should be baked by contract (at a potential savings of 1 6th of the flour used); Private contracts (let under the tender process) to supply the hospitals with bread, meat and vegetables have proven to be of advantage to those establishments; both changes result in considerable savings to government'.

The report confirms that in 1820, those victualled in NSW numbered 5,135 to whom 7,027 rations were issued daily (some convicts were on 1½ regular ration because they were considered to be in heavy manual labour). In total, the numbers victualled, including military and civil officers, rose from 8,716 in August 1820 to 9,326 in December 1820. Bigge reported 'I see no reason for not applying the former rule by which the rations of those officers whose salaries exceeded £90 per annum were taken away. I recommend that they be taken off the stores and a compensating amount be paid to them from the Colonial Police Fund.'[9]

The British Government constantly reminded colonial governors of the growing cost of running the colony and the need to take people 'off the stores'. During 1800-1803 more than 2000 convicts were transported, adding to the number dependent on the store: there was also a significant increase in the number of small farms allotted, mainly to the growing number of convicts whose sentences had expired. At that time, a small 30-acre land grant, achieved at least three benefits for the new owners: they generally improved his social status (and therefore their mindset towards crime and property ownership); they were taken off the stores and told to be self-sufficient; and they became eligible to sell produce to the store thus becoming an important cog in the colony's food chain.[11]

---

[10] Bigge, J.T. Report # 3 Agriculture & Trade in NSW (1823)- p.132
[9] Bigge, J.T. Report # 3 Agriculture & Trade in NSW (1823)- p.149
[11]. Butlin, N.G 'What a way to run an Empire, fiscally' (Working Papers in Economic History (ANU)

In his 'Working Paper', Butlin offers some interesting numbers with respect to the growth in farming activity, for the period 1800-1810. 'Excluding the holdings of civil and military officers, the number of farms grew from 400 in 1800 to 600 in 1804 and 700 in 1807. Thus, even though grain production had reached a reasonably satisfactory level by 1804 and 40 new farms were coming into production each year; the number of mouths to feed was increasing by only a few hundred annually at this time. However, meat remained scarce. Cattle were preferred to sheep because they were less prone to attack by wild dogs, thrived better in the wet and humid climate and were more suitable for salting down; whereas in 1801 the ratio was 6 to 1 in favour of sheep, by 1809 the ration was reduced to only 3 to 1'[11] The 'Epitome of the Official History of NSW' suggests the numbers of livestock in 1800 was 1,044 cattle and 6,124 sheep; in 1810 the number had increased to 12,442 cattle and 25,888 sheep; by 1821 cattle numbers had grown to 102,939 and sheep to 290,158[12].

This series of events before 1810 set the foundation for the future direction of the pastoral industry in the colony. Although there were troubling but isolated incidences of military officer domination of trade and profiteering, the colonial economy was growing and settling into a pattern of life suitable for self-sufficiency and growing independence and local governance. From 1811 to 1815, the pattern changed and turned into a commercial depression in the colony, brought about by a number of internal and external factors. 'Sealing vessels were having to sail further to find grounds not already picked bare by Colonial, British and American gangs, and in 1810, news reached Sydney that the British Government had imposed a duty of £20 per ton on oil caught in the Colonial waters.'[14] Further, in England the price for sealskins fell from 30/- to between 3/- and 8/-. Between 1810 and 1812 the British economy suffered a downturn and the financial troubles, brought on by a long drawn-out war in Europe, were soon transmitted to NSW. Indian and English merchant houses called up debts and refused to underwrite further speculations and the British Government pressed the colonial administration to further reduce running costs[15]. Locally, the Commissariat's venture into money operations helped intensify the shortage of money in the settlement and, to add to these distractions; in 1813 local duties were

[12] 'An Epitome of the Official History of NSW' compiled from the Official and Parliamentary Records of the Colony in 1883, under the direction of the Government Printer, Thomas Richards.
[14] Linge 'Industrial Awakening' op cit
[15] To these circumstances, Briggs and Jordan, writing the 'Economic History of England' adds the Malthus observations on a rising population (8% between 1808 and 1812) and the effects of the industrial revolution.

imposed on sandalwood, sperm oil, skins and timber, whether intended for home consumption or export. The English Government weighed in with another cost cutting exercise by reducing the military numbers in the colony from 1600 in 1813 to 900 in 1815. Steven concludes that by 1815, 'Sydney's commerce had almost totally collapsed'[16] She also suggests that one side benefit of the commercial downturn was that, because individuals and partnerships could no longer see easy openings in trade, commerce, land and livestock, they may have turned their attention to industrial activity, establishing a profitable base for further local production of manufactured items and import-replacement industries.[17]

Summary of Chapter One
0
One of the supplies carried by Governor Phillip on the First Fleet was a 'forge'. Such an item would have been considered necessary to make or shape a metal object by heating and hammering e.g. for use by farriers and vets, but for the First Fleeters' there were no horses and very little metal objects, so Phillip must have had a repair use in mind for broken axes, adzes, hammers etc. However, they were to come in handy later during the Phillip administration when, first Phillip then Hunter and finally King required small metal items specifically adapted to colonial conditions. The local environment was much harsher than originally anticipated by Phillip when ordering supplies for the first voyage, and few items adapted well to the new surroundings. Thus it was time thought King to put the forges to good use. Ordering new supplies took at least twelve months before receipt, and the quality, of even the most expensive items was inadequate, so the decision was made to save time, to be in receipt of suitable items by making them locally. Obviously there were side benefits – 'no direct cost' and thus a saving of foreign exchange; developing a local secondary industry and developing local skills.

This was the beginning of the network of government-owned and sponsored industries, other than public farming. The novel concept of government owned and operated farms, (as opposed to full privatisation) had been a bi-product of necessity undertaken by Phillip. Without public farming of grain, vegetables livestock and fruit trees, private settlers would not have been able to support the settlement's needs for many years. However it was not long before having gotten the basics of food production for the settlement, Phillip commenced the privatising approach, by making land grants to suitably enterprising

---

[16] M. Steven 'Merchant Campbell 1869-1846' p.136
[17] Steven *ibid* p.142

emancipists and military officers who wanted an alternative to trading in speculative cargoes. Thus the scenario became one of a directed economy, the acceptance of prisoners as unpaid but supported labour, and the usage of that labour to underpin private and public farming. But farming also needed access to roads and public infrastructure, so some of the convict labour had to be set aside to make roads (really cart tracks, build barracks, build a water supply system and develop a system of public buildings as hospitals, churches, commissariat store and wharves, bulkheads around Sydney Cove, gardens etc. All this need stretched the usage of thew few prison labourers, and Hunter appealed for further transfers.

A small settlement, struggling to feed itself, receiving significant number of prisoners, and being watched for every penny it spends, and therefore struggling to find an export commodity. Such an export can't be manufactured, but instead must be a primary or basic industry. Meat is not exportable, nor grain, since both are in limited supply, but natural resources are a possibility. The items that come to mind are timber and coal. These are always in demand in Britain, and Britain is the only available export market. Fisheries are explored but a local market exists for fish; however, seals are a multiple product source and their by-products of skins and oil are much in demand. Finally a staple capable of being exported from the settlement – an industry that is not too labour intensive and capable of employing a number of skills and of being associated with other industries. The shipbuilding and provisioning industries are young and in need of support. Visiting ships will also be supportive of these two industries. The commissariat can't get involved in these commercial type businesses, other than by providing financial services in the absence of a treasury. What the commissariat needs is some basic routine industry that is capable of employing a growing number of convicts and of producing a relevant product for the settlement. If the commissariat can't directly contribute to generating export income, it can contribute in another important way and that is to save on import expenditures, and that is exactly what operation is available. Instead of importing many standard items, why not produce them locally. If man hours were valued, and if raw materials were priced, then these items may well be more expensive that their importation, but the system does not work this way. In the mind of the British Treasury officials who make the rules, prison labour is not costed nor is extracted resources priced. So if other needs are identified, such as timber frames for housing, doors, windows, trusses for roofs, etc, then by matching supply and demand, the commissariat can meet production needs of all types of building products. This in turn will require a great deal of labour, up-skilling of many trades, a lot of supervision but most of all, a public works program can be got underway for little cost.

CHAPTER 2

THE ROLE of the COMMISSARIAT in ECONOMIC PLANNING

Introduction to Chapter Two

In 1813, these and other circumstances led to a revamping and restructuring of the colony's commissariat operations. After 1813 Colonial Commissaries were appointed from Britain (such appointments being on recommendations contained in the Report of the Commissioners on Public Acts of 1792) All financial business of the army abroad was conducted by the Commissaries of Money and Stores, appointed on warrant of the King, and directed to obey all instructions given by the Treasury.

Before 1813, the governor was in direct command of the commissariat functions, and this local knowledge and direction led to planning and regulation that appears to have kept adequate supplies in the stores and allowed fast adjustment to ration issuing, essential in keeping the growing population fed on a regular and routine basis. A brief outline of commissariat functions and operations between 1788 and 1813 will serve to show how the commissary established itself as a prime economic functionary within the government and the settlement.

Governor Phillip had declared in a memorandum to the Colonial Secretary - 'The country has no treasury' [18]. The first financial institution was the government store or commissariat, based in form and function on the military commissariat responsible for provisioning troops[19]. Commissariat stores were established in Parramatta by 1792 and Hawkesbury (Windsor) by 1794[20]. In 1794 Commissary Palmer asked Governor Hunter for additional staff and stationary as the storekeepers were overworked? When King arrived to take up duties in 1800, he noted that at no time had proper instructions been prepared and issued on how to manage the commissariat. He therefore drafted a series of detailed instructions and issued them to Commissary Laycock, who had succeeded Williamson; an outline of these regulations appears in the appendix of this study.

---

[18] A paraphrase of Governor Phillip's pronouncement was used by N.G. Butlin in 'Foundation of the Australian Monetary System 1788-1851
[19] T.G. Parsons 'Colonial Commissaries' – (Chapter 1 of Australian *Financiers – Biographical Essays* - Appleyard & Schedvin (Eds)).
[20] SRO records of the Colonial Commissariat (Research Group NC-11)

Williamson had been appointed on a temporary basis whilst Palmer was on leave[21] in England. The British Treasury had also felt the need for a comprehensive set of Commissariat regulations, for Palmer returned to the colony with a set of instructions for his guidance[22]. The Treasury regulations were more general in nature and were therefore not at odds with Governor King's instructions. However one area of the Treasury instructions did differ from King's and created a new policy, the drawing of Treasury Bills; the Commissary was now authorised to draw Bills directly, without the approval of the governor. This new procedure came as a surprise to King who, upon receipt of the Treasury instructions from England, wrote to the British Colonial Secretary pointing out his (the Duke of Portland's) earlier official direction to 'draw Bills for all public purposes through the governor and by no other person'[23]. King concludes his despatch with what appears to be reluctant approval 'whilst awaiting your Grace's commands, I am giving the Commissary an order to draw Bills, using every precaution'. The commissary had also been directed to pay the salaries of its storekeepers from funds held by the Colonial Agent rather than the Treasury. King's precautions were probably because, in actual circumstances, the commissary was becoming of considerable importance in the colony as a market and exchange, as revealed in a Report on the '*State of His Majesty's settlements in NSW*' dated 31 July 1801:

> *The Commissary officer is charged with the provisions, stores and every other article or concern wherein the public expense or expenditure is included. To assist him one deputy has charge of the stores in Sydney and one at Parramatta; another storekeeper has charge of the dry stores in Sydney, and a third is in charge of the store at Hawkesbury. As there are only two storekeepers provided for in the estimates, this third person is a superintendent. The deputies and storekeepers make weekly returns to the Governor. No article whatsoever is received into or issued from the stores without the Governor's written order, which duty is perplexing and occupies one entire day each week. Those orders and returns are checked on the Commissary's accounts, and inspected quarterly by the Governor, and transmitted to the Commissioners for Auditing Public Accounts, which from September 1800 are forwarded with the Governor's despatches. In addition to regular duties, the Commissary is also charged with exchanging such articles as are sent by Government with the settlers, for grain or animal food, and disposing of the whalers' investments in the same manner, which effectively destroys all monopolies. These duties require the constant attention of four clerks in addition to the two provided by Government.* [24]

Further duties were added to the Commissary by an Order of August 1802 whereby, under certain conditions, the Commissary was authorised to sell surplus perishable goods to free settlers at a profit, fixed at 50%. Palmer was allowed to retain a percentage (described

---

[21] HRA 1:20:675 and 632-6 (the complete copy of the instructions)
[22] HRA 1:3:5
[23] HRA 1:318 King despatch #3 to the Duke of Portland
[24] HRA 1:3:419 This statement is Para 5 from the 'State of His Majesty's Settlements in NSW' being enclosure # 1 to despatch by Gov. King to Duke of Portland dated 1st March 1802. The note 615 to this statement refers to 'these annual statements reported the yearly transactions of the colony in detail'.

only as 'small') as compensation for the extra bookkeeping - he was instructed to pay any additional clerks out of his private purse. When Bligh was overthrown, Lt Foveaux declared the commissariat department was riddled by corruption and he dismissed Palmer, who, in turn, indicated the stores were now being rapidly depleted by the military officers for their own gain. This resulted in a series of personnel changes in the Commissary Administration; Palmer was dismissed and replaced by Williamson, who, after less than six months, was arrested and replaced by Wiltshire. Wiltshire lasted less than three months to be replaced by D.C. Fitz. When a charge was levelled against Fitz, William Broughton was appointed Commissary.[25]

Parsons offers a partial explanation of this high turnover of personnel[26] : 'although commissaries had immense responsibilities for which most of them were untrained, their recruitment was a haphazard response to times of crisis. Military officers constantly complained about the calibre of the department. Wellington himself observed 'the prejudice of society against a commissary almost prevents him from receiving the common respect due to the character of a gentleman'.

Palmer and his successors may not have sought respect but they certainly created a great deal of personal wealth, far beyond what a salary of £150 per annum would have achieved. Palmer accumulated one of the finest homes in the settlement, as well as a huge estate at Woolloomooloo Bay (100 acres of land grant), investments in land, livestock, mills for grinding government grain, and eventually a fleet of whaling boats. He did well for himself by being the Commissary-General, and having the governor's ear on so many matters, with the added advantage that his brother-in-law (Robert Campbell) was the biggest independent trader with the commissariat[27]. Palmer offered an interesting insight into his schematics. The ex-purser had come a long way in a very short time when he boasted to the 1812 Select Committee 'I had more ground than anybody else, and I farmed more than any other person does' [28]. Parsons concludes, 'Palmer was a competent, if unexciting administrator who believed that public funds were for private use. His failure arose from an attempt to reserve the trade of NSW for Campbell and himself. His

---

[25] HRA 1:7:179
[26] T.G. Parsons 'Colonial Commissaries - Chapter 1 of 'Australian Financiers' - Appleyard & Schedvin (Eds)
[27] Margaret Steven 'Merchant Campbell' p.143

administration of the commissariat during the 1790s had assisted the privatisation of the colonial economy; these years were personally profitable and socially rewarding.'[29]

Before 1813, the main role of the commissary was to feed and clothe the convicts, the military and the civil officers. It also victualled all the settlers, mainly emancipists, who were supported for at least the first two years of their freedom and provided them with tools and clothing. The commissariat was the principal market for colonial produce, buying grain and other products from settlers, who relied on the commissaries for a secure, stable income. The commissaries in turn relied on the settlers for a regular and adequate supply of product to meet the commissary needs. During the period between 1788 and Macquarie's recall in 1821, the commissariat played a key role in the socio-economic development of the colony. Commissary bills and store receipts were the currency of the colony and the commissariat dominated colonial finance. At least until 1817, it acted as a bank, controlled and administered the flow of foreign exchange in the shape of treasury bills issued to pay for the cost of the colony, provided loans and credit, and encouraged the establishment of enterprises that could meet its demands. The essential personnel of the department were intimately involved with the emergence and maturing of colonial Australia.

Fletcher offers an interesting observation on the philosophy of the 'middleman' or commissariat in the colony. 'The gaol could not feed itself; whilst the private sector, composed of civil and military officers and emancipated convicts, started to produce surpluses of agricultural products in the early 1790s. A mechanism had to be found to transfer the surplus from the private sector to the government and gaol economy, and it was the commissariat that came to occupy the key role in this exchange relationship'.[29]

The other observer of commissary enterprise was S.J. Butlin:

> '*A currency was needed to provide a means of payment. The commissariat store receipts became the internal currency of the colony, dominating its monetary system until the end of the Macquarie administration. These receipts could be consolidated into a Treasury note, payable in sterling, along with paymaster's bills (the salaries of civil and military officers), which provided the colony's supply of foreign exchange. Access to sterling enabled imports to be obtained; access to the commissariat provided store receipts that could be*

---

[29] Parsons *ibid*
[29] B.H, Fletcher 'Landed Enterprise & Penal Society' (SUP)

consolidated. The commissary was the key to the system; the opportunities and temptations were considerable. [30]

Summary of Chapter Two

In his introduction to Fitzpatrick[31], Dr. Evatt observed that 'a close analysis of all the legal contests between 1788 and 1820 has not yet been made, but in my opinion the result will be to corroborate the essential truth of the Fitzpatrick thesis that there was no worthwhile economic history to write, in any detailed, business history, sense'. Dr. Evatt observed that, instead of the Shann & Fitzpatrick style of economic history, these other historians seemed to be writing political and administrative history. Evatt however, added a further dimension to the interpretation of the early governors' despatches[32], and rightly predicted the most reliable records of the pre-1820 period were those court papers such as affidavits, documents used in evidence and the evidence of the witnesses. Dr. Evatt opined that these cases would prove a major historical source.

This economic history of the commissariat cannot be responsibly based only on the HRA records. Other than for the terms of the instructions to each governor and to the commissary himself, the main sources to be relied upon should be the series of three Bigge Reports and the in-house accounting records of the Commissariat.

The commissariat's formative period occurred during the administration of Governor King and, coincidentally, that was when the most significant fiscal misdemeanours took place. Hainsworth reminds his readers, 'between 1800 and 1806, the commissioned Military officers received less than an eighth of the Treasury Bills drawn by Governor King, and not all of these bills were for grain or meat put into the store'.[33]

According to the SRO which retains most of the King records, the King papers show that most store receipts for grain and pork were received by 'dealers' of one kind or another and that only a small proportion of the receipts went to officers. In contrast; during the

---

S.J. Butlin 'Foundations of the Australian Monetary System 1788-1851' (MUP)
Fitzpatrick, Brian 'British Imperialism and Australia – An Economic History of Australia'
Evatt claims that the 'magnificent collection of dispatches that are contained within the HRA contain an inbuilt weakness: the despatches, at best, contained what the governors believed to be true and more importantly what they believed to be relevant or important: at worst they told what the governor's wanted Whitehall to believe although he knew better. As James Stephens wrote to Earl Grey in March 1850 'Commentators on colonial or any other history who confine themselves to official documents are as sure to go wrong as if they entirely overlooked them' (Quoted in Historical Studies, ANA Vol 13, No. 52, April 1969)
Hainsworth, D.R. The Sydney Traders – Simeon Lord & His contemporaries 1788-1821 p. 35

1790s it is reasonable to suppose that a majority of the receipts went to officers directly or indirectly.[34]

Hainsworth concludes that the settlers of NSW were not in economic subjection to two dozen officers and officials[35] because there was already a commercial community with numerous trades and a variety of backgrounds including convicts, and this group became fiercely competitive, especially in seeking sub-contract work from the Lumber Yard and other divisions of the commissariat. The enterprise group included Simeon Lord, Henry Kable, James Underwood, Mary Reiby, Andre Thompson, Isaac Nichols, and it was apparent that most of these traders started as an adjunct of officer enterprise[36]. At the same time, two observations should be made. Firstly, lawsuits became a local pastime as alliances, partnerships and factions formed and reformed, changing their purpose and membership at the dictate of circumstance[37], and secondly, the absence of any account of the rise of these men is one of the serious deficiencies of the pioneer histories of the period. Their appearance is a vital chapter in the history of Australian commerce and, while more recent historians have noted the development, they have not sought to explain it[38].

Having outlined the role of the government store in the colony, the theme of expanding the operations of the store in order to optimise its service to the colony is developed and numbers are provided for the convicts victualled, the locations of various stores in relation to the spread of settlement, and the changes recommended by Commissioner Bigge. The commissariat was constantly in a state of change, not unlike the economy which was during the first 30 years in constant transition from penal to free market or directed economy.

---

[34] Commissariat Records for the King period 1800-1806 are also located in the SLNSW MSS A2018
[35] A situation perceived by Fitzpatrick, The Australian People 1788-1949
[36] The rise of these men suggests that officer domination was being eroded before Governor King 's administration was forced to deal with it
[37] Hainsworth, *ibid* p.36
[38] The same conclusion could be drawn about the commissariat. The commissariat is always noted in the main texts as being an adjunct to the economic growth and wellbeing of the settlement, but rarely is it explained in terms of how it operated, its governance or its importance.

3

DETAILING THE ENTERPRISES

Introduction to Chapter 3

• The basics of a new commissariat-controlled business enterprise would be a policy directive supporting public investment in such a plan, a strategy of creating a public works program and its associated needs for architects, designers, builders, skilled labourers, supervisor and underlying need. What a huge plan; what a gigantic undertaking; production planning, market planning and a comprehensive business plan of the finest sort. A mammoth undertaking in an advanced economy, but for a small settlement of relatively few permanent free settlers, an unwilling military, and the challenge could easily seem overwhelming. The needs were not extravagant – a building, plenty of labour, raw materials, some limited equipment and off the project could go. Of course, a small number of basic government sponsored operations were already underway. A brick and tile site was initially built in the *Brickfields* area of Sydney and then Phillip commenced a second site in Rosehill on the east side or southern bank of the Parramatta river; the first stone yard was commenced just off the eastern side of Observatory Hill and the main timber harvesting site had been developed east of the Lane Cove River in Castle Hills. In addition to the small secondary industries, the early government-sponsored business enterprises included the building activities of the prisoners, the government farming activities and the livestock management. So there was some precedent for planning a convict labour driven commercial operation. The first step was the planning aspect. Lieutenant G.TWB Boyes experienced in the British Commissariat, was transferred to the colony of NSW to take control of the Finance, accounts, and planning branch. But we have jumped ahead to the time of Boyes' arrival in the colony in about 1820. Our story commences in about the middle years of the Macquarie Administration when the first surge of prisoners arrived in the colony. Macquarie appointed two Principal Superintendents of Convicts – the first being Major Druitt, and the second a Major Ovens. Both men were dedicated to the task and made giant improvements in convict work practices. During the early days of the Macquarie Administration, one of the benefits of Druitt's planning was more output from fewer labourers. With assignment under way, almost 50% of the arriving prisoners were sent into the employ of 'masters', who had grazing and agricultural properties to work. Druitt commenced work of the land clearing gangs and the road-making gangs. This harsh work was usually left to the more unruly of the prisoners. So when the big rush of prisoners commenced arriving shortly after the Napoleonic Wars ceased in 1815, some work was available for them, but the real planning for growth commenced. Whilst the commissariat was planning to upgrade and expand the government business enterprises, Macquarie himself was planning for the extensive public works program. One needed the other. Macquarie's program badly needed the GBEs for cost reasons as well as the practical supply side, whilst the commissariat needed to plan its production around specific guidelines and objectives. Thus the GBEs commenced with the Lumber Yard, and a variety of subsidiary operations – the Timber Yard, the Stone Yard, an expanded Brick and Tile Yard, a Dock Yard. The Lumber Yard's site was selected in a prominent location. Most raw materials used were despatched to the main commissariat store on George Street North, in a three storey brick building fronting George Street. Logs were floated down the Lane Cove and the Parramatta Rivers and then onto the main commissariat wharf before being moved to the Timber Yard and onto the Lumber Yard. Metal strips were brought on ships travelling from, England and transferred to the Lumber Yard. Convicts were initially housed in private quarters until the Hyde Parks Barracks were completed at which time they were marched to the Lumber Yard and other work sites each morning at 5 AM.

●

Growth in Number and Size

The lumber yard was a catalyst for economic growth in the colony. Instead of thousands of unemployed prisoners wondering the streets of Sydney, 2,000 of them were behind the 8 foot exterior wall of the facility working productively. They were contributing to the GDP instead of living off the government.

The obligation on the lumber yard was, in a year such as 1817, to service and support over 16,000 convicts. Half of them were 'assigned' to private service. About 1,000 were under the control of the Female Factory in Parramatta. The balance, one way or another were in government service. They may have been gardeners in the governor's domain, or street repairers, or night watchmen, or land clearing gang members or working in one of the GBEs. There were over 11 GBEs ranging from the lumber yard to the stone yard, the timber yard, the dockyard, the shipbuilding yard, the provisioning division, the commissariat, the government farms and the livestock management division, the lime-making (mortar) facility, or the brick and tile yard, or the hauling service, or the ferryboat service across the harbour or up to Parramatta.. The construction gangs and the road-making gangs also employed many convicts and supervisors. So the 8,000 convicts assigned to public (or government) service are not difficult to account for.

Perhaps more important is the output from these sources. There was very little in a, for instance, government building that was not or could not be made in one of the GBEs.

Output included: Meat (Livestock), grain for flour and bread, and then the building products – bricks and tiles, stone blocks, hinges, nails, timber, hand carts, culvert piping, bridge strapping, wharf components, clothing, and furniture. In fact from the foundations up, the local production filled just about every need. Foundation stones, timber frames, timber cladding, brick exterior, window frames, roof framing, tile roof, interior wall frames and cladding, floor joists flooring boards, Furniture, nails hinges, metal vents, lime mortar. All items were made in the yards, and transported to the site. Finished inventory, other than for a few hard to handle items were transferred to inventory and despatched from the store, with proper paperwork being completed. The lumber yard had clerical assistants at the main gate for keeping records of production and despatch, labour in use and raw materials on hand.

Employing Convicts

It has been demonstrated above that in 1817 over 16,000 convicts were under the overall control of the Superintendent of Convicts, Major Druitt, and of these, 8,000 or more were in government service. The balance of almost 8,000 was under the control of private masters and supervised, and fully maintained by them. This was a huge financial burden off the government, but the British Treasury never counted the benefit derived from the convicts being put to productive work., By not recognising the colony as a production centre or a future gem of the realm, they saw no value in improving the local environment.

Convict Population of NSW 1788-1847

Year	Males	Females	Total	% of Popln
1788	529	188	717	74.2
1790	297	70	367	62.1
1800	1,230	328	1,558	31.6
1805	1,561	516	2,077	29.8
1819	8,920	1,066	9,986	38.3
1828	16,442	1,544	17,986	46.4
1836	25,254	2,577	27,831	36.1
1841	23,844	3,133	26,977	20.6

Source HRNSW various

Gangs and Supervision

The term 'gang' is often misused. In this context, it refers to a team of convicts working as a unit. An earlier context referred to members of a convict gang as being shackled, but this is generally not the case. The term gang was generally used in connection with a group of land clearing convicts or a road construction team of convicts e.g. a road making gang. All convict workers were generally supervised or in the least overseen by a supervisor. Generally the supervisors were 'trustee' convicts, and placed in nominal charge of 'peers', a usually unhealthy and unwise approach. A convict ordering another convict generally produced negative results.

Weidenhofer in *The Convict Years: Transportation and the penal system* 1788-1868 (Lansdowne Press 1973) writes (p.46) 'At first they [the convicts] were fully occupied in establishing the necessities of life: constructing buildings and roads and clearing public land. All of this work was performed with a great inefficiency due to lack of proper supervision and the inexperience of the felons themselves'.

'Regardless', Weidenhofer writes (p.48) 'of whether a convict labourer was employed in government service or assigned to a settler, he was required to complete a specified task each day or each week. This minimum was known as his 'government task'. A week's work was set at nine hours a day for five days and five hours on Saturdays. Sunday was observed as the Sabbath. During the first twelve years of settlement, a convict who completed his government task before the end of the day or week, was permitted to use the remaining time to work for the government or for his master either for wages or goods in kind, such as rum, tea, sugar, tobacco. Settlers who wished to hire their labour on a time basis could do so for ten pence a day, six shillings a week, or £10 a year, plus free board'. Weidenhofer also confirms the use and role of supervisor (p.50) 'Convict labourers working in the government service were divided into gangs in charge of an overseer, who was usually another convict appointed because of his good record. His job was to ensure the convict's attendance at his place of work each day, assign the tasks and supervise their completion. From 1819 convicts in government work were housed at Hyde Park Barracks; they were taken each day to the work site and returned in the evening'.

Output and Outcomes
Weidenhofer concludes (p.12) 'The first years of settlement in NSW were marked by shortages of food and equipment as the First Fleet had come largely unprepared for Australian conditions. The construction of buildings and the commencement of agriculture

went ahead slowly and inefficiently and the convicts were not skilled in the works which needed to be done. By the 1830s, humanitarian opposition was fierce, particularly to the assignment system under which convicts were put in the charge of free 'masters'. Critics and social reformers branded the convict system as thinly-disguised slavery and a source of moral corruption not only for the convicts but for the people who used their labour'.

Sydney GBE locations

Table 5.1 Commissariat services and output [5]

Food (Govt. Store)	Manufactured Items	Other
Mutton	**Clothing**	**Brickyard & stone quarries**
Beef	Slops	Quarry stone
Pork	Straw hats	Quarry gravel
Vegetables	Bonnets	Bricks & tiles
Potatoes	Shirts	**Dock Yard**
Cabbages	Trousers	Small boats
Cauliflower	Shoes	Unloading ships
Carrots	Boots	Loading ships
Turnips	Caps	Provisioning
Beans	Cloth	Repair work
Onions	**Building products**	**Financial services**
Grain	Iron bolts	Issue store receipts
Wheat	Building materials	Consolidate store receipts into bills
Barley	Nails – hand forged	Issue bills
Maize	Timbers – pit sawn	Payroll – civil & military
Oats	Timbers – sized & dressed	Petty banking
Fruit	Furniture	**Other**
Oranges	Tools	Issue rations
Lemons	**Other**	Buying from visiting ships
Ancillary	Tobacco	Issue purchase orders for imports
Tea	Candles	Pay for goods purchased
Coffee	Soap	
Sugar	Hides	
Processed Flour	Livestock	

Table 5.2 is a partial list of items produced by the Commissariat using convict labour, mostly from the 20 locations around the Sydney and Parramatta areas (the County of Cumberland). However, some products such as tobacco were produced at penal

---

[5] These items of foodstuffs are compiled from issues of '*The Sydney Herald*' which listed vegetables grown by the Government Farms and their market prices

settlements at Port Macquarie and later Moreton Bay, whilst items such as tea and sugar were imported under licence from the East India Company. Until 1820, these centres employed over 50 percent of the convict population. Their output was directed to agricultural products, livestock supply, import replacement manufactures, materials required for the construction and building industries, materials required in the public works and infrastructure construction program, and the transport and storage requirements of the government.

Table 1.2: Commissariat business centres and operating divisions 1814

Centre	Operation
	Business Centres
1	Lumber Yard and Timber Yard
2	Female Factory
3	Government Farms
4	Timber cutting
5	Stone quarries – building materials
6	Dockyard
7	Livestock compound
	Operating Divisions
8	Financial Services Division
9	Transport Services Division
10	Accounting Services Division

Table 1.3 Locations of Farming Enterprises

Locn	Name & Location	Purpose	Acres	Superintendent	Operating
1	Longbottom	Timber& grain	700	E. Knox	1819-1821
2	Emu Plains	Grain	3,000	John Jamieson	
3	Grose Farms	Grain	280	Capt. Gill	1819-1821
4	Cow Pastures	Livestock	25,000	E. McCude	
5	Bathurst	Livestock	20,000	J. Maxwell	1814-1828
6	Castle Hill	Cattle & timber	34,539	R.Fitzgerald	
7	Pennant Hill	Timber	2.500e	Kelly	
8	Rooty Hill	Grain	8703	Murdoch	
9	Dundas		3500e		
10	Emu Plains	Vegetables	700e		
11	Toongabbie	Livestock	10,000e	G.T. Palmer	1793-1804
12	Field of Mars	Timber , grain	1,000e	T. Dovenay	
13	Cawdor (Camden)	Grazing	3,500	John Wild	
14	*Green Hills* Hawkesbury	Grain & crops	5,000e		
15	Gov't House Parramatta		260		1790-1818
16	Liberty Plains, Concord	Cattle, grain	500e		
17	Rose Hill	Timber	1,500e	J. Smith	
18	Canterbury	Cattle	50		
19	Pt Macquarie	Grain, tobacco,	1,500e		

20	Iron Cove/Five Dock	Shells for lime	2	W. Hutchinson	
21	Moreton Bay	Grain	1,500e		
22	Lane Cove	Gov't Sawing Establishment	20	J. Wright	
23	Wellington Valley	Cattle/grain	7,000	P. Simpson	1823-1830
24	Canterbury	Cattle & hay	50	Rented from J. Campbell	1807-1821
25	*Cornwallis* Hawkesbury	Grain	171	Rented @ 15s acre	1801

Government Business Enterprises

Operation	Purpose	Convicts employed
Lumber Yard	General production	1,000
Timber Yard		200
Female Factory		300
Government Farms		1,200
Stone Yard		200
DockYard		100
Livestock Management		75
Brick & Tile Yard		150
Services division	Haulage, boat ferries	100
Road gangs		50
Construction gangs		1,500
Land-clearing		250
Supervisors	Supervision and overseeing	1,500

The GBEs in Operation

Not surprisingly, and probably by default rather than intentional policy, the Commissariat became the prime producer of materials and supplies used within the Colony. Out of necessity, the demand for timber products, bricks, tiles, stones, rude furnishings and carts needed to be and could be supplied locally. There was a need for local building materials, because of the length of time it took to order and receive supplies from Britain, and the urgency of building accommodation for military and civil personnel, a secure storehouse and essential infrastructure such as wharves, bridges, and housing for both settlers and convicts. Suitable local materials had been identified, including good clay deposits for brick and tile manufacturing and grain suitable for liquor production was being produced All that was needed was labour and basic equipment. Thus the government business enterprises were assigned as a responsibility of the Commissariat and, in conjunction with the Superintendent of Convicts, Commissariat personnel planned for equipment, materials, transport and the provisioning of remote convict camps.

These Commissariat business enterprises covered a great deal of activity ranging from the making of bricks and tiles, basic forged tools, slops (clothing), shoes, furniture and timber frames for buildings to timber felling camps, vegetable and meat production, abattoirs, boat building, provisioning visiting ships and stevedoring. In addition, convicts were organised into gangs to clear land and build cart tracks. Ferry services were established to cross the harbour from north to south and link the Sydney and Parramatta settlements by river.

The Commissariat was not only about producing goods; it also became responsible for business services, and a means of exchange was created by way of barter of store receipts, negotiated payroll bills and consolidated bills for remittance overseas. A foreign exchange facility was also created, and it became a catalyst for a local free market for agricultural products for settlers and emancipists.

Location of facilities

Early maps show the location of the various Commissariat stores, warehouses and operating facilities. The Commissariat went to the Castle Hill area to find the best trees to harvest and drag to the Lane Cove River for transport to the Lumber Yard. The largest of the government's initial garden plots (adjacent to the First Settlement) was immediately to the south-east of the Governor's mansion, facing South Harbour; a further four smaller plots were located on either side of Sydney Cove, obviously to utilise fresh water from the spring (or Tank Stream) which entered the Harbour there. The Commissariat was responsible for the planting and encouragement of these gardens, which were originally intended to supply grain and fresh vegetables for the settlement. Phillip planted fruit trees on Garden Island, the most fertile location within the original settlement. The government farms, which replaced these small gardens, were eventually located in the most fertile areas of the outer settlement.

The first store was a canvas tent located on the east side of the Cove adjacent to the Governor's temporary dwelling, a prefabricated house brought in pieces with the First Fleet. A second store for baled goods on the west side of the Cove adjacent to the military camp was erected, also under canvas. Collins records[1] that by May 1788 a 'large store-house had been completed, and a road made to it from the wharf on the west side [of the Cove], and the provisions were directed to be landed from the victuallers, and proper gangs of convicts were placed to roll them into the store'.

Amongst the convicts, some tradespeople had been located – for example a bricklayer.[2] They led a convict team in building a number of huts in areas cleared for this purpose. 'Carpenters were now

---

[1] David Collins: *Account of the English Colony in New South Wales – Vol 1*

employed in covering in that necessary building [the Hospital], the shingles[3] for the purpose being all prepared; these were fastened to the roof [which was very strong] by pegs made by the female convicts.'

By July 1788, further land had been set aside for a larger storehouse,[4] the first step in Phillip's contribution to town planning. A series of grids was laid on a scale map designating roads and sections for the military section, housing for civil officers, courthouse, hospital and government offices as well as the Governor's residence. This new store location was on the west side of the Cove between the proposed hospital and church. By this time, the Parramatta settlement had commenced including provision for a storehouse. By 1792, the maps show streets with names such as Back Row, Chapel Row, Pitts Row and Barrack Row. High Street was prominently located and in 1812 it was renamed George Street. These early Phillip-designated names remained in existence until Macquarie rewrote the street names in 1812, naming them after former Governors (Phillip, Hunter, King and Bligh Streets), prominent Secretaries of State for the Colonies (such as Castlereagh and Pitt) and Kings and Queens (George and Elizabeth). The 1822 Greenway map shows that the government storehouses were built where Phillip had originally planned them, but the church had been replaced by the county gaol. A second government store was also shown as a log-cabin type building on the east side of the Cove. This may well have housed dried provisions of a longer-term nature and some of the stores designated for the Governor. This facility became known as the dry-store, so named to differentiate the facility from the grain stores and the perishables store (fruit and vegetables).

By 1802, the map shows that the majority of development had taken place on the western side of the Cove and a large area set aside for the Commissariat dockyard adjacent to the wharf, which in turn was adjacent to another new brick store. These buildings and establishments fronted High Street North, which ran parallel to the Tank Stream. Robert Campbell, whose home and large warehouses were located at the top end of High Street, had encouraged the Governor to make High Street a prominent retail and factory thoroughfare. It took a further eight years, until the arrival of Macquarie, for further developments to take place. Macquarie changed the name of High Street to George Street and located the Convict Factory on the corner of George and Bridge Streets. This convict factory was renamed and became the Lumber Yard. The *Sydney Gazette* had made much of the poorly named Female Factory in Parramatta, and the resulting disrespect shown to its occupants. The 1807 'Plan of the Town of Sydney' by James Meehan, confirmed this status quo, as did the 1808 plan prepared for Governor Bligh.

---

[3] Shingles were still preferred over tiles. The tiles being made at Rose Hill had not been perfected and failed in any strong winds or a hail storm

By 1811 Campbell had built a substantial store and wharf further around Sydney Cove, from the Hospital Wharf and John Cadman's cottage. The main wharves were The Government Wharf on the south side of the Cove and the Governor's Wharf on the east side of the Cove, giving access to the Domain and Government House. The Hospital Wharf was initially used to unload supplies for the hospital but it became the main wharf for the new three-storey Commissariat-built brick and stone store adjacent to Sydney Cove. By 1821, the Dockyard had expanded to the south and was given direct access to the King's Wharf (the renamed Hospital Wharf, originally called the Public Wharf).

The Lumber Yard was shown as occupying 3 acres on the corner of George and Bridge Streets, running down to the Tank Stream, which was marked on the 1821 map as being, 'dry at ½ ebb'. Macquarie had also completed the straightening of the town roads and the removal of encroaching houses from the road reserves. By this time too most of the windmills had been removed as Macquarie considered them an eyesore on the landscape. In addition to the Dockyard and Lumber Yard, the Commissariat controlled a third area for stonecutters, located in the main and largest quarry on the west side of George Street North directly opposite the Commissariat store. This quarry, worked by a convict gang, supplied most of the sandstone blocks used in early Colonial buildings, especially those commissioned by the team of Macquarie and Greenway. This first quarry was not large enough to supply the entire requirement for sandstone and two more quarries were opened on Bennelong Point and off Farm Cove, east of the (Governor's) Domain.[4]

Organisation of Government Business Enterprises.

Under the guise of controlling the activities and rehabilitation of convicts, Macquarie decided that, rather than placing all convicts on assignment and thereby removing any financial obligation for their maintenance, a percentage should be put to work on behalf of the government. This would be accomplished in two ways. Firstly, direct convict labour, rather than the preferred contractor program, would be used for infrastructure development and other public works programs, specifically government building. This resulted in a great concentration of convicts in Sydney employed in two big workshops, the Lumber Yard and the Timber Yard, both located on George Street, together with the stone yard (across from the Lumber-Yard) and the three-storey Commissariat store, wharf and dockyard, fronting the western side of Sydney Cove. The convicts worked on a task or piece system. In the Lumber Yard, surrounded by an 8 foot high brick wall for security purposes, forges were used

---

[4] Many original names changed by being abbreviated over the years. The Governor's Domain changed to Government Domain and was then shortened to The Domain, whilst Semi-Circular Quay was shortened to Circular Quay. The Botanic Gardens was part of the Domain and became the public vegetable patch for Macquarie Street residents before being converted into a horticultural museum

for making nails, hinges, wheel irons and other metal products. Other sections were set aside around the outside walls of the factory for boot-making, cabinet and furniture-making, barrel making, and the making of coarse wool and cotton for slops and hats. In the centre of the large factory the two saw pits were manned by up to 25 men who cut the timber taken from the kiln after the drying process. In the timber yards, beams and floor-boards were sawn and prepared from the timber drawn from the Lumber Yard. The brick and tile yard was built around a huge kiln (22 ft long by 18 ft high) producing 24,000 bricks at one raking. The stone-yard not only produced large building blocks from stone but also flagstones, hearth-stones and mantelpieces. Within the Lumber-Yard were stored all the tools required for the various business enterprises and for each work site. Each item was recorded going out and coming in while all materials – both raw material and finished product – were recorded equally carefully at the clerk's office located at the main gate. The Superintendent of Convicts, Major Ovens, had set a piecework productivity rate; for instance, the shoemaker's gang of about eight men was supposed to produce a pair of shoes per man per day from leather tanned at the government factory at Cawdor; the brass-foundry and the tailors' gang each had their own production goals. The carpenter's gang usually consisted of 50 men, made up of cabinet-makers, turners and shinglers; the bricklayers' gang, generally between five and ten men, were expected to lay 4,500 bricks each week; the sawyer's gang was usually 25 men. Other gangs based in the Lumber Yard were also sent out to garden, cut grass, dig foundations and carry grain. The Lumber Yard was responsible for over 2,000 men in all. The government business enterprises were comprehensive and massive undertakings, and Macquarie took pride in their output and accomplishments.

Manufacturing is only part of the story in any study of economic development of the period. Economic development drove public finance in the same way that the growth in population, farming, decentralisation and land utilisation impacted on the source and use of public funds.

Other factors to be considered are that the Commissariat established multiple stores and supplied foodstuffs and materials (at government expense) for convicts as well as civilian and military personnel, and the Commissariat also established work centres for convicts:

Lumber Yard	Timber-Cutting camps	Stone Quarry
Timber Yard	Land Clearing camps	Boat Yard
Dockyard	Government farms	Government Stores

A summary of their output is quite extensive for a small and young Colony

Table 5.1 Commissariat services and output [5]

Food (Govt. Store)	Manufactured Items	Other
Mutton	**Clothing**	**Brickyard & stone quarries**
Beef	Slops	Quarry stone
Pork	Straw hats	Quarry gravel
Vegetables	Bonnets	Bricks & tiles
Potatoes	Shirts	**Dock Yard**
Cabbages	Trousers	Small boats
Cauliflower	Shoes	Unloading ships
Carrots	Boots	Loading ships
Turnips	Caps	Provisioning
Beans	Cloth	Repair work
Onions	**Building products**	**Financial services**
Grain	Iron bolts	Issue store receipts
Wheat	Building materials	Consolidate store receipts into bills
Barley	Nails – hand forged	Issue bills
Maize	Timbers – pit sawn	Payroll – civil & military
Oats	Timbers – sized & dressed	Petty banking
Fruit	Furniture	**Other**
Oranges	Tools	Issue rations
Lemons	**Other**	Buying from visiting ships
Ancillary	Tobacco	Issue purchase orders for imports
Tea	Candles	Pay for goods purchased
Coffee	Soap	
Sugar	Hides	
Processed Flour	Livestock	

Table 4.2 is a partial list of items produced by the Commissariat using convict labour, mostly from the 20 locations around the Sydney and Parramatta areas (the County of Cumberland). However, some products such as tobacco were produced at penal settlements at Port Macquarie and later Moreton Bay, whilst items such as tea and sugar were imported under licence from the East India Company. Until 1820, these centres employed over 50 percent of the convict population. Their output was directed to agricultural products, livestock supply, import replacement manufactures, materials

---

[5] These items of foodstuffs are compiled from issues of '*The Sydney Herald*' which listed vegetables grown by the Government Farms and their market prices

required for the construction and building industries, materials required in the public works and infrastructure construction program, and the transport and storage requirements of the government.

Colin White[6] has concluded that the Colonial government controlled the local economic mechanism. There were three main elements to the mechanism: (1) The government provided the social infrastructure to mitigate risk to individuals, and, further, (2) guaranteed a market, at fixed prices, for the output of the private sector. This government action also provided (3) grants of free land, inexpensive credit and cheap labour with the return of any redundant labour to government service when needed.

The following is a declaration by Governor King of convict work undertaken in the settlement

'Public Labour of Convicts maintained by the Crown at Sydney, Parramatta, Castle Hill Hawkesbury, and Toongabbie, 1805
Cultivation - Gathering, husking and shelling maize from 200 acres sowed last year - Breaking up ground and planting 1230 acres of wheat, 100 acre of Barley, 250 acres of Maize, 14 acres of Flax, and 3 acres of potatoes - Hoeing the above maize and threshing wheat.
Stock - Taking care of Government stock as herdsmen, watchmen etc
Buildings -
At Sydney: Building and constructing of stone, a citadel, a stone house, a brick dwelling for the Judge Advocate, a commodious brick house for the main guard, a brick printing office
At Parramatta: Alterations at the Brewery, a brick house as clergyman's residence
At Hawkesbury: completing a public school
A Gaol House with offices, at the expense of the Colony
Boat and Ship Builders: refitting vessels and building rowboats
Wheel and Millwrights: making and repairing carts
Manufacturing: sawing, preparing and manufacturing hemp, flax and wool, bricks and tiles
Road Gangs: repairing roads, and building new roads
Other Gangs: loading and unloading boats
Public Works: various'.[7]

Investment in public works infrastructure was a major challenge. Britain essentially saw the settlement as little more than a tent town with the prisoners as inhabitants, under guard, transported out of sight and out of mind and who had no need of money or coins, public buildings, fancy housing or amenities. Under the early Governors from Phillip to Bligh, only the minimum amount of work was done and, therefore, expense was limited, and, by the time Macquarie arrived, there was a deferred maintenance and construction schedule which dumped all of the expense and workload on his Administration. Commissioner Bigge recorded for his enquiry that 76 buildings had been completed under Macquarie. Some of these were extravagant, such as the Governor's Stables, the Rum Hospital and the toll booths on the Parramatta Road. Bigge directed that they be revamped and

---

[6] Colin White *Mastering Risk-Environment, Markets and Politics in Australian Economic History* OUP 1992 P 52
[7] HRNSW -Vol 6 P43

put to alternate, less extravagant use. He made no comment on the provision of water or the sewerage and drainage measures made for a town with a growing population; Macquarie had drained the marshes in the present Centennial Park as the town water supply and had outlawed the use of the Tank Stream for animal grazing, washing and as a waste sewer.

In 1826 Governor Darling, as part of his structuring of the Colonial public service, established the first Office of Inspector of Roads and Bridges with charge over the Engineer's office; from April 1827, his title was changed to Surveyor of Roads and Bridges. The office remained active until 1830 when, in an economy drive, Sir George Murray, Secretary of State for the Colony and War Departments, passed these responsibilities to the Surveyor-General. In 1832 the Colonial Architect's Department was established to take responsibility for the planning, repair and construction of public buildings but in 1833, in another economy drive, this department was also transferred to the Surveyor-General. Later, the duties of Colonial engineer for superintendence over roads, bridges, wharves and quays were added to those of the Colonial Architect and all planning came under the Surveyor-General. It was this concentration of workload in such a few hands that led to an increasing public investment in public works.

Another effort by Governor Darling to centralise planning and control in a new public service bureaucracy was the establishment of the Clergy and School Lands Department in 1826. This corporation was to receive a seventh in value and extent of all the lands in each county in the Colony, out of which it was to be responsible for paying the salaries of clergy and schoolmasters and for the building and maintenance of churches, school and minister's residences.

Governor Darling had centralised the planning for all public works into one department, the Land's Department, which in turn employed the Surveyor-General and provided for the Lands Board. This balance assisted in prioritising and funding all public works and brought order to the chaos of Macquarie's policy of building as he saw fit. A by-product of this new policy was that all convicts were now on assignment and 'off the stores', and a competitive contracting arrangement was used for tendering for all public works.

Having reviewed the Commissariat business enterprises, it remains to further examine the convict work arrangements and outcomes and this chapter details the role, organisation and output of the Commissariat's six main operating centres. The most important reform or change to Commissariat operations under Macquarie was his addition of the role of Supervisor of Convict Work. Although there was already a Superintendent of Convicts, the role was that of discipline, in all its forms.

Macquarie asked of the Commissary that this establishment prepare a work schedule, supply the tools and equipment required, clothe and house the convicts allocated to government work. This imposed on the Commissariat a huge responsibility and burden; it was now their role to plan ahead for materials required for both government building works and what could be expected from private sales. The Commissariat had to estimate the timber, the brick and tile, stone and furnishings usage requirements of government programs and ensure the manufacture and preparation of all these articles. It was a mammoth role and was based on the speedy completion of a vast number of government projects, a role that was accomplished with credibility.

The work gangs had an important role within the transportation program and the Commissariat's work organisation. According to James Broadbent[8], 'Macquarie's public work can be grouped into four categories. Firstly, the purely utilitarian structures and engineering works: the storehouses, the markets, roads, bridges and wharves. Secondly, there were the buildings that had official government functions. Thirdly came the Greenway type civic buildings (with adornments) and then fourthly, there were the buildings of the urban type of architecture by Greenway'. [9] The Macquarie/Greenway team made a huge contribution to life in the early settlement and created much organisational work and planning for the Commissariat.

Were the convicts to be viewed as Manning Clark classified them, as an 'alienated working class...with no spiritual or material interest in the products of its work... driven or terrorised into labour',[10] or as 'a distinctive workforce, organised, directed and controlled in the performance of their labour',[11] or even as 'coerced labour emanating from a professional criminal class' [12] and members of the urban criminal class?[13] Meredith and Oxley go on to quote a vague, rather meaningless and unattributed statement from the unidentified *British Monthly* 'Australia's Colonial workers became the most murderous, monstrous, debased, burglarious, brutified, larcenous, felonious and pickpocketous set of scoundrels that ever trod the earth '.[14] It would make more sense if these attributes were applied to convict workers rather than Colonial workers, who were workers directly recruited, mainly in Britain, and imported under sponsorship or as free immigrants. It is doubtful that free labour should be or can be labelled in such an invidious way. The organisation of convict labour

---

[8] Broadbent, J and Hughes, J.(Eds) *The Age of Macquarie* MUP 1992
[9] Francis Greenway was a convict transported to the Colony for seven years for breaching bankruptcy laws in England. He was an architect working in his father's firm and after his arrival in the Colony Governor Macquarie appointed Greenway the first colonial architect.
[10] Clark, Manning, *A History of Australia*, Vol 1 p.244 MUP-1988
[11] Nicholas, Stephen *Beyond Convict Workers*, UNSW 1996
[12] Meredith, David & Oxley, Deborah *Beyond Convict Workers* p.21
[13] Nicholas *Beyond* p.3
[14] Meredith, David *Beyond Convict Workers* p.21

directly contributed to most of the problems associated with forced labour. Even penal labour today, in China or the USA, is renowned for its lack of productivity, and these prisoners are supervised by salaried administrators or contractors and protected from abuse by strong laws defining prisoner rights. The Colonial convicts enjoyed no such rights and could not be simply coerced into working as hard as a free worker. Using on-time release as an also meaningless as few records existed or arrived with the convict ships detailing the release date of each individual. There are two distinct phases of convict alienation in the workplace. The first came under King when convicts were supported by the Commissariat for food, clothing and general provisions, and were remunerated lightly by the master. The second phase came when Macquarie assembled the forced workers into an assignment system, whereby the government disqualified itself from any financial support of the convicts and passed all responsibility, supposedly other than punishment, for the convict workers to the master. With Macquarie picking the most skilled convict workers for government service and assessing the desired level of subservience and productivity in each newly-arriving convict for assignment to the government work gangs, it is little wonder that the remainder were considered dregs and failed to meet productivity levels attributed to free workers. It is not hard to understand the lack of incentive in these assigned workers – they were generally ill-treated throughout the settlement, herded for counting at least once each year and often on a more frequent basis. Their provision allowance was generally less than optimum for a workingman and they had the lowliest of tasks to complete, ones in which productivity levels were generally difficult to set and more difficult to measure. For example, Convict Superintendent Ovens allocated 8 convicts to clear one acre of ground of trees and re-growth each week. We know from our own experience even today that every acre is different – some land is super dense, with tall, ancient hardwoods, whilst an adjoining acre may be lightly treed with the softwood already thinned out. Keeping in mind the aboriginals would run a fire through much open land to regenerate the bush and grass-lands; the country-side was always at different stages of re-growth and condition, depending on drought and rains. Coghlan claims that convict works were only 50 percent as productive as a free worker, but one wonders if he has considered all aspects of the problem of such an assessment. Convicts were mostly used on piecework, where goals were difficult to set. Building workers and work-gangs for clearing land and road formation were the majority, work which free workers were rarely sought for or encouraged to carry out.

Even today it is not difficult to find a council or shire work gang of 5 or more men with two or three men digging and the remainder resting on their shovels. Coghlan's generalisation is not hard to understand but closer inspection makes it an unreasoned conclusion. The answer as to productivity and commitment is probably found in the attitude of superintendents of work. Any man is resentful of being chained like a dog and treated as inhuman, being underfed, abused both physically and mentally and having nothing to look to the future to. Due to a shortage of free workers with people skills, superintendence by a peer was the normal arrangement, and most overseers would only have been willing only to stand aside and verbally abuse the convict group or team rather than be a working-supervisor. Why should we expect a different set of standards for the convicts in 1788-1832 than we accept today? Human nature has not changed that much. Obviously there were exceptions, such as Greenway, Simeon Lord, Edward Eager and others who were self-preservationists, wanting to stand out from the crowd, embarrassed at being in such circumstances and intending to revert to their former social and economic standing. However, such people were rare amongst the 160,000-odd convicts transferred to the colonies.

The earliest convict gangs were employed on timber harvesting, timber dressing, brick and tile making and construction. Construction crews were engaged in building barracks (military as well as convict barracks) storage facilities, hospitals, paths, roads, bridges and wharves, military fortifications and observation points. A full list of Macquarie's construction work is included in the Appendix to this study. Macquarie's initial dilemma was the creation of sufficient work to keep all the newly arriving convicts employed, but this situation was quickly reversed, the demand for skilled workers grew and it could only be met from newly arriving convicts and/or specially recruited immigrants. At the same time, as newly skilled workers became available, the new manufacturing operations took shape. The construction crews, wherever located, were to be victualled and fitted out with clothing and tools by the Commissariat and this need, together with the spread of settlement, led to a diversification of Commissariat locations – Parramatta, Liverpool, Windsor, and Government Farms at Castle Hill, Pennant Hills, Toongabbie, Rose Hill, Emu Plains and Rooty Hill. Under pressure from settlers wanting to contract for convict labour, Governor King set work and task work rates:

Table 5.2: Setting Task Work Rates per Unit/Per Week

Task	£	Unit
Felling of forest timber	0.10.0	1 acre
Burning off fallen forest timber	1.05.0	65 rods
Breaking up new ground	1.04.0	65 rods
Chipping in wheat	0.06.8	1 acre
Reaping wheat	0.08.0	1 acre 60 rods
Threshing wheat (per bushel)	0.00.7	18 bushels
Planting corn	0.06.8	1 acre
Pale splitting (5 ft per hundred)	0.02.0	1000 (using 2 men)

(Source: HRA 1:3:37 March 1801)

John Ritchie, in his study of Bigge's Enquiry and the his reports to the House of Commons, quotes Major Druitt, the 1817 Convict Superintendent, confessing: 'I have had more trouble with the Sawyers than any other description of convicts, and I attribute it to my obliging them to do a greater portion of work than they ever did before'. Druitt had increased their weekly target from '450 feet per week per pair of convict workers, to 700 feet but also demanded they work on more demanding types of timber such as Iron Bark, Stringy Bark, Blue Gum and cedar'.

There was no conflict between capital and labour. Labour efficiency was under constant review, as was the manning numbers within the Yard. Equipment was well used and technological advances were transferred from Britain to the Yard as need arose. Dr. Meredith writes; 'As time passed the authorities in Britain decided that assignment [system] itself was inefficient',[19] so, by the end of 1837, it had been decided to scrap assignment and, in fact, bring an effective end to the transportation program[20]

A brief synopsis will now be given about each of the key operating areas under Commissariat planning jurisdiction:

The Operations of the Lumber Yard

The operations of the Lumber Yard are generally unrecorded, yet, as the manufacturing centre of not only the Commissariat but also of the Colony generally, the Lumber Yard was responsible for a number of significant activities It gainfully occupied over 2,000 convicts, trained younger offenders to provide them with skills for use at the end of their sentences, and built or manufactured a wide range of locally required supplies and stores. It also facilitated a transition arrangement for many manufactured items, from government enterprise to free private enterprise. It was located on the corner of George Street and Bridge Street, which had earned its name from having the first wooden bridge constructed over the Tank Stream. According to De Vries [21] the lumber or timber storage yards were a standard feature of British Colonial penal settlements. They were, in fact, convict work camps, and the Bridge Street Lumber Yard contained workshops for blacksmiths, carpenters, wheelwrights, tailors and shoemakers. There was also a tannery where the convicts made their own leather hats and shoes. Nails, bolts, bellows, barrels and simple items of furniture for the officers' quarters and the barracks were also made there. Convicts wore identification on their uniforms –**P.B.** for Prisoners of Hyde Park Barracks or **C.B.** for Carter's Barracks. They worked from sunrise to sunset, and if they failed to fulfil their allotted tasks, they were flogged at the pillory, conveniently situated nearby, also on Bridge Street.

[19] Meredith, David *Full Circle? Contemporary views on Transportation,* in Nicholas
[20] Dyster, Barrie *Why NSW did not become Devil's Island (or Siberia)* Beyond Convict Workers UNSW 1996
[21] De Vries *Historic Sydney* Doubleday Australia 1983

The Lumber Yard continued in use as a convict workshop until 1834, at which time it was subdivided and sold for up to £25 per front foot (for the best lots). Contracting for government work was a common path to independence for building craftsmen. Convicts or emancipists employed as supervisors of the government building gangs seldom wished to remain in service longer than they had to and there was always a shortage of reliable men to take their place[22]. Macquarie, in his efforts to retain his supervisors in government employment, permitted them to combine their official duties with the business of private contracting. The supervisor would undertake the management of a building project to which the government contributed labour and materials from the Lumber Yard. Major Druitt, the Superintendent of the Yard at that time, was unable to suppress the open practice of government men and tools being borrowed and government materials from the Yard being diverted elsewhere.

'Already by 1791 the government (Lumber) Yard had been established on the western side of the Stream to collect and prepare timber for building and was the recognised meeting place where the gangs picked up their tools and materials and were assigned to work. Here building materials were collected, prepared for use and distributed to the various work sites, tools were issued and gangs allocated and checked. It became the core of the government labour system after the devastating Hawkesbury floods in the winter of 1809. Lt-Gov Patterson had the Sydney working parties gather there for victualling before going to the relief of the settlers.'[23]

Under Macquarie's expanding work program the Lumber Yard became the centre of the largest single industrial enterprise in the Colony. Captain Gill, as Inspector of Public Works, exercised the general direction of the working gangs and controlled the issue of tools and materials, while William Hutchinson, Superintendent of Convicts, distributed convicts to the work gangs.

'With so much activity the Yard was an easy target for thieves and by September 1811, the loss of tools, timber, bricks, lime, coal, shingles and nails from the government stocks had become so great that a General Order was issued directing that offenders, including conniving supervisors, would be punished as felons. The same order directed that all tools had to be handed in and counted at the end of each day and prohibited men from borrowing tools or doing private jobs in the yard after normal working hours.'[24]

Gill's successor, Major Druitt, expanded the Yard to cope with Macquarie's work program. He took over the adjoining land in Bridge Street (by then abandoned by the debt-ridden merchant Garnham Blaxcell who had fled the Colony) and built new covered saw pits, furnaces for an iron and brass foundry and workshops for blacksmiths, nailers, painters glaziers, and harness makers. He raised the walls surrounding the Yard and built a solid gate to discourage truancy and pilfering; he built moveable rain-sheds for jobs around the town and provided two drags drawn by draft animals to

---

[22] De Vries *Historic Sydney*
[23] *Sydney Gazette* September 1811
[24] *Sydney Gazette* Sept 1811

replace the 90 to 100 men previously employed on the laborious task of rolling logs from the dock to the Yard.[25]

Men were selected off the convict transports on the basis on their skills and experience and were told to find lodgings in the Rocks area. Each morning a bell:

'...would call them to the Lumber Yard where they were set to work according to their trades or capabilities. Some went to the workshops, others to building sites or the Brickfields where they dug and puddled clay and pressed it into moulds for firing in the kilns. Unskilled labourers were allocated according to their physical condition; the fittest went to the gangs felling trees and cutting logs to length, others to barrowing heavy stones or dragging the brick carts to the building sites, with assignments often used as punishment for the recalcitrant. The unfit were not spared; weak and ailing men went to gangs tidying up the streets or weeding government land, a man without an arm could tend to the stock and a legless man could be useful as a watchman'.[26].

The day's work started at 5 am. There was a one-hour break for breakfast at 9 am and at 1 pm for lunch. At 3 pm the men were free to go and earn the cost of their lodgings. In 1819, Macquarie tightened the convict system, by housing all convicts in the new Hyde Park Barracks, and the working day was extended to sunset. Only married or trusted convicts were allowed to live in the town. The men from the Barracks were marched down to the Yards but 'control was lax and as they went through the streets, some would slip away to follow their own devices'. [27]

'As a result of Macquarie's building activities, and partly as a means of employing more and more convicts, the range of activities expanded in the Lumber Yard'. [25] Every kind of tradesman was gathered: carpenters, joiners, cabinet makers, wood turners, sawyers, wheelwrights, cart-makers, barrow-makers, blacksmiths, whitesmiths, shoeing smiths, agricultural implement makers, tool makers, nailers, bell founders, iron and brass founders, brass finishers, turners and platers, brass wire drawers, tool sharpeners, steelers, tinmen, painters, glaziers, farriers, horse-shoers, saddle and harness makers, bellow makers, pump borers, tailors, coopers and many more.

The organisation was simple: the big work-sheds faced the central log yard where logs and sawn timbers from Pennant Hills and Newcastle were stacked. The Lumber Yard was the source of many of the Colonial-made goods and the centre of the Government's engineering and building activities. It was the first step in the creation of the Public Works Department in 1813. Although the Lumber Yard serviced most of Macquarie's building needs, he badly required the services of a skilled architect. He found those skills in a convict – Francis Greenway, who had a solid background of practical

---

[25] HRA 1:9: 832; ADB 1-324-5
[26] Bridges, Peter *Foundations of Identity*
[27] Bridges, Peter *Foundations of Identity*
[25] Bridges, Peter *Foundations of Identity*

experience as well as theoretical training. He became influential in translating Macquarie's aims and ideas into reality. Major Ovens, in his report to Governor Brisbane, described work in the Lumber Yard: *'In the Lumber Yard are assembled all the indoor tradesmen who work in the shops such as Blacksmiths, carpenters, sawyers, shoemakers, tailors etc. The workmen, carrying on their occupations under the immediate eye of the Chief Engineer are probably kept in a better state of discipline than those, who working more remote, are dependent on the good behaviour of an overseer for any work they may perform.*

Whatever is produced from the labour of these persons, which is not applied to any public work or for the supply of authorised requisitions, is placed in a large store and kept to furnish the exigencies of future occasions; the nature of these employments, also renders it much easier to assign a task to each, for the due performance of which they are held responsible.'

In the Timber Yard adjoining the Lumber Yard was kept an assorted range of the timber, scaffoldings, etc, required for the erection of public buildings; whatever materials were carried away from the Timber Yard for building purposes and the different works, the same had to be returned or the deficiency accounted for. The storekeeper of this Yard had charge of such timber as was brought from the out-stations or sawn and cut up in the Yard, such as flooring boards, scantlings, beams, etc; some timber was also brought as ballast on ships arriving from Britain. When these supplies exceeded the demand for government purposes, the excess was sold by public auction with the proceeds credited to the government Commissariat. The Crown owned all standing timber in the Colony, and revenues derived from its sales also belonged to the Crown and were used to offset expenditures in the Colony. The Ovens' Report to Governor Brisbane lists the workforce by category as well as their expected output. [26] Table 5.3 shows the structure of the Lumber Yard workforce:

Table 5.3: Manning Schedule of the Lumber Yard in 1823

Carpenter's Gang	50 convicts + free apprentices
Blacksmith's Gang	45 convicts
Bricklayer's Gang	10 convicts
Sawyer's Gang	25 convicts
Brick-maker's Gang	15 convicts + boy apprentices – Carters barracks
Plaster's Gang(lathing, plaistering, whitewashing)	8 convicts
Quarrymen	15 convicts
Loading, carrying, clearing the Quarries - 3 bullock teams + 5 horse trucks –	19 convicts
Wheelwright's Gang (wheel, body and spoke-makers	23 convicts
Cooper's Gang	6 convicts
Shoemaker's Gang	8 convicts
lor's Gang (cloth is made at the Female Factory in Parramat	8 convicts
Dockyard Labourers on repair work	70 convicts
Stonecutters and setters	13 convicts
Brass Founder's Gang (casting iron for all wheels, etc.)	9 convicts

---

[26] HRA 1:11:655-7

Other occupations in which convicts were employed included: foundation diggers, rubbish clearers, Commissariat store gangs, grass cutters, boats' crews, boat conveyance crews, and gardeners.

The plan of the Lumber Yard (Appendix C) shows a recreation of how the Yard was laid out. Convicts were marched from the Hyde Park Barracks along Macquarie, Bent and Bridge Streets to the entrance to the Yard, which faced High (George) Street. Inside the entrance, which was two large solid wood gates set into a high brick wall, there was a supervisor's office, with room for clerical staff. A tool shed was located near the front gate so that convicts could be issued with tools and have them collected at the end of the working day. It may be assumed that there was some form of inventory control of tools, otherwise the Governor could not have been advised that tools were missing (assumed) stolen. In the centre of the half-acre area under roof (of the three acre total site), there was a large open, but roofed building, under which the logs were stored, debarked and sawn.

Along one side of the site, probably the back fence, the five operating divisions were housed, probably also under an open-sided, roofed building. These five independent areas included workshops for blacksmiths, carpenters, wheelwrights, tailors and shoemakers.

Sawpits were located in the central area (Ovens reported two in the Lumber Yard and one each in the Timber Yard and in the Dockyard.) The sawpits were recorded by Ovens to be each of about 70 feet in length. For safety reasons, furnaces would have been located, on a third boundary wall. Materials were stored along the fourth boundary wall, whilst bricks, tiles and sawn lumber were stored in the general Yard, ready for issue to local construction sites. Fire in the Lumber Yard would have been a constant threat, but there is no record in the HRA of any fire event.

Items maintained in the various Commissariat stores included:

Table 5.4: Lumber Yard Stores and Products

Stores Maintained	Products Manufactured
Bricks	Sawn timber for framing and flooring
Lime	Window and door frames
Coal	Nails
Shingles	Bolts
Nails	Bellows
Tools	Barrels
Timber in process of drying	Wheels
Logs awaiting cutting	Furniture

Employment was considerable, and was categorised into at least these groupings for control purposes:.

Table 5.5: Employment Categories within the Lumber Yard

Construction & Work-site gangs
Construction gangs for building, houses, public buildings, wharves, bridges
Gangs for land 'clearing'
Gangs for felling trees in the selected timber harvesting areas (Pennant Hills and Castle Hill)
Gangs for Road making
Work facility gangs
Gangs working in the Stone-yard on the west side of High Street
Haulage Gangs
Gangs for moving logs from the wharf behind the Commissariat, further up High Street, to the Lumber Yard
Gangs for dragging materials carts from the Yard to building and construction sites
Gangs for dragging the portable rain-sheds to the various construction sites
Cart dragging gangs for bricks, tiles and stones

In all, over 20,000 convicts were organised from the centre of manufacturing (the Lumber Yard), with about 2,000 employed within the Yard itself at the time of the Ovens' Report. Many government-assigned convicts were employed on government farms at Emu Plains, Castle Hill, Rooty Hill and Sydney Town. Their work ranged from ground clearing, cultivation, weeding, picking and storing, whilst the range of produce included vegetables, fresh meat and grain growing. and clerical assistants in the Commissariat.

Table 5.6: Commissariat Work gangs and Convict employment -1809

Vegetables	150
Cattle	11
Hay/charcoal	110
Wheat/maize	269
Timber cutting	73
Lime preparation	27
Road making	362
Land clearing	386
Stone quarries	69
Cart operators	268
Brick/tile makers	124
Boat navigators	12
Official boat crews	120
Dockyard operations	47
Lumber Yard	1,000
Construction work	1,450
Convict Supervisors*	1,500

*There were over 1,500 convicts employed as supervisors, foremen, leading hands at and its work gangs as well as in the Governor's office and other official government offices.

The hierarchy carrying out the convict work supervision was equally as simple in structure to the convict work organisation itself. The Governor was ultimately responsible for supervising and assigning the convicts to the various tasks whilst the Chief Engineer, Major Druitt, had overall responsibility for the works program – planning and completion. The Commissariat was closely involved and recommended the production schedule, and made available the raw materials, tools and equipment. In 1814, Macquarie made three new appointments to assist Major Druitt. William Hutchison, an ex-convict, as principal superintendent of convicts; Francis Greenway, another ex-convict, as chief architect of public buildings, quality control and convict productivity; and Lt. Watts of Macquarie's 46th Regiment as the design chief for military and civil barracks and police posts. .

The Stone Quarries

With knowledge of local building materials so limited, the more traditional British building materials were sought and encouraged in use. Sydney town was a fertile source of soft sandstone building blocks also suitable for sculpturing. The Commissariat used four locations for sourcing Sydney sandstone for its public building program. A number of stonemasons were located within the ranks of the convicts assigned to government service.

In Francis Greenway [27] Ellis writes of a visit he made to Liverpool, at the request of Macquarie, at which time he saw a few stones delivered and showed Gordon, the mason, how they should be worked. Greenway remarked on the excellent quality of the stone and commented further 'if a proper quarry were opened on the site from which the specimen came' then there would be unearthed the finest stone yet found in the Colony. Greenway was very disappointed to find that there was no quarry; what he had seen were only some loose surface stones. By letter dated 10th April 1818, Greenway recommended to Mr. Lucas (a contractor and the Liverpool property owner) that he should open 'a proper quarry, and good white stone should be obtained'. This was not to be, as the *Sydney Gazette*[28] recorded a few weeks later that Mr Nathaniel Lucas, a respectable builder, was found dead near Moore Bridge, Liverpool.

Greenway wrote to Sir John Jamison on 8 November 1822 that a preliminary estimate for renovation work on the Jamison house included '16 enriched blocks' at 16/-. Without a private contractor able to extract and supply building stone, Greenway recommended to Macquarie that the Commissariat establish and supervise various sandstone quarries to supply government and private building sites around Sydney. Four town quarries were located at Cockle Bay, the Domain, the gaol-site quarry off Pitt's Row, and the High Street quarry.

A submission was made by John Oxley to the Bigge Commission in Sydney in 1821 and included a return of the number of buildings in Sydney in 1821:

---

[27] Ellis, M.H. *Francis Greenway* p.95
[28] *Sydney Gazette- report dated 9th May*

Table 5.7: Stone building constructions in Sydney 1821

Location	Public Buildings	Private Buildings
Macquarie Street	2	1
Bent Street	1	0
George Street	3	21
Macquarie Place	2	3
Charlotte Place	1	1
Elsewhere	0	33
Total	**9**	**59**

The Macquarie Tower and Lighthouse on South Head used stone specified by Greenway to be 'not less than 4 feet long by 2 feet 6 inches in the bed, joggled and cramped in the same way as the stones in the basement'. The problem confronting Greenway at this time was that no masons were obtainable, since there were only two or three government men who even pretended to call themselves such. Greenway therefore selected twelve young men and lads and gave orders that they should be taught to face a stone, to handle their levels, plumb rules, trowels, hammers and chisels. The foundation stone was laid for the Lighthouse on 11 July 1816 and it was completed on 16 December 1817.

Macquarie was being advised on one hand that the Colony 'was a devil's island, with no need for public buildings', whilst on the other hand there were hundreds of convicts coming into the Colony, to be put to work, and an expanding Colonial revenue, supported by taxes, which was providing local resources not very closely watched over by the British Treasury. Some of these Colonial funds were used to build churches in Sydney, Windsor and Liverpool. Macquarie was not acting secretly, for he wrote to Lord Bathurst in April 1817 'In regard to public buildings still required in Sydney, and in other parts of the Colony, I shall avail myself of the discretionary power provided by your Lordship to build as required and pay for them from Colonial revenues'. Early reports identified a few stonemasons in the Colony – such as Thomas Boulton, a free settler who arrived in 1801. By 1810 he was well established and in that year won a government contract to build a 950 feet stone wall in the Domain for which he received £481.12.0. Macquarie established the structure for civil engineering in the Colony, especially for public buildings and works projects. Lt-Colonel Foveaux designed the Commissariat stores and military barracks, but successive Governors soon delegated responsibility to a single superintendent for each bridge, road, building and public works project.

The map appended to this study (Appendix C) shows the location of three stone quarries in Sydney Town. The first and oldest, in use, was on George Street (High Street) opposite the Commissariat

Store and adjacent to the Military watch-house; the second was on the point now known as Bennelong Point (where the Opera House is now located) and the third was on the east side of Sussex Street North. It was the Pyrmont Quarries that built Sydney, and which supplied virtually all the sandstone for every major construction in Sydney.

a.   **The Timber Yard**

Directly associated with the Lumber Yard was the Timber Yard. Although there were sawpits within the Lumber Yard, they were used for sizing sawn timber. The main function of the Timber Yard, and within it the sawpits, was to extract sawn timber of varying sizes and lengths from the large number of logs brought into the Yard. These logs were floated down the Lane Cove River and across the harbour to the Commissariat landing where they were hauled from the water and stacked to enable a drying process before being moved over the sawpits. The logs, having partly dried in the sun, were then rough sawn into a variety of sizes and lengths before being placed for further drying on racks under weights, designed to minimise the twisting and splitting that naturally occurred when native Colonial timbers were dried. The natural moisture content of native timbers was high and best reduced through kiln-drying, but this method was untested until the 1830s. Governor Phillip had used timber cut directly from standing logs and found to his great cost that the timbers twisted, warped and split after a short time in the sun. All his early work had to be rebuilt after allowing the sawn timber to naturally dry before being nailed into place. It took many years for the Colonial building supervisors to understand the characteristics and nature of the native timbers and how different they were to English timbers.

The third main function of the Timber Yard was to cut the rough-sawn timber to preferred sizes and, after the drying process, to rack them until required for construction purposes. From early records it appears that there were never sufficient sawn timbers and demand always outstripped supply, so much so that many British ships were still bringing in timber from Britain and the continent as ballast. Also, local supplies were used in growing quantities for transfer back to and sale in Britain. Although an import tax had been imposed on timber originating from Colonial NSW, it was still in great demand for specific uses, especially for naval purposes and as hardwood.

The Timber Yard was the main timber operation in the Colony but, as the source of most timbers was in the Castle Hill and Pennant Hills area, a second but smaller timber yard was built adjoining the Pennant Hills forests. Ralph Hawkins in a study of the convict timber getters of Pennants Hills for the Hornsby Historical Society, has detailed the names and occupations of both convict and non-convict workers employed at the timber-getting establishment in the Hills area from the 1828 census (the first complete census following the last of the musters). In all there were 166 active convict workers who were employed as timber-fellers, wood and post splitters, sawyers, shingle makers, carpenters, charcoal burners, sawpit clearers and basket makers. A number of the convicts (10 in total) were working with animals as bullock drivers, stock keepers and grass cutters, whilst another sub-operation consisted of metal workers – i.e. blacksmiths and wheelwrights. As the finished products or cut timbers were moved by water, there were boatmen and wharf workers. As it was a self-contained camp, there were also hut-keepers, barbers, shoemakers and tailors. Convicts were used on the administrative side, including approx 40 men acting in a capacity as superintendents, overseers, watchmen, constables, clerks and a school teacher. The Commissariat victualled and provided supplies for a grand total of 166 convicts and provisions would be taken by boatmen returning from the Timber Yard after delivering a supply of product from the Pennant Hills establishment.

The Timber Yard was an important aspect of the Commissariat operations and underpinned the substantial quantity of timber supplies necessary to the Colonial building program commencing under Macquarie.

b.   The Female Factory of Parramatta

Both male and female convicts arrived in the settlement but, as far as balance between the sexes was concerned, the numbers seemed to be of little interest to the authorities in Britain. Upon arrival in the Colony, male prisoners were housed in barracks in Sydney, Parramatta, Liverpool or Windsor. Female prisoners were expected to be retained under government supervision for a short period before assignment into the private sector as housekeepers or manual workers. Whilst awaiting assignment they were temporarily housed in the female barracks in Parramatta. Governor King changed the name of the facility from the House of Industry to The Female Factory in 1800.

In his report on the Parramatta Gaol for Governor Macquarie, Greenway recommended that the existing female factory be removed and rebuilt on a new site as early as possible, since the 'factory had a very bad moral tendency'. Governor Macquarie had included a new factory and barracks for female convicts in his 'List of essentially necessary Public Buildings' of January 1817[29] and in March 1817 he identified to Greenway[30] the 'intended site for the new Factory and Barrack'. However, it was not until 1818 that he instructed Greenway to 'make a plan and elevation of a factory and barrack, sufficient to accommodate 300 female convicts, on an area of ground of 4 acres enclosed by

---

[29] HRA 1:17:255 *Governor's despatches*
[30] Greenway had been appointed Colonial Architect and had responsibility for building what he had designed

a stone wall, 9 feet high'[31]. The site chosen lay between the old Government millrace and the river, opposite the Governor's Domain. Greenway based his plan on a design submitted by Samuel Marsden, and the contract was let in April 1818 for completion within 18 months. Macquarie laid the foundation stone in July 1818 but, due to numerous delays, the building was not completed until 30 January 1821.

Commissioner Bigge described the building, in the following way: [32]

'The design for the building consists of a basement story containing two large rooms (for the females to take their meals), two upper stories with large sleeping rooms. Each sleeping area will contain 20 double beds (containing accommodation for 172 females). The rooms are separated by a staircase and landing places, and in the centre of the roof is a cupola for ornamental purposes and ventilation. In the outer yard are the principal entrance and the porter's lodge, and rooms for the superintendent and his family. In the inner yard is the hospital, a room for weaving cloth and four very small lodges for constables or overseers. Other buildings include the bake-house and kitchen, provisions and stores, storing wool, a spinning room, a carding room and a large storeroom for wool and cloth. No washrooms or privies had been included in the original design and these were added later with drainage to the river.'

Samuel Marsden, who Governor Macquarie had appointed a Trustee of the Female Factory, [33] had advised Macquarie of some background to the commencement of the original Female Factory:

'Nine looms had been operating since 1804 at the Government factory at Parramatta, where 50 women and 18 men were employed. At that time only a small proportion of the Colony's sheep grew wool that was worth shearing, let alone exporting, so the course crossbred-wools, which predominated until the early 1820s, had from the King period been manufactured into slop clothing for the convicts, under the arrangement that the grower received 1/4th of the cloth as payment for the wool supplied.'

In 1814, Marsden told the Secretary of State in England that the absence of barrack accommodation for female prisoners had forced many into prostitution in order to find shelter. In the absence of a favourable response, he wrote to Wilberforce in 1815 complaining of Government inaction and seeked his support in building a new Female Factory.[34] Later, in 1815, he reminded Macquarie of the appalling conditions at the Parramatta Factory.

Early in 1816 Marsden pointed out that the lack of proper accommodation for the convicts employed by the government at Parramatta not only subverted morality and law in that district, but also destroyed the most distant hope of reformation. The female convicts who were not assigned to private service were employed by day in the Government clothing factory at Parramatta. However,

---

[31] HRA 1:17:255 *Governor's despatch*
[32] Bigge, J. T *Third Report on the Colony of NSW* (1823)
[33] Yarwood, A.T. *Samuel Marsden*
[34] Yarwood, *Samuel Marsden*

only 30 of the 150 women and 70 children slept there amongst the litter of wool, grime and machinery, while the remainder were forced to 'cohabit with wretched men or earn lodging money by prostitution' (Yarwood). Yarwood writes that:

'Marsden's water mill was on his land adjoining the female factory grounds. The female factory was a controversial establishment and was reconstructed to Greenway's design with carding, weaving and looming rooms, three storeys high, including single-storey wings to accommodate 300 female convicts. The four-acre site was enclosed by a high stonewall and moat to conserve the morality of townsmen and impose a long-deferred constraint on the inmates.'

Macquarie's explanation for the delay in building the new factory was demonstrably untrue. He claimed he was waiting for Westminster approval, but many of the Macquarie buildings had been commenced and completed without any official approval. Bigge wrote that 'Marsden's lack of criticism of Macquarie's inaction was due to his effort to achieve reform, and not the embarrassment of the Governor.'

The Executive Council Minutes of 15 August 1826 confirm that it was Darling who proposed a change in the Female Factory operations. The Female Factory Board, established by Darling to examine the overall Convict operations, especially those of the Female Factory at Parramatta, included Major Ovens and William Lithgow. The Board's recommendations included a change to rations for female prisoners. Convicts had been assigned rations based on their classifications. For first and second class prisoners, rations included tea and sugar and slightly higher quantities of meats and greens but instead of being issued rations as if female factory workers were in the third or penitentiary class, they were to now have even less. On a weekly basis, they were to receive:

¾ lb of bread (half wheaten and ½ Indian corn); ½ lb fresh meat; 1 lb green vegetables or ½ lb potatoes; 1 oz corn meal to thicken soup; 8 oz corn meal for breakfast and supper; 1½ oz. sugar; 1 oz. salt.

No milk was authorised and corn meal was the substitute for flour.[35]

Personnel arrangements were revised so that salaries were paid to supervisors instead of a percentage as was previously the case. Average percentage payments had been added to a salary base in order to set overall salaries at no less than the previous six-monthly average payments. In fact after over three years of no increases, salaries were adjusted by about 20 percent [36]in 1825. The Board acknowledged how difficult it had been to replace the Factory Storekeeper (the previous occupant of the dual role of Storekeeper and Factory Secretary having resigned). Allowances for this position had previously been £180 per annum, but the replacement was only to receive a fixed salary of £100. Since there had been no applicants at that salary, the Board decided to revise the overall salary scale so that the

---

[35] HRA 1:12:255 Record of rations
[36] Salary table with comparisons HRA 1:14:526 Minute by Darling

matron would in future receive £200, the Storekeeper/Secretary £150, and the Master Manufacturer £150.

The Board had made this latter appointment in the previous year when the original Operations Report was completed, in order to co-ordinate manufacturing standards and output with the Commissariat. The Female Factory had also reported a lot of waste in washing the wool, spinning and carding and then weaving. The Master Manufacturer was now responsible for machine maintenance, productivity, materials management and transporting finished product to the Commissariats responsible for issuing convict blankets and clothing.

A Government Notice set out in the HRA and dated 27 June 1826 encouraged matrimony for Female Factory inhabitants, in order to remove them from the Factory and to create room for newcomers and take more off the store. The Notice encouraged assignment for good behaviour:

'To husbands who were newly arrived in the Colony (for women who had married in England)
To free men who married prisoners, since their arrival
If both husband and wife were prisoners, they would be assigned to the same master
No female prisoner being married to a free man or ticket-of-leave male was to be kept in the Factory
All prisoners who sleep out of barracks would be allowed to work for themselves on Fridays and Saturdays.
All prisoners who sleep out of barracks are to be regularly mustered before proceeding to the gangs to which they belong
To assist in the public accounts it is planned to issue rations, to those who sleep out of barracks in arrears instead of in advance and such rations will be issued at the controlling barracks and not directly from the Commissariat.'

Obviously bookkeeping simplification was required to keep records of rations issued and to stop these types of prisoners receiving double rations from different issuing points.

William Lithgow and Alexander McLeay responded to Governor Darling's request for financial information on 23 November 1826. Whitehall had enquired as to the actual cost of maintaining convicts in the Colony, and Lithgow, as Colonial Auditor-General, responded with typical detailed accounting. For his response, he included the costs of running:

The office of 'Principal Superintendent of Convicts'
The prisoner's barracks at Sydney, Parramatta, Liverpool and Newcastle (including Carter's Barracks for Boys)
The Female Factory at Parramatta
The penal settlements at Port Macquarie, Moreton Bay, Norfolk Island and King George's Sound
The Agricultural Establishments at Grose farm, Long Bottom, Rooty Hill, Emu Plains, Bathurst and Wellington Valley
The Medical Departments at all stations, where Colonial hospitals had been established
The Police & Gaol Establishments and the Judicial Department

According to the Lithgow Report, also set out in the HRA the actual cost of these seven operational areas for convicts came to £15,500. These expenses were defrayed from the 'proceeds of bills drawn on H. M. Treasury'. The cost of the Female Factory at Parramatta was £850 per annum for an average of nearly 500 female prisoners. Food and rations costs were borne by the Commissariat so the establishment cost referred to was simply salaries and minor maintenance work. The result was a rather meaningless figure that could not be benchmarked to any other costing or, in fact, as a guide to efficiency by any British Treasury directive.

c.   The Dockyard

King advised the Victualling Board in London on 16 May 1803:

'...the Commanders of Ships are requested to sent Boat Bills (i.e. Bills of Lading) of the articles sent in each boat, since a person belonging to the Commissary Department is constantly on the landing wharf, and he gives receipts for the specific quantities landed. Bills are delivered to the Deputy Commissary, who accounts finally to the Commissary-General, and the masters of the ships' expenses in charge of the provisions produce the receipts, when the whole are landed. On producing those receipts, the numbers of casks stated by the Commissary were found to be deficient or rather no receipt was produced by the Purser.'

d.   The Government Farms

Governor Hunter had set the pattern for later government farming when, in June 1797, he wrote to his Lt.-Gov and stated, 'I trust I shall soon have as much ground in cultivation on government account as will prevent the necessity of purchasing to such an extent from individuals, grain of any kind'. So Hunter accepted the role and necessity of government farms and passed this same philosophy onto his successor, Governor King:

'Your shortage of public labourers to cultivate the extensive quantity of public land set aside for such purposes (Hunter had previously advised the public land to be cultivated is one-third more that that land in possession of all civil and military officers) will mean that the many buildings you are in need of will not be constructed if you use labour for cultivating rather than building. Your approach calls for such radical reform as may affect a system of real and substantial economy, and confine the issues from the stores such as to eliminate individual production'.[37]

King took a particular interest in agriculture – not as an academic exercise but as a necessity of life in the Colony namely, the regular production of foodstuffs, grain and meat in sufficient quantities to meet projected demand in a growing settlement together with strategic reserves for emergencies when floods and droughts impacted on the settlements. King also took a forward-looking approach to the use of Crown timber. He could envisage the productive use of the enormous quantities of standing timber that was being carelessly axed to open up land for grazing when a better system of timber preservation and a grazing use of naturally open pastures could be adopted.

---

[37] Hunter had corresponded frequently with his Secretary of State for the Colonies – The Duke of Portland and in August 1797, the Duke responded to Hunter: -

Timber of useable quality was not to be found around Sydney Cove, so Phillip brought pine from Norfolk Island until he found good stands of eucalypts, blue gum, black-butt, flooded gum and box around the upper reaches of Lane Cove River and Middle Harbour. These logs were so heavy (and unable to float) that they had to be cut to length on site for moving by boat.

There was plenty of good stone and clay for building purposes, but again the shortage of skilled labour made these materials unusable in the early days of the Colony. Bricks came more into use in 1789 when the early timber constructions were decaying and in need of replacement. Roofing tiles became necessary to replace grass or reed thatching previously used for storehouses as less flammable materials were needed to protect the valuable foodstuffs and other stores. Collins recorded that the living huts were constructed from pine frames with sides filled with lengths of cabbage palm plastered over with clay to form 'a very good hovel'.

In the Colony, close confinement was neither necessary nor practical and, except for hospitalisation, most convicts before 1800 had to find their own shelter. Building huts for convicts had not been part of official building policy, although some huts were built especially for convicts; in Rose Hill, for instance, Phillip designed and built huts as part of his town layout. Since the sawn timbers were used for officer accommodation and public buildings, convicts building their own huts would use saplings covered with a mesh of twigs and walls plastered with clay (mud and daub). Convicts were not given any special access to the limited quantity of building supplies, such as ironmongery and glass, which had been brought from England so that windows were covered by lattices of twigs. The best buildings in the town were those for government use, such as the stores, the barracks, the hospital and housing for officials. Only when convicts became free or went on ticket-of-leave status was there any call or need for private building and a building, industry began to emerge.

King again wrote to the Duke of Portland in July 1801, trying to re-state his position on government farms:

'Although I have been obliged to rent a large farm to employ the government convicts on, and the rent is to be paid from the produce, I have no doubt of its turning out very advantageous. I have previously described how very circumscribed government cultivated lands are, and the cause of it. I am now beginning another farm for the Crown and shall take care the grants of land are not made so as to exclude government from the ground cleared by the convicts at public labour, which had been the case at Toongabbie and Parramatta, to the great accumulation of expense to the public'.

Later in August 1801, King reminded the Duke[38]:

'As the land at Toongabbie and Parramatta (being only 380 acres) had been improperly leased and granted to individuals, perverting Gov. Phillip's plan of concentrating the labour of government servants to one place, which would have greatly facilitated the public work and interest, instead of employing the convicts at public labour in detached situations, and not having people to direct their labour and secure the produce of it without incurring much additional expense.'

Governor King had also prepared a comprehensive report on the state of the Colony on 12 August 1806, [39] in which he described the status of the government agricultural farms.

'Cultivation on the public account is confined to the agricultural settlement at Castle Hill, where only 177 convicts are employed, the remaining 1,774 full rations victualled being composed of the civil, military, stockmen, artisans, and others employed at necessary public works, with the women, children, invalids and aged (who) do not productive labour in agriculture on the public account; nevertheless that object has continued on the part of the Crown, which goes to prove the disadvantage of any cultivation on the part of the public. By the annual muster, taken August 1806, the land in cultivation for the Crown was 330 acres, and 854 acres being worn out by repeated and constant cultivation, and the want of labourers to till it. The government herds will in time remedy the first evil, but the others will continue to diminish or increase in proportion as the convicts now in the Colony sand those sent in future may be appropriated to public labour or assigned to individuals. It seems advisable to encourage the latter, which eases the public of a very considerable expense; but relinquishing public cultivation entirely, and depending on that of individuals, will be far from beneficial to the interests or safety of the Colony.'

Summary of Chapter 4

The Commissariat was the manufacturing centre for the Colony and the Lumber Yard was its hub. In terms of physical output through both convicts and supervisors employed, the Lumber Yard was the key to the success or failure of the Commissariat in the Colony. Its overall operations were earlier discussed in Chapter 2, but in this chapter its detailed operations, output and staffing of this key work centre have been discussed, especially in the context of the Commissariat being an economic driver in the Colony. In addition to the highly influential financial services role played by the Commissariat, the government store maintained responsibility for food production planning and supplies, a wide range of manufacturing operations from equipment to tools, to clothing, building materials and commodities.

The Commissariat was the powerhouse of economic activity in the Colony, as well as the catalyst and facilitator for large amounts of public investment. Without the Commissariat acting so responsibly, the Colony could not have grown and matured as it did. Neither the private nor rural sectors could have developed as they did, mainly, without assistance by its loans of breeding stock to farmers and pastoralists so that livestock would be suitable for the export market.

---

[38] King to Portland HRNSW Vol 6 p.134
[39] HRNSW Vol 6, page 135

CHAPTER 4

INTRODUCING THE COLONIAL ECONOMY

Introduction to Chapter Four

The   hre are two truisms to be considered here. The first is that the history of NSW is the history of Australia, at least between 1788 and the mid-1840s – and therefore for the period covered by this study. The second truism is that the history of Australia is the economic history of the country again for at least the period covered by this study. The importance of these revelations is that an endeavour such as this to study the economic conditions cycles and outcomes of the colonial economy is largely a history of the country with an economic slant.

It would be a mistake to conclude that in 1788, there was neither an Aboriginal economy nor a basic structure for a domestic colonial economy. Although our interest is not directly in the Aboriginal economy, there is obviously an initial linkage and a transition between the two. It may also be thought that the removal of the Aborigines from the traditional hunting grounds around the foreshores of the harbour might have stifled part of the Aboriginal endeavours. Phillip carved an economy out of the bush around the harbour foreshore and went on to found a magnificent city. The transition can be followed by his efforts towards basic town planning, the initial provision of water for the occupants of the settlement, the construction of housing and barracks, and the first planting of future food supplies – all the ingredients of an economy in its earliest stage of development. It is accepted that the second third and fourth naval governors of the colony made little new contribution but settled for more of the same, which policy was acceptable because the major distractions to progress within the economy was the monopolistic activities of military officers traders and the influence of the trade in spirits. That there was no treasury in the colony and the elemental transition from penal to free settlement as the highlight of these three administrations, and it was thus left to Macquarie as the first of the military governors to carry the burden of putting convicts to useful employment and settle on a public works program of eminent suitability to future generations. The question to be raised later is, was the early economy, controlled, directed, guided or free market, or as one economic historian argues, was it a closed economy for the first 30 years?

Thus this study commences with a discussion of the Phillip policies for the new settlement and follows government policies through to the Gipps and FitzRoy administrations. The stated goal;

of this study is to follow and interpret the numerous policy changes of the first 50 years and expand on the causal link of the government business enterprises being an important economic driver of colonial growth and development. Fitzpatrick by comparison using his first chapter – entitled *Genesis of Australian settlement* to fully explore conditions in Britain as being the catalyst for populating and expanding the penal colony[1]. Abbott and Nairn on the other hand [2] trace the progress of the economy along functional (constituent) lines such as agriculture, pastoral industry, industry, trade and government works. This Abbott & Nairn approach makes for easier reading but their sections lose the time-scale so desirable in considering inter-linking economic events.

The Epitome of the Official History of NSW published in 1883 provides a convenient timescale of important measures and non-economic events can be compared in overall context and time frame.[3]

I referred (in the introduction to this chapter) to the Aboriginal economy of 1788 and need only to add that at first the natives submitted peacefully to the encroachments by the colonist visitors; but on discovering the true state of affairs they became distrustful, shy and treacherous. Their hostility increased as the scarcity of food became greater, owing to the disturbance of the wild animals on which they relied for sustenance.[4] The circumstances of the food shortage was the result of poor planning, optimism on an early arrival of the second fleet and misplaced optimism on the quality of soil around Sydney Cove but most of all a lack of any skills in farming and horticulture. One of the first explorations was in February 1788, led by Lt P.G. King to Norfolk Island where the visitors found ideal conditions for cropping. A new settlement commenced in March 1788 much to the benefit of Phillip and those people remaining in Sydney. An early historian writing in the 1870s reflects on Phillip's power as governor 'He could fine £500, regulate customs and trade, fix prices and wages, remit capital as well as other sentences, bestow grants of land, and create a monopoly of any article of necessity. All the labour of the colony was at his disposal; all the land, all the stores, all the places of honour and profit and virtually all the justice'.[5] This reflects the economic transition during the five Phillips years for he operated the economy much like he ran the administration. The anonymous historian offers a further insight 'under the absolute government described, the settlers were crowded together on a narrow space – a promontory cleared of dense forest. The soil was barren sand; every yard required for cultivation had to be gained by removing enormous trees of a hardness that tried the temper of

---

[1] Fitzpatrick
[2] Abbott and Nairn
[3] Richards Epitome
[4] Epitome p.20
[5] Epitome p.23

the best axes, wielded in skilled hands'. Much can be made of Phillip's sanguine expectations but there is no doubt that he was the right man for the difficult role of defining the future economic conditions for the settlement.

As one sign of Phillip's contribution, at the close of 1792, the quantity of livestock in the colony was 182, land in cultivation 1,703 acres and the population was less than 3,500.

Although the Hunter administration (1795-1800) offered much of the same with little originality, his main claim to fame must be the encouragement of the Bass and Flinders expedition of 1796. The history of the press also dates back to the Hunter days. Phillip had brought out a small printing press and types but had not been able to find a printer. One was at last found and one of Hunter's first official acts was to establish a small printing office, initially for official work but soon for the use of the *Sydney Gazette*, which for the next thirty years was the government organ.

PHILLIP

The most immediate challenge for Phillip, upon his arrival was to construct a temporary settlement and attempt to be in command of his charges to act as an operating unit, over which he had control. The psychological impact of appearing to have matters under management was an important first step, but was to be followed very quickly in ensuring his future survival. The contingencies to a second fleet arriving were to have on hand an internal supply of foodstuffs and provisions. This would be accomplished initially by locating fertile soil capable of growing grains and fruit trees. Such a place was not the Sydney Cove area, so Phillip looked further a field until he found such a location. The longer term strategy required dedicated farming, both public but for stability purposes, private farming. The British Government had instructed Gov Phillip and his successors to emancipate well-behaved prisoners and grant them small blocks of land. The choices had been to create a peasant farming community, with ex-convicts and their families living on small subsistence farms and working only for themselves. To reduce the costs of food production to the settlement, to encourage good behaviour and make them less anxious to return home, the policy of peasant farming was commenced, rather than relying on a penal colony supported by Britain. A selection of ex-military for receiving land grants was also allowed to encourage a more respectable element to stay in the colony. They all lacked capital and agricultural knowledge, but in time they could have become numerous. In 1803, just ten years after Phillip's resignation, emancipist farmers numbered 464 and in 1819 the number was 808, with an average holding of 46 acres (HRA). In time they came to provide the bulk of the community's labour.

Phillip's second most immediate challenge was to provide a basic infrastructure. Already from a tight settlement centred around Sydney Cove, there was private farming at Rose Hill, accessed along the Parramatta River, but numerous outlying activities such as the brick and tile manufactories all required access by cart-track, barracks, housing, store facilities and general buildings for a hospital etc. With so few men available but where so many were needed, the progress of public works and public buildings was very slow. The labour shortage held back the colony's progress and although it struggled successfully against famine, the lack of buildings had a negative impact as well. After Phillip's departure, Governor Hunter needed men for necessary works so urgently that he had no men to spare for public farming. He wanted granaries, storehouses, churches, windmills, prisons, a new hospital, schools, court-house, new barracks and houses for senior civil officials. As originally conceived the Botany Bay settlement was an immediate and economical way for England to dispose of its surplus prison population. Less than two years 'supplies were to be sent with the First Fleet to tide the settlement over until it was able to raise its own food requirements. Governor Phillip was instructed that as soon as possible after his arrival he was to 'proceed to the cultivation of the land, distributing the convicts for that purpose in such manner as may appear to you to be necessary and best calculated for procuring supplies of grain and ground provisions'[6]. Such supplies were to 'be considered as a public stock' to be used for the 'subsistence of the convicts and their families, or the subsistence of the civil and military establishments' with any surplus being reserved as ' a provision for a further number of convicts, which will shortly follow you from hence'.[7]

Construction of a new settlement can be considered as the first step in economic development. Building public services and permanent structures are a suitable use of both natural resources and labour. Processes of economic development can be identified in a number of ways, whilst change can be defined in terms of aggregate economic expansion, i.e. productivity changes, population changes, standards of living, development of trade, market structure and organisation and infrastructure development. The story of the colonial economy commenced with the white-man transfer to a supposedly vacant country, carrying but a few peaceful natives. This was certainly not the case if Phillip had taken time to examine the circumstances he found. The Aborigines were proud possessors of the land and lived within a splendidly organised economic system, transparent and fragile, and the foreign incursion wreaked havoc on that economy, such that the two could not co-exist.

Although the government had made no provision for anything but basic food and clothing requirements for the convicts, fortuitous circumstances arranged for speculative cargoes brought by the ships which arrived during Governor Phillip's administration to be sold readily at inflated prices. In this way the military and civil officers found a readily exploitable opportunity. At this stage (the first half of the 1790s) few if any of these officers planned to remain in the colony and so were an unlikely source of entrepreneurship rather than mere speculators. The officers monopolised the system of foreign exchange made available by the commissariat purchasing system. Some Treasury bills were sent back to England by those wishing to build up savings there but most were used for the purchase of imports for trading. But officer-traders faced a problem from such trading. Profits were made in the form of 'local currency', a medium which could not be remitted to England. The enterprise system being developed within the colony, based on settler's need rather than a free market, was not to receive further consideration or encouragement until an underlying industry of boat building, boat provisioning and repair was established. The thinking behind this move was to determine a staple industry that could

---

[6] HRA
[7] HRNSW

support an export arrangement and bring into the settlement foreign currency. Secretary of State Dundas wrote to Phillip in 1792 whaling 'may eventually become an object of great consequence to the settlement'.[8] Sir Joseph Banks gave his support to sealing. Pressure from the British whaling interests helped whittle down the monopoly position of the East India Company in the 1780s. By 1802, British whalers were allowed to work in local waters as far north as New Guinea. These same concessions were not extended to colonial whalers.

This became a period of transition within the settlement, albeit with many headaches for Phillip. The inflow of convicts with an increasing supplement of free arrivals and the move from public to private capital inflows suggests a tying together of the British and colonial economies. Obviously there was a special link, but the willingness of Britain to allow the colonies a high degree of flexibility in accessing the British Appropriations gave a degree of peculiar independence. Butlin asked about the motivation for the transfer of private capital.[9] Was it for gain from the colonial economy or was it in response to the growing trade situation between the two countries? Were there strings tied to this capital formation? For example, were private capital transfers encouraged by the British Treasury to ensure the colony could take responsibility for supporting the growing number of convict transfers? Butlin also estimates that the NSW economy expanded at about 9% per annum between 1788 and 1830. Questions that arise from this Butlin estimate include: Are such growth rates consistent with stability; Do they give way to inefficiency; Are they feasible with simple patterns of production and easy access to resources?

Back in Britain there was much discussion and debate as to the cost benefits of the colonies, especially at a time when relatively scarce appropriations were needed more for defence of the realm than for pursuing altruistic trade opportunities. One outcome of the 1810 Commission of Inquiry into Transportation was that the transfer rate of convicts to the colony be stepped up. This was to result in two significant periods of acceleration–the first between 1820 and1825 and then between 1830 and1835. After 1831, there was a major reorientation of the labour market, wherein the level of local births increased and the high level of expirees provided a free labour force, and a market-determined mode of labour allocation and use. This same period of increased convict transfers and an enlarged private labour supply coincided with a shift from a predominantly public to a strongly private capital transfer. In all, although Phillip faced an enormous challenge in developing a new settlement with all the physical challenges of having

---

[8] HRA

[9]

sufficient materials and labour to do so, he succeeded and left in 1792, the sound basis for a future colony.

HUNTER

The Secretary of State in 1793 (Duke of Portland) instructed governor-elect Hunter to revert to the former system of public farming and the public use of convicts. But on his arrival, Hunter realised that 'if government were to continue to cultivate land sufficient for the maintenance of its convicts there would be an effectual stop to the exertions of industrious farmers for want of a market for their crops'. Hunter's solution was to privatise farm production, assign convicts to private farming and for the commissariat to buy from the private farm sector. Hunter's purchases provided a ready and ample market for the expanding agricultural sector, but since these purchases created an ample supply of Treasury bills, the income derived from this production was drained from the colony.

Hunter had been a much better and more pro-active administrator before his appointment as governor than afterwards. Three social problems which were not covered by the governor's instructions presented themselves and demanded resolution. Firstly the welfare of a growing number of orphans – children of convicts required much attention, but he failed to find resolution because of the appropriation system and a shortage of funds for general purposes[10]
Secondly the replacement of the Sydney Gaol burnt by its occupants required replacement.[11]
Thirdly the consumption of spirits had grown rapidly and was in need of control, and one such mechanism was to impose a fee for access. Hunter's successor King imposed a more direct charge on imported spirits (1/- per gallon of spirits and 6d per gallon of wine plus wharfage charges). Officially the use of the revenue was for 'the jail and other public works'. Then in September 1800, King announced the purchase of Lt Kent's house in Sydney for the use of orphans[12].

A continuing but orderly flow of new arrivals eased the same burden faced by Hunter from Governor King. King was able to revive public farming and to begin manufacture of hemp, flax and wool, begin coal mining and to keep up the dockyard for repairs and building colonial vessels. He began a granary and school at the Hawkesbury, a goal and brewery at Parramatta, a printing office, wharf, salt works, guard house and Fort Phillip in Sydney and began the church. However a lot remained to be done. King had about 9% of the population in government employment – 181 on government farms, 39 in boat crews, 48 in the dockyard, 40 flax-drawers and wool-weavers, 111 acting as servants to officials and military officers, 96 in sundry work and 45 sick, but only 197 were engaged on public buildings and 97 engaged in miscellaneous

---

[10] HRA 1:2:536
[11] HRA 1:2:355 and 1:2:588
[12] HRA 1:2:525

employment. From 1806 until December 1810, only 917 male convicts arrived and twice as many had completely served their time in the colony, and so Macquarie opined 'male convicts are much wanted to carry on the agriculture of the country'. However, the British government was only concerned with the crime rate at home and the labour requirements of the English dockyards, and not the desires of an obscure colonial government. Between 1810 and 1813, only 1,463 males arrived in NSW or 415 men per annum, only few more than the average 345 men who had arrived during the previous decade. By 1810 only a very small number of persons, either convict or free, had been transferred to Australia. The great inflow of migration took place after 1815 and kept accelerating up to 1840. Macquarie was logistically challenged in handling and managing the surge of transportees in the middle of his administration. Little planning had been undertaken for further receptions and Macquarie was caught without barracks, work plans or victualling plans. Hastily he co-opted Greenway, for town planning assistance and his chief Commissary officer (in charge of government business enterprises) to put into effect a range of creative opportunities within the colony.

Butlin calls it 'intellectual baggage' that accompanied both the convict and the free migrants, because they came with various parts of an understanding of how the British economy and British society operated. This implied a degree of understanding of the most advanced market system and of self-interested behaviour, of the value of private property, of the importance of accumulation and incentive. Butlin is linking a transition towards a market economy with personal values being both a catalyst and a standard. Butlin is also suggesting that Nicholas is incorrect in claiming that most crimes were work related, which if they were would bring another type of worker rights values to the colony rather than the values of a free market economy.[13] It may be that their crimes were industrial revolution related, such as job dislocation, failure to update skills, redundancy and elimination of old industries. What Butlin doesn't comment on is the other benefits that the human capital brought to the colony. They arrived in the colony with basic skills, intuition, and a familiar lifestyle, their physical and monetary capital – all of which was of considerable benefit to the fledgling economy. His human capital was the basis of new industries, general entrepreneurship and a private enterprise drive. On this point Butlin takes issue with Linge, on the topic of entrepreneurs. Linge implies in *Industrial awakening* that entrepreneurs were in short supply but enough to suit the early economy - a skill that needed intuition and motivation rather than schooling and training.[14] Butlin however takes the position that in contrast with the North American pioneer model, there was very restricted scope in

---

[13] Nicholas (ed.)
[14] Linge, G. *Industrial Awakening*

Australia for self-sufficient behaviour. Butlin claims that accessing natural resources and establishing farms required a different set of skills and mode of organisation and was therefore not an encouragement to entrepreneurship. Hainsworth on the other hand suggests that the full story of the colonial entrepreneurs has not yet been told.[15]

One resolution to predicament facing Governor Hunter in helping orphans, rebuilding the goal, and controlling the consumption of spirits was local taxation, illegally imposed but kept in good standing from 1801 to 1819 when an Imperial Act ratified its impost. Until 1810, there were two funds handling these illegal charges (the Orphan Fund and Gaol Fund) – with each fund having separate revenue sources and distinct expenditure objectives much along the lines that the names imply. Although Phillip had considered imposing a cost recovery system to raise revenue as early as 1792, Hunter only initially proposed local imposts in 1796 (again not as revenue but as a charge on access to imports) but not as a duty on goods as such.[16] It was left to Hunter's successor, P.G. King to impose a duty on imports, plus harbour charges and provedore charges for supplying water and provisions to visiting ships.

Hunter determined that the incentive for inducing free workers to labour was wages and due to the shortage of free workers, workers demanded high rates. To bring this under control, he laid down standard rates for piece work and set the first general wage-fixing order in the colony. Hunter created a scale of labour rates, designed to limit the bidding war between employers for labouring, but high wage rates continued under both Hunter and King. Macquarie set another scale in 1816 which was almost exactly the same as King's and he ordered magistrates to settle disputes between Master and servant based on his scale., but free labour was in a stronger bargaining position than the employer and was able to demand and receive wage rates far in excess of authorised rates. In 1798, Hunter was ordered to adopt a system of assigning convicts on a fully maintained basis, even though officers were still allowed two convicts maintained by the government. Initially all convicts had worked for and were fed and clothed by, the government, but then when free settlers arrived, convicts were 'assigned' to them but still maintained by the government. In addition to the prescribed rations and clothing, many masters offered 'incentive' payments of money, plus other indulgences of special foodstuffs such as sugar, tea and tobacco, but with rum being the most popular. S.J. Butlin writes in *Foundations* 'for nearly forty years rum was part of the wages received by a considerable section of the population'.[17] Samuel Marsden had written in 1798, *without rum, the dispirited indolent convict*

---

[15] Hainsworth, D *Sydney Traders*
[16] HRA 1:1:593 & 1:2:437
[17] Butlin, S.J. *Foundations of the Australian Monetary System* 1788-1851 MUP 1953

cannot be excited to exertions.[18] Then in February 1803, Lord Hobart, the Secretary of State, was 'induced to recommend', that 'every convict who shall have conducted himself in a proper manner during the week, shall be given a pint of grog on Sunday'.[19] Thus up to about 1820, spirit consumption in the colony per head was four times as much as in Britain. Convicts were given prescribed hours of work, outside which they were to be paid. It was only by such extra pay that convicts could afford their hired lodgings. Macquarie paid convicts working at the commissariat stone yard, a gallon of rum for every 100 hundred feet of fine stone they cut. The working day traditionally ended at three o'clock. In 1800 King ordered that 'day work is nine hours per day for 5 days and 5 hours on Saturday'. Any additional time was to be paid at 10d per day.[20]

Primarily it was the officers' covetousness which led to their concentration on trade, but at the same time it must be remembered there was a dearth of investment opportunities in the colony. The opportunities outside agriculture, which was dependent on the government market, were negligible. Those with the ability to organise economic activity in the 1790s considered themselves as temporary residents and therefore sought maximum short-run profits. The search for a staple was fundamental to the stability and progress of the settlement. It was essential that foreign exchange be earned, and a balance maintained. Once it was recognised that there was no natural produce available for export, the eyes of NSW commerce turned to maritime ventures. Lack of innovation was supported by mercantile attempts to assemble export cargoes for the colony. Thought was now given to the opening of new trade routes for the exchange of commodities, which required capital skill and knowledge Campbell and Company opened and maintained a sealing industry. Richard Jones promoted a local whaling industry, but it was not to reach its peak before 1821. Initial dependence on the commissariat and government contracts was broken down by the establishment of the colonial fishing industry and soon led to a flourishing and independent free sector. Fisheries gave employment to local labour and encouraged the growth of linked industries such as ship refitting production of salt, barrels and ship provisioning. Commissioner Bigge reported that there were 21 merchants in business in Sydney and 12 mercantile houses, 3 of them controlled by emancipists.

(102)Growth can be recognised from various indicators, for instance GDP and GNE per head of population are the preferred, although other indicators such as labour market growth, trade statistics and government revenue are just as reliable.

---

[18] Yarwood, *Samuel Marsden*
[19] HRA
[20] HRA

KING

The tragedy of the third naval governor was that little innovation was forthcoming, although compare to Hunter King appeared spirited and emboldened in his endeavours. With little positive coming from the Bligh administration, it was left to Macquarie, the first of the military governors to inspire financial and social change and growth. From early in the King administration an important aspect of the economic system was the purchase from local sources of food, grain and produce by the commissariat. Such purchases represented the main agricultural market in the 1790s and until 1800, as well as the main source of foreign exchange which, in the form of Treasury bills, was needed to obtain the imports which formed the material basis of the trading 'monopoly' of the period. So long as the government continued to purchase large amounts of farm produce, this agricultural trading system could continue, with the earnings of agriculture being converted into the foreign exchange required to prosecute the highly profitable trading in imports. When Governor King reduced the government purchases of local farm production it necessitated changes in the internal colonial trading arrangements and encouraged the colonists to assess the need for staple export production.

By 1800 there were more than 600 males 'off the store'. Masters were to feed and clothe their men and pay them £10 per annum in wages as well. After the end of the Napoleonic wars, the number of convicts arriving increased substantially, with about 1000 males arriving each year from 1814 to 1816 of whom 60% were assigned to the private sector. This plus a local drought relieved the labour shortage. The drought caused farmers generally to delay their planting and harvesting, whilst slowing the plans to acquire and clear new land. Then from 1817 to 1820, 9,317 males arrived, an average of 2,524 males per annum. Macquarie was overwhelmed and complained 'the consequence of so large an importation of male convicts was there is no immediate employment for them. I have no alternative but to employ gangs of them on government works in Sydney and on building roads'.[21] He also re-opened the government farm at Emu Plains to absorb a number of previously unplaceable convicts. Government employment in 1819 was 1,840 compared with 346 in 1810 and 500 in 1817.

The Treasury was obsessed with comparing gross expenditures and hard as it seems, overlooked the additional population demands in the colony. However, the paucity of information concerning the levels of Hunter's Treasury bill expenditure was replaced in the King period by an abundance of data. Treasury bills were drawn by the governor locally for purchases from

---

[21] HRA

local residents; for purchases from visiting ships' masters; and for purchases made in India, Batavia, and elsewhere on the authority of the governor. The maximum volume of imports obtainable with Treasury bills was therefore represented by the total of the bills received by local residents for sales to the commissariat, salaries etc, and the bills paid to ships' masters for wheat; these two sources totalled £39,772 for the whole King period , with £34,315 being in favour of residents. In 1798 the import market had for a few months shown signs of glut when the supply of imports arriving had tempor5arily exceeded the means of purchase. During the following years, 1801, 1802 and 1803, the import market continually remained glutted. The *Sydney Gazette* of 18 December 1803 referred to 'the scarcity of money that prevails' and trade 'appears to suffer depression'. Governor King claimed that this glut was distributing 'a great part of the private trade among different dealers'.[22] King had reduced the volume of commissariat purchases within the colony from the high levels they had reached during Hunter's governorship and at the same time had resorted to means other than the drawing of Treasury bills to pay for these purchases. Grain was now the main, if not the only, item of locally produced foodstuff purchased, and King purchased an increasing proportion of the government's requirements by bartering the supplies of merchandise sent from England, or by paying with dollars and other coins.

Commissary Palmer had admitted to the 1812 Select Committee on Transportation that the officers had 'a large proportion' of the supplies and that they retailed them, and 'the supplies were retailed by officers at up to 500 percent profit'. However, the abuse of the supplies arrangement would not have provided the much-needed foreign exchange for the colony, which could have only been obtained in the form of paymaster bills. The officer supply system had only been tolerated by government as a means of breaking the officer's monopoly over foreign purchases.

The colony continued to receive transportees as well as free settlers, but in particular the local birth-rate of both legitimate and illegitimate births was also growing. Shaw explains the basis of population growth in the colony.

> In the first three fleets, there were only officials and convicts with military to guard them. With family females and female convicts, there were plenty of local births, and so with expiring sentences and free births the free population grew, even though the number of free immigrants was negligible. In 1800, NSW had a military and civil population of 469 with only 82 other free men and settlers. Of the remaining 3,414 in the settlement, 60% were supporting themselves. In 1810 Macquarie reported 10,452 people in the colony which included 2,078 officials, soldiers and their families, 1,132 male convicts in government employment and 2,928 other male inhabitants, including settlers, convicts assigned to the private sector, altogether making an adult make workforce of 4,060. Even in 1814, the potential workforce was only about

---

[22] Sydney Gazette

40% of the community. This low participation rate didn't seem to worry Macquarie who kept skinning the best convict arrival off the top for government employment. Convict labour was considered(in evidence to Commissioner Bigge) to be about 1/3rd less efficient than free and on that basis adult male labourers might be regarded as composing only about 30% of the community.[23]

The economy was growing, assisted largely by the growing population and new enterprises were under way. During the administration of Governor King, there were significant changes in the NSW economy, in particular in the appearance and development of export industries. By the end of the King period, all the elements of the private sector of the economy as it was in 1821 had appeared. To the construction activities, were added other labour intensive activities such as arable farming, pastoral farming and basic trade in coal and timber which formed the private sector of the 1790s and to which had been added (by 1806) whaling, sandalwood and trepang. Only further basic new industries appeared after that until 1821 (such as tallow, soap, leather, cloth and blankets) so that any change in the output of the private sector was a change only in its constituent elements. The high levels of commissariat spending during the last three years of the 1790s had attracted many speculative cargoes, the volume arriving in any given year being related to the volume of purchasing power created by the government in the preceding two years. When King reduced commissariat expenditures in 1801, the volume of cargoes attracted previously by Hunter was in excess of the colony's purchasing capacity in that year. W.C. Wentworth traced the origin of this diversification into these three new export industries (sandalwood, trepang and whaling) as a response to cut-backs in King's official expenditure, and his commencement of import replacement manufacturing. This was also the point where the colony became self-supporting in grain production (King achieved this significant event in 1804). This, he claimed, marked the beginning of the colony's independent progress since capital was being withdrawn from agriculture and invested in pastoral farming, manufacturing, retailing, sealing, whaling and sandalwood. Before 1800 imports came mainly in the form of cargoes brought as speculations and were bought on arrival by the officer group; in a few instances the officers chartered a ship and sent bills for the purchase of a cargo overseas. The situation which then developed was to reappear on subsequent occasions in the early history of NSW. Overseas suppliers extended credit to Sydney merchants who in turn extended credit to customers; a system which could only continue as long as the original suppliers did not press for payment. An article in the *Sydney Gazette* of 1 May 1803 reported

'A staple commodity must be raised by the industry of the inhabitants, before a preponderance can be hoped; and manufacturing, however obvious its necessity, does not at present seem inclined to rear its head...A spirit of trading has so universally insinuated itself, that the mechanic, instead of applying himself to the occupation he was reared in, sacrifices his genius to the prevailing impulse of truck and cavil'.[24]

---

[23] Shaw, A.G.L. *Convicts & Colonies*
[24] Sydney Gazette

The plethora of Treasury bills drawn during the Hunter period had fostered the growth of internal trade, but in the light of reduced government expenditure it was apparent that another source of foreign exchange was necessary for its continuance. W.C. Wentworth in his analysis of the economic development of NSW contrasted the first 15 years of the colony's history 'when the necessities of the government were greater than the means of the colonists to administer to them, so the productive powers of this settlement developed themselves with a degree of rapidity', with the subsequent period when for the want of a sufficiently large market for grain 'the colony may be said to have continued stationary, with respect to its agriculture'. Wentworth, following Adam Smith's analysis, considered agriculture as the natural and best basis for the colony's development; and hence he considered the early appearance of manufacturers due to the lack of a sufficient market for grain to be unnatural.[25] The combination of increased costs, decreased returns and diminished control over the commissariat's purchase of grain would have been sufficient to bring about the lessening of the officers' agricultural exertions in 1801 but the huge grain surpluses of 1803-4 quickened the process begun by King's economy measures in 1801, except that King also dropped the buying price of grain per bushel from 10/- to 8/-. Commercial agriculture thereupon became less viable, with the potential of further pressures impacting on the agricultural productive capacity. Pastoral farming as an alternative did not offer any significant immediate market but in terms of avowed government policy to attain self-sufficiency in meat, such grazing potential could offer advantages. The government did not make any purchases of meat during King's administration but obtained its requirements from the government's herds. There was a private marketplace in central Sydney for fresh meat of a limited size between July 1804 and August 1805, which was popular and attracted many individual buyers

John Blaxland's study *Remarks on the state of the colony of NSW* offers some interesting commentary on the Hunter/King period.

> *Hunter granted lands, assisted the cultivator with labourers and bought their corn, by which they acquired capital to rear hogs and sheep as well as to pay for the clothes they wore and for other comforts. Cap't King became governor in 1800 and from his lack of knowledge in the laws and customs of civil society, agriculture and commerce and from his mistaken notions of economy, evils of great magnitude arose which have occasioned large and unnecessary expenses to this country, and distress and poverty in the colony.* [26]

---

[25] Wentworth, W.C.
[26] Blaxland, John

MACQUARIE

Macquarie economic policies

Macquarie arrived in late 1809 to a disturbing scene in the colony. His predecessor had been forcibly removed and was sailing around the Pacific somewhere, the settlement had stagnated during the inter regnum and was run down and rudderless. Macquarie's choices were obvious – to continue the failed policies of Hunter, King and Bligh, and essentially follow his official instructions to the letter or strike out and place his own imprimatur on growth and development. The upsurge in revenues for the Orphan and Goal funds gave Macquarie the reputation of a builder. Before 1810, despite the Gaol Fund, the provision of infrastructure was concealed and disbursed in public convict gangs. It was Macquarie's fiscal leverage(through his command of a growing local Treasury) and a greatly enlarged supply of convicts that allowed him to use both direct public delivery of infrastructure and to use the private market top deliver flexibly the types of infrastructure he chose to emphasise.

One does not push hard for change without stepping on more than a few toes. Macquarie's taxation regime was seen as an endless means of raising revenue, much of which disappeared into projects that free settlers questioned. Just who was this revenue meant to benefit - the free settlers or the convicts? Macquarie thought he was working for the greater good of all, but a few in the colony declined to accept his assurances on that point. They couldn't challenge a principle without having a good cause, thus the cause became the misuse or rather misallocation of public monies, whilst the principle became this illegal taxation. Naturally the taxation being raised was illegal – that was common knowledge, but leave something like this in place for long enough and it becomes accepted, except where a lawyer is involved. A challenge to the fiscal system was made in the colony by Judge Bent and Judge Field. The tax revolt was not only against Macquarie but also against the blinkered approach of the British Government. British officials were well aware of what was happening and the colonial office accommodated the local behaviour without seeking parliamentary approval. After all it was a direct saving to the British taxpayer.

Macquarie faced another mini-crisis, when the business sector of the economy suffered a relapse and slumped into recession for a short period. The commercial slump of 1812-1815, was as much a result of external factors as the scarcity of local money. The domino effect of pressure for payment moved from Britain to India, to Sydney and onto Sydney customers. The flow of capital in the form of credit extended to local merchants was cut off, and the volume of imports fell during this commercial slump from the high levels it had reached immediately before its onset. It was from wool exports that the local market sought salvation. Sheep numbers were expanded, rising from 34,550 in 18140 to 74,825 in 1814, a total not exceeded until 1819. Exports of wool to England, began with 3-4,000 pounds shipped by Marsden in 1812, 35,000 in 1813, 17,000 in 1714 and 35,000 in 1815

The early economy revolved around three courses of adaptation (1) declining public sector and rapid escalation of the private sector (2) acquiring access to natural resource and utilising them for beneficial economic purposes (3) evolution of urban-oriented trades, commercial and services activities. Constraints within the economy at that time included settlement containment; insufficient early use of the sea; reliance on private interest, the search for profit, capital inflow and local capital accumulation. It is estimated that rate of return on capital invested was extremely low, often losses. However, the build-up of these pioneering investments necessarily looked to long-range rather than short-term yields. So long as Britain supplied considerable funding to the colony, a substantial contribution was made to sustaining the standards of living. Hence effective demand for a wide range of goods could be exercised on the expenditure side. Inflows of capital further enhanced this capability

The paradox of promoting long-term economic growth gives rise to the observation by Wentworth in 1820 'the colony has been in a state of retardation for the last 15 years; an assertion not easily reconciled with the increase in population, and in the cultivated lands and in the number of sheep and cattle'.[27] Wheat had trended upwards in total production terms but needs to be weighted by annual increases in yield per acre. Yield initially was estimated at 12.5 bushels per acre in the Parramatta region but had climbed steadily in the Hawkesbury region to 25 bushels according to Bigge. Sheep numbers steadied reflecting an increase in the consumption of sheep meat, and a tendency to breed lighter carcasses. Because of the lack of precise data concerning changes in agricultural and pastoral yields only a broad indication of the rate of growth of real output in the farming sector can be made For the period 18/10 to 1820, indications are that wheat production increased at a rate of 5%whilst meat and wool, rose by about 10%. Before 1808 most of the colony's meat needs were met by imported supplies. This rate of growth in physical output would have been consistent with the observed growth in the capability of the colony to supply its own food requirements. From a dependency on imported grains and meat until the mid-1990s, the King period worked towards and met self-sufficiency in grain by 1802 and meat by 1810

---

[27] Wentworth

The Industrial evolution in Britain had certain impacts on the colonial economy; although not all of the traditional views can be sustained. There were claims by certain early academics that there was a large transfer away from the agricultural sector into the manufacturing sector. Mainly, in practice, the situation was one of much greater production off the land with the same number of workers. Another impact was on the cost of internal transport costs, which came down in cost and opened up more internal markets. Incentives were given to improve roads and develop canals and waterways. The beginnings of railways in Britain, in the 1830s opened up new opportunities in raw materials, iron and steel factories and carriage manufacturing. Mobility of goods and persons increased together with the carriage of greater tonnages of goods throughout an increasingly unified national market. This internal mobility was linked to the development of port facilities and through them the growth of British international commerce, thus the 'commercial' revolution. An overall demographic change took place with the transfer in respect of urban populations between 1801 and 1851 – this jumped from 15,500,000 to 27,371,000 in those 50 years. It was from these towns that most of the convicts and pauper migrants came to the colony, particularly after 1810. Accompanying this urbanisation was an upsurge in commercial and service activity and in urban building. London's population jumped in that period from 2,496,000 to 7,660,000 a tripling of population. Finally, recalls Butlin, the success of the American Revolution helped to break down, for Britain, much of the internal and colonial trappings of centralised mercantilist policies.[28] Then followed the destruction of the Navigation Acts and the change of policies to ensure colonial development served the interests of Britain. There was a breakdown of monopoly companies with the exception of the East India Company. Its presence did inhibit some activity for a time in the colony, though less in reality than in form. Its monopoly was much in question in 1788 and by 1815 its control of trade and shipping in the Indian and Pacific Oceans were largely eroded.

The replacement of the NSW Corps by the 73rd Regiment and the continued influx of convicts and free arrivals helped to update local awareness of evolving British policies and practice.

Butlin considers that four markets were operating in the colony (*Forming*)
1.   The Aborigine market
2.   The land market
3.   Capital markets – money credit and banking
4.   urban business –goods and services

---

[28] Butlin, N.G.

Market behaviour developed on two fronts. One arose in relations between colonial governments and private individuals. The other emerged between individuals within the colony and individuals outside Australia.

Migration during this period came largely from towns, most having experienced the full flood of the restructuring in the Industrial Revolution. The towns of Britain were the locale for specialisation and interchange. What Butlin is now suggesting is that migrants came with sufficient awareness of parts of the market behaviour to make feasible its rapid application, subject to modifications, in the new territory. This so- called 'market' was a mosaic of personal assumptions and understandings, of behavioural patterns, rules and institutions that were not consciously created but grew together, sometimes in harmony, sometimes in conflict

Enterprise

One essential ingredient to expand an economy is entrepreneurial skills and associated new enterprise. Macquarie tried to supply these ingredients by himself, assuming that he remained and would continue to do so, and a 'dictator' and omnipotent governor. However, the weight of evidence suggests that the colonial governments played a positive and active part in encouraging economic enterprise, whether trading, pastoral, agricultural or experimental. It seems justifiable to dispute the validity of statements in the British government's instructions to Commissioner Bigge in January 1819, for even if it could be argued in 1788 that the colony 'had not been established with any view to... commercial advantage, its economic growth up to 1821 had frequently not been regarded by governments as 'secondary consideration' to its function of 'receptacle for offenders'.[29] The range of private enterprises in 1810 was very broad. These enterprises were rarely specialised, often depended on agency or partnership arrangements and frequently carried through the range of buying and selling of local products, imported goods and spanned wholesale, retail and auctioning. After 1810, shipbuilding, milling, textiles, metal products, tanning, glass etc largely transferred from the public to the private sector. Abbott & Nairn quote Wentworth as writing 'over £250,000 had been invested in private Sydney factories by 1820).[30]

There were also a growing range of technical skills on hand –publicans, private teachers, boat builders, butchers, tanners. Entrepreneurial skills were essentially linked to growth in the manufacturing sector – the secondary industry area. To these skills was linked a requirement for

---

[29] Bigge Reports
[30] Wentworth, W.C., *Statistical, historical and political description of NSW*-1820

capital, a market study and worker recruitment. Manufacturing before 1821, except for Simeon Lord in the production of cloth and a few domestic articles, attracted little capital. There were notable exceptions – brewing and flour milling. Perhaps the greatest restraint on manufacturing arose from the way in which capital was raised for colonial enterprises. Few settlers brought actual capital to the colony. Most depended on mercantile credit, which merely encouraged the decision to persist with trade. Once capital had begun to accumulate, its transfer to pastoralism was more attractive since the otherwise heavy investment in land could be avoided through lease or grant or a modified form of squatting. Perhaps it was the difficulty in getting large grants of land that channelled a large proportion of emancipist capital into manufacturing. Though most raw materials were available, manufacturing was restricted to replacing imports by an absence of skills and sometimes of equipment. A transition of manufacturing from the public to the private sector was a further encouragement to investment in and contributing capital to manufacturing. Abbott concludes 'overall it remained more profitable to import goods than to make them'. This conclusion is questionable, although obvious. The cost-benefit rationale would include a decision on timeliness of the need for the item being purchased. Even in 1821, the turnaround time was at least six months-a length of time that was unnecessary if that item could be obtained locally, at any cost. The commissary was in a continual squeeze between the governor and the end user. The governor's regular and routine cost cutting measures included minimising inventory in the commissariat. What generally happened was that the items kept in stock were not always the one s required most urgently and so the commissary's judgement was questioned time and again. Britain obviously benefited from economies of scale in its manufacturing output, but how was a young colony on the threshold of manufacturing to reduce its costs, if it did not support its labour training and throughput for reducing overheads.

Numerous emancipists and ticket-of-leave persons carried out craft activities, both processing and selling their wares as cottage industries-they used special skills in jewellery, watchmaking, file-making, gunsmith, garment-making, and tobacco processing and even in law and education. After 1810, the productive role of the government contracted as the number of persons supported directly by government declined to be replaced by positive public support for private activity and the successful development of private enterprises. Up to 1810 and into the next decade, large landholders tended to combine farming interests with commerce and maritime ventures. After 1815 an increasing separation of investment took place. The pastoral industry was moving further away from the ports and was facing transport problems.

e.   **Economic Growth during the Macquarie Administration**

Governor Macquarie arrived in the colony in December 1809 and commenced his administration on 1st January 1810.

In 1812 a select committee of the House of Commons was appointed to enquire into the colony of NSW. The circumstances related mainly to the disposition of former Governor Bligh and the many complaints received in England regarding the hardships caused by the monopoly of the favoured class".[18] A new Charter of Justice was conferred on the colony as a result of the committee report in 1813[19]. The Governor's Court was a 'modification of the previously existing tribunal'[20]. The Supreme Court was to consist of a judge, appointed by the Governor – the first Judge Jeffrey Hart Bent arrived in July 1814 but following a dispute with Governor Macquarie, Bent was recalled by Earl Bathurst and replaced by Mr. Barron Field, an English Barrister who arrived in 1817.

Macquarie oversaw a period of agricultural expansion and a series of explorations in order to open up new grazing areas in the inland. In 1813, the first crossing of the Blue Mountains took place and the Bathurst Plains were discovered. This search for new, more fertile land was made necessary because of the repeated droughts and the unsuitability of the coastal plains for agriculture or pastoral purposes. The three explorers Wentworth, Blaxland and Lawson "affected a passage across a chain of mountains clothed with dense timber and brushwood, and intersected by a succession of ravines, which presented extraordinary difficulties – not so much from their height as from their precipitous character".[21] Within fifteen months from the discovery, Governor Macquarie ('with characteristic promptitude'[22]) caused a road to be made; sand many new settlers quickly transferred their flocks and herds to the newly discovered country.

In 1817, Captain P.P. King (son of former governor King) sailed from Sydney to survey the east coast to Cape York. In the same year Surveyor-general John Oxley explored the Lachlan River following it for more than 400 miles. During his return he came across an extensive and fine pastoral country, which he named Wellington Plains and he finally reached the Macquarie River.

The following year Oxley traced the Macquarie River and reached the Liverpool Plains and discovered the Hastings and Manning Rivers. In 1818 Hume discovered the pastoral district of the Monaro of which Goulburn is now the centre. In the following year Hume traced the Murrumbidgee River, and the Riverina district.

With these discoveries, the known area of the colony grew by twenty times its former extent, and 'the new sources of wealth, of incalculable amount, were thrown open to the industry and enterprise of its inhabitants'.[23] With the new agricultural lands had to come a new agricultural policy and this came in the form of minimum prices for produce purchased by the Commissariat. But the colony was experiencing a new lease of life as was expressed by a correspondent to the *Morning Chronicle*, printed in September 1825. The nom-de-plume of 'Austral-Asiaticus' supposedly belonged to Lt. G.T.W.B. Boyes, who had been appointed during the Macquarie administration to head up the Commissary accounting and audit systems. The letter was a response to printed criticisms of Macquarie policies, and the incredible deterioration since the resignation of Macquarie and read in part:

'Under Macquarie's judicious administration, commerce and agriculture flourished, because they received from the Executive Government that fostering protection and encouragement which, in turn, in the infant state of the colony, were indispensable for their growth. The farmer received for his corn, the grazier for his cattle, such a fair equitable price from the Commissariat, for the large purchases made on account of government (namely 10/- per bushel for wheat and seven-pence per pound for beef) as enabled them respectively to support a state of decent mediocrity, suitable to their sphere of life and encouraged increasing industry and perseverance in their pursuits. The merchant was not embarrassed in his commercial speculations by the difficulty of making his remittances, but could, at all times obtain Treasury Bills for that purpose without paying, as at present, a premium of from £15 to £20 per centum for the accommodation. Under the change of system, introduced on the accession of the present governor, an entire and distressing alteration of affairs took place...'[24]

However successful Macquarie was with his encouragement of exploration and his agricultural policy, the most remarkable feature of Governor Macquarie's administration was the number of public buildings erected, the total reaching 250. His roads policy almost must also be noted for the benefits it produced.

Commissioner Bigge had been directed by Earl Bathurst to 'examine all the laws, regulations and usages of the territory and its dependencies, and into every other matter or thing in any way connected to the administration of the civil government, the state of the judicial, civil, and ecclesiastical establishments, revenue, trade and resources'.[25]

Macquarie did little to defend his administration other than writing an extremely long letter to Bathurst which commenced" I found the colony barely emerging from infantile imbecility and suffering from various privations and disabilities; the country was impenetrable beyond 40 miles from Sydney; agriculture was in a languishing state; commerce in its early dawn; revenue unknown; threatened with famine; distracted by faction; the public buildings in a state of dilapidation and mouldering to decay; the population in general depressed by poverty; no public credit nor private confidence; the morals of the great mass of the population in the lowest state of debasement and the religious worship almost totally neglected – Such was the state of the colony when I took charge in 1810. When I left the colony it had reaped incalculable advantage from my extensive and important discoveries. In all directions, including the supposed insurmountable barrier called the Blue Mountains to the westward of which are situated the fertile plains of Bathurst; and in all respects enjoying a state of private comfort and public prosperity"[26]

Exports slowed in 1820 due to:

1 A large array of allocative demands were pressed on the colonists

2. The East India Company's monopoly limited trading in the Pacific until 1819.

3. The rapid influx of convicts after 1812 added many more mouths to be fed rather than human capital to generate exports.,

A consequence of large meat purchases by the commissariat was they encouraged livestock activity and supplied large landholders with access to commissariat resources either through barter or access to foreign exchange. The scale of these purchases kept natural increase in check, limiting the expansion of livestock populations, particularly of sheep. This loss would have impact on the production of wool for export and the breeding of fine woolled sheep

(182) To measure the flow of new investment into the colony, we need to combine estimates of balance of payments with direct British outlays from two sources – one is the direct British subvention to the colony in the early years- this continued into the 1820s when some, but very little private capital inflow occurred. It was during the mid-1820s when Britain began to reduce its fiscal commitment to the colonies, whilst seeking alternatives such as to colonial revenues to support the colony and the private employment of convicts as a means of budgetary constraint by

the British Treasury. Colonial export capability built up rapidly during the 1820s with both balance of payments and real capital dependence relative to GDP shrinking. The place of Government appropriations was taken by private capital inflow which approximated official support to the colony. External capit6al appears as a primary driver of colonial expansion during the 1810-1840 periods. Total capital inflow rose faster than local domestic activity until the early 1820s but declined from the late 1820s.

(183) External capital, firstly public and then jointly public and private, appears as a major contribution of the ability of the colonies to sustain a high level of activity in the process of forming the early substitute for the original Aboriginal economy.

NSW, in addition to the major investment by the AAC in 1824, attracted a significant inflow of free immigrants with capital and also absentee investors during the 1820s. Land grants continued, especially along the Hawkesbury and Hunter Rivers in NSW. One of the conditions of pastoral development in NSW was the dependence on imports of crops, particularly grain crops. The linkage between agriculture and pastoral activity went through three phases

1. During the 1810s the settlement was constrained in the vicinity of the local bridgeheads, the two industries were divided by the size of landholding.

2. During the 1820s agricultural and pastoral activity was widely conjoined particularly in the expanding riverine valleys, each providing income flows to given producers and large landholders.

3. During the 1830s, coastal and mountain agriculture supported the specialisation of pastoral producers in the interior

As reflected by Fletcher, during the 1820s, meat sales surpassed incomes from wool. NSW was unlikely to have been self-sufficient in meat until at least 1835.

The maritime industries were the first colonial staple and became a major source of export income up to the 1830s. The Blue Books for 1827 show that whaling products for that year exceeded pastoral exports. There is little information on the whaling industry before 1820.Shipbuilding in the colony was a catalyst for maritime activities. Capital was always a limiting factor – in sealing, shipbuilding and export trade, also until 1819, the East India Company monopoly restrained colonial deployment of ships of any substance for whaling purposes Into the 1830s whaling establishments were dotted along the NSW coast south of Sydney and whaling 'factories' were established as boiling down plants.

As late as 1832 maritime exports exceeded pastoral exports but the trend reverses and the gap widened until in 1845 wool exports reached over One million pound sterling and fisheries were still under One hundred thousand pound, and by 1850, wool was nearly 100 times as large as fisheries.(which had slipped to under £30,000.

The colonial economy, because of the introduction of attitudes, mores, institutions, market practices and rights that existed in Britain, benefited from this transference of knowledge and values such that the colony was in fact British-driven. The scale of the market was all different. It was a pioneering process, carving (after transplanting) out an economy from the wilderness.

Migration

Butlin suggests that British retention of rights to crown lands in the colony and an early adoption of a system of land grants, did not supply the circumstances for specialised, flexible conditions for allocation. Next, British restrictions on particular activities such as shipping and trade again seem to present strong constraints on freedom of behaviour. Learning by doing was another limiting factor, by most of these were overcome by 1840. The conventional dividing year between the directed and free market economies is 1821, but 1810 is more relevant because of these other influences.

Sundry Economic Policies

Macquarie's building program seems to have been necessary for both skilled and unskilled labourers. The government was in 1820 employing 3300 out of 8900 male convicts in NSW, whilst the remaining 5600 were assigned, but the greatest demand was still for farming men. It was these that the government could not supply – it only had about ¼ of the number request6ed. In addition to the 9000 convicts there were a further 5000 male emancipists and about 1300 who had arrived free or who were born free in the colony. Thus in 1820, the participation rate had grown from 40% to over 60%, adjusted to about 45% if adjustment for productivity is included and this is compared to only 30% in 1814 and 40% in contemporary England.

(116) 'Assignment' appealed to the civil servants of Whitehall, who considered the inducements of special rations for good behaviour and 'tickets'. Macarthur told Bigge, 'being involved in rural work, there is much time for convicts to reflect and self-examine themselves'. On the other hand, in government work, threat of punishment was greater, though the skilled man was often put on piece work. Bigge recorded 'a convict servant costs his employer between £20 and £25 a year for rations, supplies and wages; the unskilled free labourer costs £40 per annum and he was often paid more. Bigge concluded that 'if the convicts were only 2/3rds as efficient as a free man he was worth having and when wages of free men were higher than those quoted by Bigge, the convict could be even less efficient and still be an economical servant.

In the 1806 muster, the number of convicts was at Aborigine 40% of the adult population, slightly less than half. Between 1806 and 1810 this proportion fell substantially because of expiry of sentences and low rates of new convict arrivals. From 1813

, convict arrivals rose rapidly to half and in spite of increasing free migrant arrivals remained at this level to the 1830s.

Why did a public market in convicts not develop in Australia as it had done in the U.S.? This appears due to changed British attitudes to the use of human beings. Within the colony itself, a very limited and partial public market had developed in 'What a way to run an Empire, fiscally'. (123) Private assignment was strongly established by 1810, at zero access cost to recipients. However, the accelerated influx from 1813 soon taxed the capacity of both the private and public sectors to absorb the flow. In the absence of a market for convicts, colonial officials were faced with decisions to distribute convicts between public and private sectors and between individuals, locations and industries and, they assumed the task of attempting to determine conditions of convict employment and terms of their release into free Aborigine. The allocation of convicts to the public sector for goods and services such as roads, wharves, bridges, buildings, exploration remained at 15 and 20 percent throughout 1810-40. Pressure for public road construction increased substantially as settlement spread into the hinterland during the 1820s and 1830s. Two British policy changes aggravated the tight Aborigine market. Firstly the British government direction to give priority to the private sector in allocating convict services; secondly, was the decision (after 1828) to withdraw convicts from clerical oppositions in the colonial public service. As a consequence, there was a tendency to substitute public roads with private toll roads during the 1830s.

(124) After 1810, there was a preference for allocation of convicts in the private sector to a 'master' capable of supervising and using larger groups of convicts, as well as to persons of wealth, whilst the majority of assignees tended to be within fairly closely settled areas so that the assignment procedures tended to favour the areas that progressively emerged as urban centres. Thus, as expansion into the country areas occurred, was less readily available to sustain the expansion of natural resource exploitation. There was a widespread practice (until the 1840s) of convicts working for pay beyond their official hours of work. This practice further reduced direct supervision and meant 'accommodation' between individual employers and convict mobility.

1. Persons functioned as merchants landlords, farmers, and convicts employees functioned as semi-skilled workers in unrelated areas to the convict prime employment

2. The Sydney area still contained a substantial amount of farming

3. The Sydney area was only dominant in occupations such as commerce, food, drink and tobacco (820% of NSW total)

4. Sydney was also strongly represented in specialised industrial;/craft activities, including metalworking, leather and textiles, and goldsmith, bookbinder, glassmaker, jeweller, saltboiler, silversmith, soapmaker and watchmaker

5. The muster failed to show a significant proportion of administrative/professional occupations – reflecting a bias of omissions from the muster

6. Sydney's role as a prime colonial port was recognised, including the importance of communication by waterways eg Sydney-Hawkesbury

7. Distribution activities remained strong with Sydney remaining the dominant commercial centre in NSW, with this dominance remaining essentially private

8. Sydney in 1828 was a major centre for clothing, textiles, timber products, production of metal goods, building products and leather working Butlin uses the term 'staples' to include the important natural resource exploitation in import substitution.

9. By 1828, 'personal service' was prominent and reflected the less skilled domestic servants including boarding housekeepers

The Land Market

(127)In contrast with convicts, land was abundant relative to employment opportunities. The abundance of land implied low prices in transfer from the government. Problems arose. The challenge for government was to try and recapture control and determine the validity of transfers made by the military after the overthrow of Bligh. There became an issue of at what rate transfers could be achieved and the appropriate speed of extending the boundaries of settlement. There came a tendency for a large proportion of the economic activity of the various settlements to concentrate in towns impacted on organisation of the urban land market.

Means of Exchange

(132)As at 1810, the settlement operated through barter and a miscellany of commissariat store notes, personal notes and a mixture of currencies, Spanish, Indian and British. Within this miscellany, sterling was employed as a unit of account despite its limited availability as a medium of exchange. Other credit instruments existed before (and after) 1810. Private transactions expanded side by side with the commissariat, but by 1830 the commissariat role was dwindling rapidly

(134) Banking institutions spread through all colonies in the 1820s., partly as colonially formed banks, partly as London-based and British chartered banks. By 1830 the basic conditions of operating a money economy were established. Barter activity still persisted on the fringes of

settlement until 1840 but basically the economy functioned as fully established monetised systems.

Structural Adjustment after 1810.

There is the division between public and private activity. The formative process had been substantially completed by 1840- there were still many developments to follow but the broad patterns based on natural resource conditions and isolation had been laid down by 1840. All this had been achieved over 3 decades at break-neck speed, and ended in a major depression. Butlin concludes that convictism was not the sole inducement to strong early government. Further consideration needs to be made of A. the movement toward urbanisation and B. the conditions of development of external economic activity versus domestic activity and C. the continuation of import replacement activity. The role of export staples was an important one as being part of the export-led growth as the basis for early economic development.

Underlying estimates of G.D P.

A.   Natural Resource and **public** sector activity

B.   Urban (part of the **private** sector) manufacturing, commerce, services and rent

C.   Agriculture including **pastoral** Industry

D.   Maritime and **non-pastoral** activities

The public sector expanded rapidly during the period 1810 to 1820. As a public sector, responsibilities included

- Inter-acting with the private sector interests, and
- The British government

Other functions included

- Reception of convicts, their housing and allocation
- Commissariat functions of provisions, supplies and finance arrangements
- Harbour administration and control
- Government business enterprises – manufacturing and farming
- Public works and construction, local development of building materials supply and infrastructure
- Provision of social provisions
- Planning development for urban communities
- Administration of land disposal, recording and titling
- Licensing of businesses and professions.
- regulation of prices, wages and working conditions
- Currency management and banking
- Exploration and surveying
- Welfare and medical services
- Provision for education and religion

- Aboriginal policy
- Law and order
- Defence

The question must be raised of the 'size' of the public service, limiting the number of public servants, using convicts in the public service, supporting the public administration – British or local revenues?

As mentioned, one role of the public sector was to liaise with the private sector, but for much of the 1810s, the private sector was constrained by government. But private interests progressively moved outside government control during the 1820s and 1830s. On the other hand, **increasing private intervention in the government process checked government growth and authority** A lot of these public functions took place early in the life of the settlement and were one off tasks. E.g. Hospitals, churches or public support for schools and churches. Butlin points out those increasing public outlays were often in the nature of transfer payments rather than increasing public output. Possibly the most important change in the areas of public action was the role of government in access to land as private expansion occurred. Beginning with land grants and urban leases, government was deeply involved in land transfers

Development of Infrastructure

(146) The earliest emphasis was on roads, wharves, military barracks, followed after 1810-1820 by laying out of towns(town planning),, provision of schools, hospitals, churches, gaols(strictly convict barracks), and construction of roads to link smaller hamlet settlements and, as a special project to push a road from the NSW Coast into the newly discovered interior. The Bigge reports referred to the broader issues such as further large-scale public infrastructure, but also led to the change in British government policy toward encouragement of public enterprise, the larger extension of the colonial settlements and the increased private assignment of convicts. However before Bigge's arrival there was an internal push towards these ends, and Bigge became the vehicle for change. Macquarie was torn between change and order and control

The commissariat activities created a joint private and public development, both before 1810 and for some years after. Public farming did not fill all of the grain or food needs for the colony and the government store bought grain from private farmers for a fixed price. As the local roads system grew and replaced water transport, a major organisation change developed with the commissariat inviting tenders for specified goods to be privately delivered into and from the store. A small step towards privatisation

(152) Butlin poses two important questions. What prompted the colony (as compared to Canada and the United States) to become quite strongly urbanised at an early stage and to persist with that urban concentration? Why did a complex of manufacturing and commercial and service activities group together in the colonies? From the beginning of settlement, the dominantly urban backgrounds of the mass of new arrivals created some predisposition in favour of concentration. This was a form of urbanisation. Butlin analyses the census of 1828 which shows that Sydney population grew rapidly but also that decentralisation was taking place with a growing number of small centres dispersed over areas of expanding settlement

Sydney Population and % of total

Year	Population	% of total
1820	7821	40.00
1828	10815	29.55
1833	16232	26.67
1836	19729	25.59
1841	29973	22.91

These years also witnessed the growth of Parramatta, Liverpool, Windsor, Newcastle, Maitland and the Hunter Valley, Goulburn Bathurst and Port Phillip.

Physical attributes supported the move to urbanisation, such as local arable land, water supply, ports and the role of Sydney as the centre of governance. Aboriginal risks around Sydney diminished with time, and free or freed persons appeared to show a strong preference for urban locations.

The Pre-1820 economy

(161)There was a strong public representation among the totality of commercial, manufacturing and professional activities. The commissariat was the largest storage agent and buyer and seller of imported and local products. The colonial government conducted the largest manufacturing enterprises especially in timber, grain milling, textiles, production of building materials, (bricks, tiles, lime and timber) and salt-making. The government also operated boat and shipping services for goods and passengers, in addition to professional services

There were many omissions and errors in recording and reporting exports before 1821, and it is implausible that colonial exports before this time attained more than 2 to 3 percent of GDP. For the same period, the annual purchases by the commissariat were twice the export earnings for 1810-11 and three times for 1821 for meat alone. During the 1810-21 period Fletcher reports that the NSW Commissariat purchased 10 million pounds weight of meat, plus 350,000 bushels of wheat and 125,000 bushels of maize for public distribution (Fletcher, B.H *Landed Enterprise and penal society – A history of farming and grazing in NSW before 1821(SUP)* Fletcher also claims that farming production had not kept pace with public pressures or population growth. NSW wheat acreage in 1812 was just less than 10,000 acres but by 1821 had risen to just over 17,000 acres – wheat production was much more successful in VDL between those same dates. (1500 acres to 13,000 acres-making export of wheat available from that colony

[Fletcher does not reveal what type of meat was imported or the country of origin]

Post-Macquarie Economic Performance

(198) As an immigrant society, whether coerced or free, were colonists benefited or otherwise by the long-distance transfer to Australia As immigrants, the colonists were 'an invading army'. As part of economic growth, land was absorbed into colonial productive activity, so was British colonisation positive, negative or zero sum experience for all those colonists transferred The Aborigines were the losers. Aggregate Aborigine output declined, Aborigine productivity fell along with Aborigine living standards

One question to be asked is: What implications were there for the structure of the British economy and its growth performance arising from the accession of Australian natural resource products? The colonists had two important bases for development – natural resources and immigrant human capital

(220) Colonial output per head rose rapidly to 1810, thereafter declining to 1840

Instability and Economic Fluctuations

The major depression of the 1840s rivals that of the 1890s and the 1930s.

There was the commercial crisis of 1810-1813, and the recession of 1826deepening in 1826-1827. These downturns reflect the problems associated with rapid aggregate and geographic expansion that contributed so strongly to the depression of the 1840s. This depression was attributed to domestic conditions but was largely dependent on the severity of the downturn in Britain

(225) The Australian economies expanded rapidly in the 1830, with the pace further reflecting the British and domestic interest in the pastoral industry.

As Fitzpatrick points out (*British Empire in Australia* p.33) the economy moved forward at a pace not to be repeated until the gold rush of the 1850s. It was a boom fuelled by wool with wool cheques 4 times as great in 1834 as in 1831 and in 1840, 7 times as great.

Another contributing factor was the British Government's policy of the sale of Crown land to stimulate migration and along with the importance of the wool industry as supplier to British manufacturers, came the extensive imports of development capital (Fitzpatrick)

A decade of depression then ensued with rapid economic expansion r5eturning after the discovery of gold

Both Fitzpatrick and S.J. Butlin reflect on the causes and contributions to the 1840s depression. Fitzpatrick offers 5 causes:

1. Fall of English wholesale prices
2. gradual fall of NSW export wool prices
3. the economic crisis in Britain in mid-1839
4. the severe drought in NSW from 1838
5. the withdrawal of funds by the colonial government to meet the costs of immigration

Butlin *Foundations* claims

1. that the primacy of external factors is questionable – evidence of wool exports showed a modest drop in prices between 1840 and 1842 but otherwise, every sign of a strong industry
2. the key issue was the emerging evidence of bad returns in the colonies as the great expansion of the 1830s had taken up all the best opportunities and increasingly what had remained 'appeared to offer poorer yields and higher costs, especially for transport'. (Butlin p. 317)
3. The great drop in capital transfer was occurring in 1842, with 1840 as the great peak (p 318)

N.G. Butlin's death interrupted the more detailed analysis of the Colonial business cycles of the 1830s and 1840s and compares it with those of Britain for the same period. These events also reshaped immigration from Britain and the public finance of the colony

Summary of Chapter 5

(59) By 1821, NSW was a diversified economy, encouraged by the government. It was also not the case, claims Joyce, that economic expansion to this time was the result of defiance of government regulations by private enterprise, or the challenge to the monopoly by the East India Company. Nor is it the case that the penal function slowed or restricted economic development. Before 1821, the role of the gov was usually positive. On occasions it restricted or opposed certain types of enterprise on the grounds it was in conflict with gov and private enterprise. The fundamental challenge facing early governors was to feed and clothe not only the convicts but also the military and many of the free settlers. Even during the Macquarie years, government despatches describe food shortages in much the same terms as earlier governors did. Ensuring a sufficiency of food against the perils of floods, drought and the excess transfer of prisoners was the immediate and immense problem the governors faced. Thus they remained concerned mostly with the short-term rather than the 'distant scene'. Whilst the governors faced the task of feeding the colony, private enterprise turned its focus on other not so necessary consumables. There became a close proximity between government and private enterprise

(64) One problem faced by the British Board of Trade in protecting the interests of the East India Company was that many boats owned partially by Campbell, Macarthur and Simeon Lord were also partially owned by British residents and registered in England. The question asked by Lord Auckland, the president of the Board of Trade of Prime Minister Grenville was: Is NSW a colony and don't its inhabitants have a right to trade. Grenville decided that British interests could not be used as an excuse to prevent the development of the colony and he sought a solution which preserved the interests of the company. However the privileges of the company were not ended by legislation until 1814, except for trade with China and trade in tea. The general colonial response was 'official policy still preferred to maintain existing British interests rather than to encourage colonial trade and commerce', but in fact colonials had gained much by these negotiations. Only on one staple could the colonial governor and the British government both completely support rival economic interests – the exception was wool. Since 1788 sheep had been underpinned for meat production, and Secretary Dundas stressed that the increase in livestock, chiefly sheep and cattle must be a primary objective. A Governor King enquiry in 1805 into the types of sheep owned in the colony concluded that income from meat production was the main goal of most owners. Each governor had to stress the need for agricultural expansion for subsistence, and no governor opposed pastoral expansion, nor can any governor be blamed for other defects in the industry such as inefficient shepherds. Hunter was aware of these

and other problems whilst Bligh gave priority to agriculture and supported grain production for food and recognised the shortage of labour. He also gave priority to sheep production for meat rather than for wool. Although agreeing that the wool trade would eventually improve.

(119) Enterprise does not lend itself statistical analysis only reinforces the tendency to 'discount the economic significance of anything that cannot be numerically expressed'. Enterprise is the catalyst that converts inert land, labour and capital into functioning factors of production. The entrepreneur is the agent of change, who with initiative and persistence exploits resources in new ways, thereby increasing efficiency. Economic development depends on the existence of the entrepreneur as much as on the availability of sufficient capital, land or labour. Because of his pioneer activities the colonial entrepreneur holds the key to the growth of a colonial economy, and it can be expected that the nature of that economy, will reflect the character and experience of the men who first accepted economic risk. There had to be the ambition to investigate and exploit the resources of the new world. Another characteristic of colonial enterprise was the spirit of economic speculation which found its strongest manifestation in trade. The glamour and consequence of the successful merchant provided a target for all men of ambition. The most alluring test was the speculator were the new settlements outside Europe.

Before the colonial hinterland had been settled fifty miles from the coast, commercial frontiers of trade had been reached with the Pacific Island, India, China and South America. Free men came to the colony to engage in trade, and convicts stood by awaiting an opening. The four classes of colonial society by 1819 were:

1. Civil and military officers and private gentlemen in mercantile pursuit
2. Transferees from England of credible habits who came free to trade
3. many persons who are householders and traders
4. free labourers and prisoners

Since specialisation was not yet economically feasible, the term merchant described a function rather than an occupation. Merchanting was a risk, but it was wiser to spread them than for one man to risk everything. Variety provided the means of dabbling in a number of small commissions. Many merchants and treaders kept a farm on which to raise grain and livestock. These piecemeal activities raised many a fine entrepreneur- those people who from the successful commercial activities amassed the capital that was later invested in the development of sealing, whaling, grazing or manufacturing. The first to indulge were the military officers of the NSW Corps but it began modestly earning the odium of *The Rum Corps*.

The masters of ships visiting the near-starving settlement found an eager demand for their goods. Minimum retail profits of 100% were the norm but up to 500% was anticipated. Practically no degree of business acumen except at a most primitive level was necessary to make a profit in such a monopolistic situation. The trade of the military and civil officers remained unenterprising, based mainly on the permanent demand for spirits.

(122)Even in retailing the officers cut their risk to a minimum. They sold to convict 'dealers' who undertook to sell the goods and guaranteed to pay for them. W.C. Wentworth writes of the process 'A subordinate class of trader started up and acted as intermediary agents between the importers and the consumers. The object of this class is not to realise large fortunes in money but to acquire landed possessions by selling to settlers using mortgaged securities, which were foreclosed promptly with the result that many dealers became proprietors of the finest estates in the colony. Circumstances provided their own opportunities. Because for the first ten years most in the colony were on government rations officers because of their access to foreign exchange, exploited the any market opportunity to come along. When officers turned from trade and speculation, to agriculture and farming, they also minimised their risk and outlay. The government provided grants of land, free convict labour and a guaranteed market by the commissariat store.

Few early 'merchant traders' other than Macarthur, Blaxcell, Chisholm and Kemp and Darcy Wentworth survived as commercial men of stature. Macarthur was the only one amongst those few to show any initiative. As paymaster of the regiment between 1792 and 1799 he invested in trading ventures more heavily than his fellow officers. He then turned to farming and wool growing but maintained interests in 6 maritime vessels employed in coastal and sealing trades, importing Pacific pork and sandalwood trade and large speculations to China. He had shared ownership in British whalers working the southern seas and imported a number of mixed cargoes into the colony. Then commercial speculation proved beyond his capital or skill and he returned to enterprise in developing fine wool. By 1800 a new breed of commercial men appeared in Sydney, and for political reasons the Americans were not allowed to settle. So agents for British, Madras and Calcutta merchants set up shop – Robert Campbell, William Campbell, James Birnie and William Trough received official sanction.

Though many immigrant merchants operated initially on the basis of government contracts, they had no intention of depending on the commissariat for ever. The military and civil officers, though they dominated the colonial source of capital had been restricted in turn by the limits of commissariat expenditure. They were able to risk larger investment through their access to external sources of capital, and in order to ensure continuity in their transactions and extension of their market they had to find some means of augmenting the limited supply of exchange available through government expenditure

(126) Most middle-class settlers, who came to the colony with s small store of capital, hoped to command considerable credit. It was not unusual or hard for an intending settler to invest his capital entirely in goods that accompanied him to the colony from which he hoped to realise a sufficient profit. One striking aspect of business activity in NSW was the comparative absence of suitable cadets to recruit and train, as well as a restricted range of persons with enough capital to make them attractive candidates for partnerships. In the 18th century partnership, where a member of a firm could act both for the firm and for himself, and when no limited liability was recognised, the recruitment of partners or agents was of supreme importance. Some convicts, such as Robert Cooper and Daniel Cooper arrived with capital, but most successful emancipists, such as Simeon Lord, Solomon Levy, William Hutchinson, Henry Kable, James Underwood and Samuel Terry accumulated their working capital in the colony. Theirs was a slow and patient progress where incredible shrewdness combined with some barefaced practices to give them the room they needed for financial manoeuvre. Often they were dealers for officers and accrued enough capital to purchase their own wholesale supplies directly

Once merchants got a foothold in NSW, ironically through government contracts and sales, their establishment automatically changed the nature of the colony. Merchants who prospered in the colony were considered a necessary evil by administrators, but their ships supplying both government and settler introduced another administrative aspect6 to what had previously been an ordered prison farm. Independent commercial activity not only prompted colonial exports and therefore a colonial income but it allowed the administration to reduce its expenses and redeploy its resources by enabling it to caste off its previous responsibility for supplies

(139) David Munro, a visitor to NSW made these comments in 1842, during a period of great depression in the colony; a condition he also attributed to 'gross over-estimate of its resources and prospects'. Whether he is correct or not in his interpretation is not important, the perception of the role of government is important. This opinion is in contrast to E.G. Wakefield's opinion in *Letter from Sydney* in 14829 that the colony's progress had 'arisen from the happy influence of penal immigration and discipline, on production, distribution and consumption. Also Commissioner Bigge and W.C. Wentworth had both acknowledged the benefits which had arisen from British government expenditure on the colony but both expressed reservations.

The Munro letter read in part as follows *The settlers of NSW found a certain and splendid market for their produce, they had abundance of labour for nothing and that labour was maintained at government expense for two years and the settlers then given cows:, pigs and other useful farm animals to form the nucleus of their herds. In short there was a great expenditure of government money; a great abundance of labour; free land grants; the farmer was started and supported at first at public expense and afterwards supported in an indirect manner by the government purchasing all the wheat he could raise... If anything could make a colony go ahead, this ought to certainly do so.*

(140) As concerned as Bigge was to increase the capacity of the colony to absorb convicts without incurring a proportionate increase in government expenditure, only the successful development of an export industry would enable the private sector to employ and maintain greater numbers of convicts and thereby save the government some expense. He reasoned that the private sector's demand for its convict labour was directly proportional to the demand for its product; that there existed only a local demand, limited by the size of its population, for its grain and meat; but the demand for an export commodity would not be limited by the size of the colony's population.

To Bigge the colonists' failure to fully respond to export opportunities was more pertinent; its explanation lying in the nature of the economy. The colony's penal nature had led to the unusual degree of government involvement, so tartly described by David Munro as constituting 'a process of hot-bed forcing' but this was not without disadvantages for the promotion of long-term growth; not so much in the administrative restrictions it involved as in the market advantages it created

(143) Whilst the colonists' readiness to concentrate on production for the government market imposed limits on the long-run potential growth of the colony, at the same time this government market formed the nucleus of the colonial economy. The economic changes which occurred before 1821 can be associated with changes in the government market by regarding it as a quasi-export market and examining the consequences using 'linkage effects', that is, the inducements the production for this market created for investment in (a) the home production of its inputs, (b) home production using its output and (c) domestic industries producing consumer goods.

(1) English wholesale prices fell from 1818 to 1833, and then rose to 1839; the largest source of national income was from the cotton industry –especially manufacture. The value of cotton goods exported was about half of total exports during the 1830s. Almost half of the exports went to Europe (44%) with 17 % going to the US of A. The British colonies of NSW and VDL made up only about $1/60^{th}$ (1.5%) of British exports. Cotton manufacturing was the only fully mechanised industry before the mid-1830s. It took a further twenty years before the power loom was in general use for the woollen industry In 1831 more than 28% of workers were still employed in the agriculture industry, with less than 14% employed in the building trades.

(2) Fitzpatrick writes 'the new empire in Australia, not much developed by British private capital investment, was insignificant to the purposes of British economy, though that was to change within a few years

(3) The British banking industry was undergoing radical change in the 1820s, 30s and 40s. In 1826, there had been 554 private banks registered, but in that year joint stock banks previously operated only in Scotland, were allowed in Britain, resulting in over 100 private banks merging into joint stock undertakings in 1826-1836.

(31)   It is *wool* finance which, from 1817 when the first colonial bank was opened and the first auction of colonial wool in London, influences Australian history. In 1821 the first wool was exported from the colony and an imperial government policy released which encouraged a steady if not considerable flow of private capital from Britain to Australia. The Forbes Act of 1834 cleared the way for English banking capital to be used within the colony; this was followed by a sharp rise in the price of colonial wool in London. By 1834, immigration rose 3 times from a base of 1817 whilst wool exports were 4 times over the same period. By 1845, Australia was to become the chief foreign supplier of the British Woollen industry. It took British capital in the 1830s to change much of the colonial exports to fine wool (from course wool), with the result a pastoral industry was established which began answering the question: What is the best economical or social use of the land in the Australian colonies? Before the new colonial constitutions of 1855-1856, rights over the colonial lands were exercised exclusively by the imperial government. This authority did little to determine the optimum or best use of the land, other than Macarthur's liaison with the colonial office, and the many thousands of convicts who were assigned by Macquarie (1809-1821) to the agricultural sector.

(32)   After Macquarie (and into the 1820s) imperial policy changed again – England was looking overcrowded and there were more criminals than ever – men with capital and families were encouraged to emigrate, employ convicts and receive large grants of land. The sale of crown land was authorised for the first time in 1824 and over the next four years, Governor Brisbane, granted and sold more land than had been alienated over the previous 34 years. By 1828, when grants to convicts ceased, 6 times as much land had been alienated as was the case in 1820. The era of peasant farmers was over. Proceeds from the sale of crown lands were to be used to finance the emigration of unemployed English workers.

(33)   In 1831, the colonial office finally laid away its old notion of NSW as a settlement for prisoners and ex-prisoners, substituting the conception of a colony in which land would be alienated by auction, instead of grant or tender, and the proceeds used to finance the emigration of unemployed workers from England. In over 8 1/.2 years to the end of 1840, 30,000

immigrants were brought to the colony, 2 out of 3 having their passage guaranteed by the emigration fund. This high level of growth created a boom, unequalled until the discovery of gold a dozen years later. Wool, on which the boom was based, seemed capable of supporting the boom. By 1840 revenue was very high. The wool cheque in 1834 was 4 times the figure of 1831, and in 1840 more than 7 times as great. The revenue from Crown land sales was 25 times in 1840 as great as 1832 the first year of the auction system.

(34)   The Forbes Act was 'an act for removing doubts respecting the application to NSW of the laws and statutes of England relating to usury and to limit and define the rate of interest, when not previously agreed to by the parties. Interest rates were limited to 8% p.a. Banks were starting to compete in the colony.

1.   Bank of NSW - 1817

2.   Bank of Australia – 1826

3.   Bank of Australasia – 1834

4.   Commercial Bank – 1835

5.   Sydney Banking Company – 1839

6.   Union Bank of Australia – 1839

(35)   The Forbes Act cleared the way for banks to become financier of the great push west, north and south of pastoral interests. The boundaries of location were reset annually by a Government Order, but kept expanding. The order of October 1829 (*Sydney Gazette 17* Oct 1829) proclaimed 19 counties of NSW, whose boundaries marked the limits of location. The 20th country was recognised as Port Macquarie in July 1830. It was after this point that squatters became involved and the 'limits' were completely open.

(36)   A NSW Return of 30 September 1843 offered current sheep statistics. There were 1.596m sheep in the twenty counties and 1.4m in Port Phillip and a further 1.8 outside the limits of location towards the Darling Downs, and down to the Murrumbidgee. Much of the capital arriving in the 1830s was borrowed so that pastoralists could buy land, within the boundaries at 5s per acre, commencing August 1831. 'Any man that has £1,000 in one of the Sydney banks will readily get credit for £3,000 worth of stock and many got his stock on terms, by which he readily clears the purchase money as it becomes due'. (*Settlers & Convicts* by an emigrant mechanic, Alexander Harris. p. 282, London 1847) These were days of easy credit, high wool prices and a rising demand for wool, so the man of small capital (with none to spare to buy freehold land) went further out and squatted.

(37)   The Act 4 Wm IV, No. 10, passed in August 1833 recognised squatting outside the 1829 limits. The legislation required the appointment of Crown Land commissioners to regulate

squatters together with grazing licences at £10 per annum. By 1840, there were nearly 5,000 free persons on 718 pastoral stations outside the boundaries and nearly 3,000 assigned servants.

(54) The introduction of private capital brought about a considerable increase of colonial revenue by sending up customs collections and land sale receipts. The colonists demanded the appropriation of these for their own purposes including importing a labour force, but the Crown had to provide administratively for these new settlements. The new development also increased the demand for convict labour, but it was not easy to administer 'assignment' of convicts to the scattered runs (3/4ths of the convicts arriving during the 1830s went to Sydney as opposed to VDL)

(56) It took until 1833 for the export value of wool to reach £100,000, but there were two differing ways of marketing, depending on the financial interests of the seller. The first adopted by most wool growers was to use the Sydney auction sales, allows the buyer to pay the freight, handling, insurance etc and allow the grower to get his money quicker. The more wealthy growers, such as Macarthur, Marsden, Jamieson, Simeon Lord, Richard Jones et al, transported their bales to England and sold either directly to a mill or sold through the English auction system. Of course they got more money but received it in London

In the period 1831-1837, convict transportation increased the colonial population by an average 6,500 per annum. The great increase in population between 1830 and 1840 in all colonies (from 70,000 to 190,000 was the result of free immigration. The squatters drew mostly from the convict resources. The importance of this is that in the 20s and 30s the pastoral owners had consistently encouraged transportation to NSW, because convict labour, in spite of its defects was cheap. And legislation limited most former convicts to wage-labour, and many colonial employers maintained that convict labour was a good labour base to which they could add free labour. In the 30s the largest number of convict arrivals was still far too small to meet the labour demand of the pastoral extension.

(60) After transportation and assignment ceased in 1840-41 the number of assisted immigrants fell from 12,000 in 1841, to 5,000 in 1842, and to nothing in 1843 but the abolition of 'convictism' was not the cause of the inability to pay for land, however, the change of imperial policy for NSW had much to do with the crisis which the colonial economy experienced shortly after.. When it became clear the old labour supply was failing, colonial employers took measures to get more free labour from Britain. They used the bounty system to get large numbers in 1839-40, by taking out bounty orders for nearly £1 million, although the source of repayment – land sales revenue - amounted to less than half this sum even in the boom years. The sudden call on colonial funds to meet dues on immigrants was more than an imperfectly adjusted financial

system can stand. But before the moment of crisis arrived internal stresses in the changed colonial society had brought about other situations.

(61) It took a Frenchman to write in 1832 (Pilorgerie) to pronounce 'a penal colony's prosperity, and the continued effectiveness of punishment by transportation to it, are two phenomena which cannot co-exist but must cancel each other' In other words an expanding colony must offer opportunities, even to bondsmen, and opportunity is not punishment.

Table: NSW Male Working Population outside limits of location 1839-45

Year	No. of Stations	Free male Workers	Bonded males	Bonded % Of total	Index no. of total
1839	694	3540	3126	47	100
1840	673	3333	2672	46.5	89
1840	718	3732	2598	41	94
941842	761	4157	2794	40	104
181044 3	806	4650	2697	37	109
1844	881	5447	2168	28.5	113
1845	907	5024	1685	25	100

(63) Assigned convicts became the shepherds and hutkeepers. Most of the permanent hands were paid about £25 a year and board. It was the shepherd's, the hutkeeper's, the general hands or the dairyman's tasks that the newly arrived immigrant was needed to fill, as the supply of assigned servants and ex-convicts dwindled and failed. In 1828, legislation from the NSW L.C. passed setting minimum regulations for labourers, but it didn't apply to the pastoral establishments. This was corrected in 1840 and created an indentured worker system binding bonded men to the employer for a minimum of six months on pain of forfeiture of loss of wages and six months jail.

(68) The bounty system was commenced by Governor Bourke in October 1835 and from 1837, bounties were paid from colonial land revenue. The system was dropped in 1856 after large-scale use over a twenty year period. It was Bourke's successor Sir George Gipps who found in 1840 that much of the land revenue was devoted to immigration in the form of bounty payments that the question arose of the direction of colonial expenditures.

Table: Bounty immigration costs had a lower unit cost than did government sponsored immigration

Item	1837	1838	1839

No. of Government Immigrants	2668	663	4096
Total Cost	43341	122318	89414
Cost per gov immigrant	16.05.0	18.18.0	21.17.0
No. of bounty immigrants	742	1622	2814
Total Cost	8585	22398	43026
Cost per bounty immigrant	11.12.0	13.16.0	15.05.0

(68) The use of Crown land revenue caused a quasi-constitutional issue. The members of the NSW L.C. demanded a say in the usage of the land revenue and the Crown issued an instruction (without reference to any parliament) that '*money raised in NSW and disposed of is not only without reference to the local legislature, but without reference to the English legislature*'. *(HRA 1:16:80)*. The 1828 Judicature Act (9 Geo IV, cap.83) gave limited rights of the L.C. to levy duties like those previously levied by the governor, but left control of the land revenue in the hands of the colonial office

CHAPTER 5

CONVICT MANAGEMENT

Introduction to Chapter Five

Having reviewed the commissariat business enterprises, it remains to further examine the convict work arrangements and outcomes. This chapter details the role, organisation and output of the six main operating centres of the commissariat. The most important reform or change to commissariat operations under Macquarie was his addition of the role of Supervisor of Convict Work. Although there was already a Superintendent of Convicts, that role was that of discipline, in all its forms. Macquarie asked of the commissary that this establishment prepare a work schedule, supply the tools and equipment required, and victual cloth and house the convict allocated to government work. This imposed on the commissariat a huge responsibility and burden. It was now their role to plan ahead for materials required on both government building works and what could be expected from private sales. The commissary had to estimate the timber, the brick and tile, stone and furnishings usage within the government programs and ensure the manufacture and preparation of all these articles. It was a mammoth role and based on the speedy completion of the vast number of government projects, a role that was accomplished with credibility.

Convicts at Work

The work gangs had an important role within the transportation program and the commissariat's work organisation. According to James Broadbent[1], 'Macquarie's public work can be grouped into four categories. Firstly, the purely utilitarian structures and engineering works: the storehouses, the markets, roads, bridges and wharves. Secondly, there were the buildings that had official government functions. Thirdly came the Greenway type civic buildings (with adornments) and then fourthly, there were the buildings of the urban type of architecture by Greenway'. [2] The Macquarie/Greenway team made a huge contribution to life in the early settlement and created much organisational work and planning for the commissariat.

---

[1] Broadbent *The Age of Macquarie*
[2] . Francis Greenway was a convict transported to the colony for seven years for breaching bankruptcy laws in England. He was an architect working in his father's firm and after his arrival in the colony Governor Macquarie appointed Greenway the first colonial architect.

Were the convicts to be viewed as Manning Clark classified them an 'alienated working class... with no spiritual or material interest in the products of its work.... driven or terrorised into labour', [3] or as 'a distinctive workforce, organised, directed and controlled in the performance of their labour', [4] or even as 'coerced labour emanating from a professional criminal class' [5] and members of the urban criminal class.[6]. Meredith goes on to quote a vague, rather meaningless and un-attributed statement from the unidentified *British Monthly* 'Australia's colonial workers became the most murderous, monstrous, debased, burglarious, brutified, larcenous, felonious and pickpocketous set of scoundrels that ever trod the earth'. [7] It would make more sense if these attributes were applied to convict workers rather than colonial workers, as other than convicts, colonial workers were directly recruited mainly in Britain and imported under sponsorship or as free immigrants. It is doubtful that free labour should be or can be labelled in such an invidious way. The organisation of convict labour directly contributed to most of the problems associated with forced labour. Even penal labour today, in China or the USA is renowned for its lack of productivity and these prisoners are supervised by salaried administrators or contractors and protected from abuse by strong laws defining prisoner rights. The colonial convicts enjoyed no such rights, and could not be simply coerced into working as hard as a free worker. The incentive for work using 'on-time' release was also meaningless as few records existed or arrived with the convict ships, detailing the release date of each individual. There are two distinct phases of convict alienation in the workplace. The first came under King when convicts were supported by the commissariat for food, clothing and general provisions, and remunerated lightly by the 'master'. The second phase came when Macquarie assembled the forced workers into an 'assignment' system, whereby the government disqualified itself from any financial support of the convicts and passed all responsibility, supposedly other than punishment, for the convict workers to the 'master'. With Macquarie picking the most skilled convict workers for government service, and assessing the desired level of subservience and productivity in each newly arriving convict for assignment to the government work gangs, it is little wonder that the remainder are considered 'dregs' and fail to meet productivity levels attributed to free workers. It is not hard to understand the lack of incentive in these 'assigned' workers – they were generally ill treated throughout the settlement, herded for counting at least once each year and often on a more frequent basis. Their provision allowance was generally less than optimum for a

---

[3] Clark, Manning, *A History of Australia*, Vol 1 p.244 (MUP-1988)
[4] Nicholas. Stephen *Beyond Convict Workers*
[5] Meredith, David *Beyond Convict Workers* p.21
[6] Nicholas *ibid* p.3
[7] Meredith, David *Beyond Convict Workers* p.21

workingman. They had the lowliest of tasks to complete, ones in which productivity levels were generally difficult to set and more difficult to measure. For example, Convict Superintendent Ovens allocated 8 convicts to clear one acre of ground of trees and re-growth each week. We know from our own experiences even today that every acre is different – some land is super dense, with tall, ancient hardwoods, whilst an adjoining acre may be lightly treed with already thinned out softwood. Keeping in mind the aboriginals would run a fire through much open land to regenerate the bush and grass-lands; the country-side was always at different stages of re-growth and condition depending on drought and rains. Coghlan claims that convict works were only 50% as productive as a free worker, but one wonders if he has considered all aspects of the problem of such assessment. Convicts were mostly used on piecework, where goals were difficult to set. Building workers and work-gangs for clearing land and road formation were the majority, work which free workers were rarely sought for or encouraged to carry out. Even today, it is not difficult to find a Council or Shire work gang of 5 or more men with two or three men digging and the remainder resting on their shovels, at any one time. Coghlan's generalisation is not hard to understand but closer inspection makes it an unreasoned conclusion. The answer as to productivity and commitment is probably found in the attitude and of superintendence of the work. Any man is resentful of being chained like as dog and treated as inhuman, underfed, abused both physically and mentally and having nothing to look to the future for. Superintendence by a peer, due to a shortage of free worker availability with people skills, was the normal arrangement, and most overseers would have been willing only to stand aside and verbally abuse the convict group or team, rather than be a working-supervisor. Why should we expect a different set of standards for the convicts in 1788-1832, than we accept today? Human nature has not changed that much. Obviously there were exceptions, such as Greenway, Simeon Lord, Edward Eager and others, who stood as self preservationists and wanting to stand out from the crowd, embarrassed to be in such circumstances and intending to revert to former social and economic standing. However such people were rare amongst the 160,000-odd convicts transferred to the colonies.

It is doubtful that the assignment system 'would create a dynamic economy'. [8] Dyster asks 'what would be the incentive to use convict labour efficiently, or for the convicts to cooperate efficiently?' [9] He concludes 'there were four ambitious and rather contradictory standards of efficiency: punishment, reformation, cheapness, and a reasonable return to the

---

[8] Dyster, Barrie *Beyond Convict Workers* p.84
[9] Dyster, Barrie *Beyond Convict Workers* p.84

Empire'. It was Commissioner Bigge's enquiry into how post-1820 New South Wales could be run more efficiently that recommended the solution of 'dispersal of convicts away from the delights of town and of each other into the service of men of capital and authority, who would grow wool for export to Britain'.[10]

Dyster records 'a genteel plan of getting money out of the British Treasury. It was in their interests [that is, the interests of the of the 'Officer's Ring' trying to monopolise importing in the first twenty years[11] that all convicts employed by government should be treated as generously as possible. Indeed as farmers and traders, it was in their interests that *private* employers should pay just as generously for their assigned convicts. The convicts would misbehave or seek to be returned to government [service] if their rations did not match those of the commissariat.

The earliest convict gangs were employed on timber harvesting, timber dressing, brick and tile making and construction. Construction crews were engaged in building barracks (military as well as convict barracks) storage facilities, hospitals, paths, roads, bridges and wharves, military fortifications and observation points. A full list of Macquarie's construction work is included in the Appendix to this study. Macquarie's initial dilemma was creating sufficient work to keep all these newly arriving convicts employed. But this situation was quickly reversed and the demand for skilled workers grew and could only be met from newly arriving convicts and/or specially recruited immigrants. At the same time as newly skilled workers became available, the new manufacturing operations took shape.

The construction crews, wherever located, were to be victualled and fitted out with clothing and tools by the commissariat. This need together with the spread of settlement led to a diversification of commissary locations – Parramatta, Liverpool, Windsor, and Government Farms at Castle Hill, Pennant Hills, Toongabbie, Rose Hill, Emu Plains and Rooty Hills

Bill Robbins, claiming to be a specialist in the 'Management of Convict Workers' in NSW between the years 1788-1830, takes the position that there was not a coercive relationship between government and convict workers, nor were the convicts powerless. He claims that there was interaction between managers and workers concerning control of the labour process. Robbins, as a former union official, suggests there is evidence that during the 1788 to 1820 period, there was a vibrant and at times fierce struggle between convict workers and colonial managers of convict labour. Robbins does not identify this evidence nor does he identify the source for his statement 'task work was the official designation of a minimum quantity of work, or quota for individual convicts or for a gang of convict

---

[10] Dyster, Barrie *Beyond Convict Workers* p.85
[11] This theme is further developed in the sub-section relating to the commissariat and the *Rum Rebellion*

workers.' Bigge obliquely referred to this policy in his first report (page 29) when he states '[the policy] was adopted more for the purpose of securing and ascertaining that a certain quantity of labour [was] performed, than of stimulating the quicker performance of it'.[12] Under pressure from settlers wanting to contract for convict labour, Governor King set work and task work rates:

Table 6.1 Setting Task Work Rates   per Unit/Per Week

£	Unit	
Falling forest timber	0.10.0	1 acre
Burning off fallen forest timber	1.05.0	65 rods
Breaking up new ground	1.04.0	65 rods
Chipping in wheat	0.06.8	1 acre
Reaping in wheat	0.08.0	1 acre/ 60 rods
Threshing wheat (per bushel)	0.00.7	18 bushels
Planting corn	0.06.8	1 acre
Pale splitting (5 ft per hundred	0.02.0	1000(2 men)

(Sourced: HRA 1:3:37 March 1801)

John Ritchie in his study of the Commissioner Bigge Reports, quotes Major Druitt, the 1817 Convict Superintendent, confessing: 'I have had more trouble with the Sawyers than any other description of convicts, and I attribute it to my obliging them to do a greater portion of work than they ever did before'. Druitt had increased their weekly target from '450 feet per week per pair of convict workers, to 700 feet but also demanded they cut more demanding types of timber such as Iron Bark, Stringy Bark, Blue Gum and cedar'.

When in another article, Robbins reviews the management of the Lumber Yard, his observations are purely quotations from Ritchie and other historians, and he makes no effort to understand the operation of the Lumber Yard.[13] It would be of interest to ask Robbins, how he can expect to understand the labour management of the Lumber Yard (a division of the commissariat) without identifying the interior layout and operating departments within the Yard, or the range of outputs from the Yard, or the labour manning schedule within each division.[14] Because of his invalid approach, Robbins concludes that

---

[12] Robbins, Bill *Contested Terrain: The Convict Task work system 1788-1830*, in Labour & Community: Historical Essays (ed) Raymond Markey p.37
[13] Robbins, W. M. *The Lumberyard: A case study in management of convict labour.*
[14] Chapter 6 of this study sets out the operations of the Lumber Yard.

convict labour in the Lumber Yard involved 'a basic conflict of interest between capital and labour'.[15]

Robbins obviously fails to understand the function of the Lumber Yard, and its attributes and great significance in the colonial setting. The Yard was the specialty manufacturing centre of the settlement as well as the major employer of government convict labour. The Yard was enhanced in importance and relevance by becoming a major import replacement facility, and offered the advantages of fast supply of many components, on time delivery, quality control over imported goods and usually a price advantage. The lead-time for ordering from Britain was well over a year, whilst production from the Yard was locally and centrally controlled and allowed for minimum inventory and better utilisation of government controlled convict labour.

There was no conflict between capital and labour. Labour efficiency was under constant review as was the manning numbers within the Yard. Equipment was well used and technological advances were transferred from Britain to the Yard as need arose. Dr. Meredith writes; 'As time passed the authorities in Britain decided that assignment [system] itself was inefficient',[16] so by the end of 1837 it had been decided to scrap assignment and, in fact, bring an effective end to the transportation program[17]

Convict Work Organisation in the Colony

The first Bigge Report states that 'the centre of colonial industry is the Lumber Yard, a large space of ground now walled in, and extending from George Street to the edge of the small stream that discharges itself into Sydney Cove. The able bodied men who are lodged in the Hyde Park barracks and the Carter Barracks are divided into gangs, and are employed in the Lumber Yard'.

Bigge saw the use of convict labour for local manufacturing was quite appropriate but it employed too many persons at the expense of the government. He preferred the 'assignment' of convicts to the private sector where they would be kept at the expense of the employer. Bigge overlooked the huge saving included in making many building items locally rather than paying to import them. But then Bigge really did not see the need for a local government-building program in a penal colony. Bigge's reports did not opine on the

---

[15] Robbins, *ibid* p.142

[16] Meredith, David *Full Circle? Contemporary views on Transportation,* in Nicholas

[17] Dyster, Barrie *Why NSW did not become Devil's Island (or Siberia)* Beyond Convict Workers UNSW 1996

quality or productivity of the Lumber Yard, nor of the timeliness of demand being satisfied within the settlement. As directed by Bathurst his primary concern was with total immediate cost, rather than the larger picture of benefit to the colony or to the future projected lower costs of operating the colony by improved public infrastructure, and having an industrial base for the colony

Other observations based on the Bigge assessment of the convict work in the colony can be made as follows:

In the seven years between January 1, 1814 and December 20, 1820, Bigge reports 11,767 convicts arrived in the colony.

Of the 11,767 convicts, 4587 were placed into government service, whilst the remainder of 7,180 were assigned to the military officers and other land grant beneficiaries, and taken 'off the store' and as such off the government expense.

The government assignees (4587) were placed into various enterprises as mechanics and labourers – they all (except for 594) were required to live in government barracks in Sydney (Hyde Park or Carters' Barracks) Parramatta, Windsor, and Bathurst

In a report on the state of the Lumber Yard to Governor Brisbane in June 1825, Major Ovens[18], who had arrived in the colony as part of the Governor's staff, recommended a 'government contract' system. Oven's introduced his report by stating that 'this colony was formed with a view prospectively of becoming in the course of years a useful appendage to Great Britain, and with the prospect of serving as a place for exercising that degree of discipline over the larger portion of its population who, forfeiting all claims to the more lenient laws of their own country, had rendered themselves fit subjects for a more coercive system of restraint. In the first case, therefore, it was only reasonable that the Colony should be indebted to the Mother country for a large outlay of capital in support of its principal institutions; and in the second, that the labours of the convicts should be rendered available for that purpose. Hence the numerous works and Establishments, that became necessary in the march of the colony's progress, were furnished from the industry and labour of that class of its inhabitants'.

Having tried to justify both the development of the colony and the use of convicts for that purpose, Ovens went on to state:

---

[18] HRA 1:11:653 Ovens' reports on the state of the Lumber Yard

'The assignment system should be temporary and used only when a benefit on the colony of accentuating it natural productions, or enhancing the value of its material by the skill and industry of the convict labour'. In other words, place the convicts into service, where they could do the most good, and for the colony to reap the largest reward. He pointed out that to that time, priority had been given to town development, but the priorities should now change and concentrated effort be given to developing agricultural and pastoral industries. Although the previous priority was not the most consonant to the principles of political economy, it was the most natural at the then existing state of society; when the extent of the agricultural resources of the country became better known, clearer and more enlightened views on the subject were entertained, and the labour of the prisoners could be applied to such pursuits as were eventually most likely to add to the wealth, comfort and independence of the community. A practical example of the happy result of such measures may be instanced in the system adopted in clearing the country by means of convict labour, and bringing into cultivation large tracts of land which otherwise would be dormant and useless to the colonist; this work has also improved the moral condition of the convicts as well as their habits assimilated to those of farming men.

Ovens then noted a new system (with incentives) for the land clearing gangs in the country areas. He recommended:

'Convict labour should be used not only for land clearing, road making, and public works in the towns (government buildings etc) but for repair work as well (rather than have contractors imposing costs on the colony). Ovens noted four commonly held objections to the privatisation of contract work. As a means of coordinating the government contract system, he recommended establishing an engineer's department, in order 'to give a systematic effect to the labour and exertions, as well as to the skill and mechanical arts of the prisoners'. Not all of Ovens' ideas were adopted. Brisbane was influenced by others on his staff, who reminded the governor of the need to keep total costs down. One Ovens idea that was adopted and then failed was the convict land clearing program, which was based on a policy that before sale took place, whereby the land (concluded Ovens) would sell at a higher price than un-cleared land, thus recovering the cost of land clearing. The theory was great but in practice, buyers felt they were paying twice for the same work. Upon purchase of the land, the buyers were entitled to request a number of 'assigned' convicts, and if they were not used to clear the land what would they be doing?

The Operations of the Lumber Yard

The operations of the Lumber Yard are generally unrecorded, and yet as the manufacturing centre of not only the commissariat, but also of the colony generally, the Lumber Yard was responsible for a number of significant activities It gainfully occupied the over 2,000 convicts at work, trained younger offenders so as to provide them with a skill for use at the end of their sentence, and built or manufactured a wide range of locally require supplies and stores.

The Lumber Yard also facilitated a transition arrangement for many manufactured items from government enterprise to free private enterprise.

The Lumber Yard was located on the corner of George Street and Bridge Street.

Bridge Street earned its name from having the first wooden bridge constructed over the Tank Stream. According to De Vries [19] the lumber or timber storage yards were a standard feature of British colonial penal settlements. They were in fact convict work camps and the Bridge Street Lumber Yard contained workshops for blacksmiths, carpenters, wheelwrights, tailors and shoemakers. There was also a tannery where the convicts made their own leather hats and shoes. Nails, bolts, bellows, barrels and simple items of furniture for the officer's quarters and the barracks were also made in the Lumber Yard. Convicts wore identification on their uniforms –**P.B.** for Prisoner's of Hyde Park Barracks or **C.B.** for Carter's Barracks. They worked from sunrise to sunset. If they failed to fulfil their allotted tasks they were flogged at the pillory, conveniently situated nearby, also on Bridge Street.

The Lumber Yard continued in use as a convict workshop until 1834, at which time it was cut up and sold for up to £25 per front foot (for the best lots).

Contracting for government work was a common path to independence for building craftsmen. Convicts or emancipists employed as supervisors of the government building gangs seldom wished to remain in service longer than they had to and there was always a shortage of reliable men to take their place[20]. Macquarie, in his efforts to retain his supervisors in government employment, permitted them to combine their official duties with the business of private contracting. The supervisor would undertake the management of a building project to which the government contributed labour and materials from the Lumber Yard. The Superintendent of the Yard at that time, Major Druitt was unable to suppress the open practices of government men and tools being 'borrowed' and government materials from the Yard being diverted elsewhere.

' Already by 1791 the government (Lumber) Yard had been established on the western side of the Stream to collect and prepare timber for building and was the recognised meeting place where the gangs picked up their tools and materials and were assigned to work. Here building materials were collected, prepared for use and distributed to the various work sites, tools were issued and gangs allocated and checked. It became the core of the

---

[19] De Vries *Historic Sydney*
[20] Scott, Geoffrey *Sydney's Highways of History*

government labour system after the devastating Hawkesbury floods in the winter of 1809. Lt-Gov Patterson had the Sydney working parties gather there for victualling before going to the relief of the settlers. Under Macquarie's expanding work program the Lumber Yard became the centre of the largest single industrial enterprise in the colony. Captain Gill, as Inspector of Public Works, exercised the general direction of the working gangs and controlled the issue of tools and materials, while William Hutchinson, Superintendent of Convicts distributed convicts to the work gangs.

With so much activity the Yard was an easy target for thieves and by September 1811, the loss of tools, timber, bricks, lime, coal, shingles and nails from the government stocks had become so great that a General Order was issued directing that offenders, including conniving supervisors, would be punished as felons. The same order directed that all tools had to be handed in and counted at the end of each day and prohibited men from borrowing tools or doing private jobs in the yard after normal working hours'. [21]

Gill's successor, Major Druitt, expanded the Yard to cope with Macquarie's work program. He took over the adjoining land in Bridge Street (by now abandoned by the debt-ridden merchant Garnham Blaxcell, who had fled the colony); and built new covered saw pits, furnaces for an iron and brass foundry and workshops for blacksmiths, nailers, painters and glaziers, and harness makers. He raised the walls surrounding the Yard and built a solid gate to discourage truancy and pilfering; he built moveable rain-sheds for jobs around the town and provided two drags drawn by draft animals to replace the 90 to 100 men previously employed on the laborious task of rolling logs from the dock to the Yard.[21]

Men were selected off the convict transports on the basis on their skills and experience. They were told to find lodgings in the Rocks area. Each morning a bell 'would call them to the Lumber Yard where they were set to work according to their trades or capabilities. Some went to the workshops, others to building sites or the Brickfields where they dug and puddled clay and pressed it into moulds for firing in the kilns. Unskilled labourers were allocated according to their physical condition; the fittest went to the gangs felling trees and cutting logs to length, others to barrowing heavy stones or dragging the brick carts to the building sites, with assignments often used as punishment for the recalcitrant. The unfit were not spared; weak and ailing men went to gangs tidying up the streets or weeding government land, a man without an arm could tend to the stock and a legless man could be

---

[21] Sydney Gazette Sept 1811
[21] HRA 1:9: 832; ADB I-324-5

useful as a watchman'.[22]. The days work started at 5 am, there was a one-hour break for breakfast at 9 am and at 1 pm for lunch and at 3 pm the men were free to go and earn the cost of their lodgings. In 1819, Macquarie tightened the convict system, and housed all convicts in the new Hyde Park Barracks, and the working day was extended to sunset, and only married or trusted convicts were allowed to live in the town. The men from the Barracks were marched down to the Yards but 'control was lax and as they went through the streets, some would slip away to follow their own devices'. [23]

'As a result of Macquarie's building activities, and partly as a means of employing more and more convicts, the range of activities expanded in the Lumber Yard'. [24]

Every kind of tradesman was gathered: carpenters, joiners, cabinet makers, wood turners, sawyers, wheelwrights, cart-makers, barrow-makers, blacksmiths, whitesmiths, shoeing smiths, agricultural implement makers, tool makers, nailers, bell founders, iron and brass founders, brass finishers, turners and platers, brass wire drawers, tool sharpeners, steelers, tinmen, painters, glaziers, farriers, horse-shoers, saddle and harness makers, bellow makers, pump borers, tailors, coopers and many more.

The organisation was simple: the big work-sheds faced the central log yard where logs and sawn timbers from Pennant Hills and Newcastle were stacked. The Lumber Yard was the source of many of the colonial made goods and the centre of the Government's engineering and building activities. It was the first step in the creation of the Public Works Department in 1813. Although the Lumber Yard serviced most of Macquarie's building needs, he badly required the services of a skilled architect and he found those skills in a convict – Francis Greenway. Greenway had a solid background of practical experience as well as theoretical training and became influential in translating Macquarie's aims and ideas into reality.

Major Ovens in his report to Governor Brisbane described work in the Lumber Yard.

'In the Lumber Yard are assembled all the indoor tradesmen who work in the shops such as Blacksmiths, carpenters, sawyers, shoemakers, tailors etc. The workmen, carrying on their occupations under the immediate eye of the Chief Engineer are probably kept in a better state of discipline than those, who working more remote, are dependent on the good behaviour of an overseer for any work they may perform.

Whatever is produced from the labour of these persons, which is not applied to any public work or for the supply of authorised requisitions, is placed in a large store and kept to

---

[22] Bridges, Peter *Foundations of Identity*
[23] Bridges, Peter *Foundations of Identity*
[24] Bridges, Peter *Foundations of Identity*

furnish the exigencies of future occasions; the nature of these employments, also renders it much easier to assign a task to each, for the due performance of which they are held responsible.'

In the Timber Yard adjoining the Lumber Yard was kept an assorted range of the timber, scaffoldings etc required for the erection of public buildings: and whatever materials were carried away from the Timber Yard for building purposes and the different works, the same had to be returned, or the deficiency accounted for. The storekeeper of this Yard has charge of such timber as was brought from the out stations, or sawn and cut up in the Yard, such as flooring boards, scantlings, beams etc; and when these supplies exceed the demand for government purposes, the excess was sold by public auction, and the amount of the proceeds credited to government commissariat. The Crown 'owned' all standing timber in the colony and the revenues derived from also belonged to the Crown and were therefore used to offset crown expenditures in the colony.

The Ovens' Report to Governor Brisbane lists the workforce by category as well as their expected output. [25] Table 6.2 shows the structure of the Lumber Yard workforce:

Table 6.2   Manning Schedule of the Lumber Yard in 1823

Carpenters' Gang	50 convicts + free apprentices
Blacksmiths' Gang	45 convicts
Bricklayers' Gang	10 convicts
Sawyers' Gang	25 convicts
Brick-makers' Gang	15 convicts + boy apprentices - Carters barracks
Plasters' Gang(lathing, plaistering, whitewashing)	8 convicts
Quarrymen	15 convicts
`Loading, carrying, clearing the Quarries– 3 bullock teams + 5 horse trucks –	19 convicts
Wheelwrights' Gang (wheel, body and spoke-makers)	23 convicts
Coopers Gang	6 convicts
Shoemakers' Gang	8 convicts
Tailors' Gang (cloth is made at the Female factory in Parramatta)	8 convicts
Dockyard Labourers on repair work	70 convicts
Dockyard Town gang loading or discharging vessels	22 convicts
Stonecutters and setters	13 convicts
Brass Founders' Gang (casting iron for all wheels etc)	9 convicts

[25] HRA 1:11:655-7

Other occupations of convicts employed included: foundation diggers, rubbish clearers; Commissariat Store gangs, grass cutters, boats' crews, boat conveyance crews, and gardeners

The plan of the Lumber Yard (Appendix No. 6) shows how the Yard was laid out. Convicts were marched from the Hyde Park Barracks along Macquarie, Bent and Bridge Streets to the entrance to the Yard, which faced High (George) Street. Inside the entrance, which was two large solid wood gates set into a high brick wall, there was a supervisor's office, with room for clerical staff. A tool shed was located near the front gate so that convicts could be issued with tools and have them collected at the end of the working day. It may be assumed that there was some form of 'inventory' control of tools; otherwise the Governor could not have been advised that tools were missing (assumed) stolen. In the centre of the half-acre site, there was a large open, but roofed building, under which the logs were stored, debarked and sawn.

Along one side of the site, probably the back fence, the five operating divisions were housed, probably also under an open sided roofed building. These five independent areas included workshops for blacksmiths, carpenters, wheelwrights, tailors and shoemakers.

Sawpits were located in the central area, (Ovens reported two in the Lumber Yard and one each in the Timber Yard and in the Dockyard.) The sawpits were recorded by Ovens to be each of about 70 feet in length Furnaces, would have been located, for safety reasons, on a third boundary wall. The fourth boundary wall contained materials storage, since bricks, tiles, and sawn lumber were stored in the Yard ready for issue to local construction sites.

The four town Quarries were located at Cockle Bay, the Domain, the Gaol-site quarry off Pitt's Row, and the High Street quarry.

Items maintained in the various commissariat Stores included:

Table 6.3 Stores maintained by the Lumber Yard
Bricks
Lime
Coal
Shingles
Nails
Tools
Timber in process of drying
Logs awaiting cutting

Products despatched through the front gate, included:

Table 6.4 Products Manufactured by the Lumber Yard
Sawn timber for framing, roofing battens, flooring supports (if used instead of bricks),
Window frames, doors and frames
Nails
Bolts
Bellows
Barrels
Furniture for the various barracks

Employment was considerable, and was categorised into at least these groupings for control

purposes:

Table 6.5 Employment Categories within the Lumber Yard
Construction & Work-site gangs
Construction gangs for building, houses, public buildings, wharves, bridges
Gangs for land 'clearing'
Gangs for felling trees in the selected timber harvesting areas (Pennant Hills and Castle Hill)
Gangs for Road making
Work facility gangs
Gangs working in the Stone-yard on the west side of High Street
Haulage Gangs
Gangs for moving logs from the wharf behind the commissary, further up High Street, to the Lumber Yard
Gangs for dragging 'materials' carts from the Yard to building and construction sites
Gangs for dragging the portable 'rain-sheds' to the various construction sites.
Gangs for dragging brick-carts to and from the Brickfields
Gangs for dragging the 'roofing tile' carts from the Brickfields
Gangs for dragging carts with large stones from the Stone-yard to building sites

In all, over 20,000 convicts were organised from the centre of manufacturing (the Lumber

Yard), with about 2,000 employed within the yard itself, at the time of the Ovens' Report.

Many government assigned convicts were employed on government farms at Emu Plains,

Castle Hill, Rooty Hill and in Sydney town. Their work ranged from ground clearing,

cultivation, weeding, picking and storing, whilst the range of produce included vegetables,

fresh meat and grain growing

Table 6.6   Commissariat Work gangs and Convict employment -1809

Vegetables	150
Cattle	11
Hay/charcoal	110
Wheat/maize	269
Timber cutting	73
Lime preparation	27
Road making	362
Land clearing	386

Stone quarries	69
Cart operators	268
Brick/tile makers	124
Boat navigators	12
Official boat crews	120
Dockyard operations	47
Lumber Yard	1000
Construction work	1450
Convict Supervisors	1500*

(*There were over 1,500 convicts employed as supervisors, foremen, leading hands and clerical assistants in the Commissariat and its work gangs as well as in the Governor's office and other official government offices.)

Convict Work Supervision

The hierarchy carrying out the convict work supervision was equally as simple in structure to the convict work organisation itself. The Governor was ultimately responsible for supervising and assigning the convicts to the various tasks whilst the Chief Engineer, Major Druitt had overall responsibility for the works program –planning and completion. The commissariat was closely involved and recommended the production schedule, made available the raw materials and the tools and equipment. In 1814, Macquarie made three new appointments to assist Major Druitt. The principal superintendent of convicts was to be William Hutchinson, an ex-convict, whilst the chief architect for public buildings and quality control as well as convict productivity was another convict Francis Greenway, and the design chief for military and civil barracks and police posts, Lieutenant Watts of Macquarie's 46th regiment.

Operating the Stone Quarries

With knowledge of local building materials so limited, the more traditional British building materials were sought and encouraged in use. Sydney town was a fertile source for soft sandstone building blocks also suitable for sculpturing. The commissariat used four locations for sourcing Sydney sandstone for its public building program. A number of stonemasons were located within the ranks of the convicts assigned to government service.

Ellis writes in *'Francis Greenway'*[26] of a visit Greenway made to Liverpool, at the request of Macquarie, at which time he saw a few stones delivered, whereupon Greenway showed Gordon, the mason, how they should be worked. Greenway remarked on the excellent

---

[26] Ellis, M.H. *Francis Greenway* p.95

quality of the stone and commented further 'if a proper quarry were opened on the site from which the specimen came', then there would be unearthed the finest stone yet found in the colony. Greenway was very disappointed to find that in fact there was no quarry but what he had seen were only some loose surface stones.

By letter dated 10th April 1818, Greenway recommended to Mr. Lucas (a contractor, and the Liverpool property owner) that he should open 'a proper quarry, and good white stone should be obtained'. This was not to be, as the *Sydney Gazette*[27] recorded a few weeks later that Mr Nathaniel Lucas, a respectable builder, was found dead near Moore Bridge, Liverpool.

Greenway wrote to Sir John Jamison on 8th November 1822 that a preliminary estimate for renovation work on the Jamison house included '16 enriched blocks' at 16/-. With the failure of any private contractor being able to extract and supply building stone, Greenway recommended to Macquarie that the commissariat establish and supervise various sandstone quarries for furnishing to government and private building sites around Sydney.

A submission was made by John Oxley to the Bigge Commission in Sydney in 1821 and included a return of the number of buildings in Sydney in 1821.

The Macquarie Tower and Lighthouse on South Head used stone specified by Greenway, to be 'not less than 4 feet long by 2 feet 6 inches in the bed, joggled and cramped in the same way as the stones in the basement. The problem confronting Greenway at this time was no masons were obtainable' since there were only two or three government men who even pretended to call themselves such'. Greenway therefore selected twelve young men and lads and gave orders that they should be taught to 'face a stone' to handle their levels, plumb rules, trowels, hammers and chisels'. The foundation stone was laid, for the Lighthouse, on 11th July 1816, and completed on 16th December 1817.

Macquarie was being advised on one hand that the colony 'was a devil's island, with no need for public buildings, whilst on the other hand there were hundreds of convicts coming into the colony, who had to be put to work, and an expanding colonial revenue, supported by taxes, which was providing local resources not very closely watched over by the British Treasury'. Some of these funds were used for churches in Sydney, Windsor and Liverpool – the expense of which was paid from Colonial funds. Macquarie was not acting secretly, for he wrote to Lord Bathurst in April 1817 'In regard to public buildings still required in Sydney, and in other parts of the colony, I shall avail myself of the discretionary power provided by your Lordship to build as required and pay for them from colonial revenues'.

---

[27] *Sydney Gazette- report dated 9th May*

Early reports identified a few stone masons in the colony – such as Thomas Boulton, a free settler arriving in 1801 and who by 1810 was well established and in that year won a government contract to build a 950 feet stone wall in the Domain and for which he received £481.12.0. It had been Macquarie who established the structure for civil engineering in the colony, especially for public buildings and works projects. Lt-Colonel Foveaux designed the commissary stores and military barracks, but successive Governor's soon delegated responsibility to a single superintendent for each bridge, road, building and public works project.

The map Appended to this study shows the location of three stone quarries in Sydney Town. The first and oldest, in use, was on George Street (High Street) opposite the Commissariat Store and adjacent to the Military watch-house; the second was on the point now known as Bennelong Point (where the Opera House is now located) and the third was on the east side of Sussex Street North.

The Appendix includes a reference to the Pyrmont Quarries as being the quarries that built Sydney, and claims 'the Pyrmont Quarries supplied virtually all the sandstone for every major construction in Sydney'.

f. The Timber Yard

Directly associated with the Lumber Yard was the Timber Yard. Although there were saw pits within the Lumber Yard, they were used for sizing sawn timber. The main function of the Timber Yard, and within it the sawpits, was to extract sawn timber of varying sizes and lengths from the large number of logs brought into the Yard. These logs were floated down the Lane Cove River and across the harbour to the commissariat landing where they were hauled from the water and stacked to enable a drying process before being moved over the sawpits. The logs, having partly dried in the sun, were then rough sawn into a variety of sizes and lengths. The rough sawn timber was then placed onto racks, under weights for further drying. The purpose of the weights was to minimise the twisting and splitting that naturally occurs when native colonial timbers were dried. The natural moisture of native timbers content is high, and is best reduced through kiln drying, but this method was untested until the 1830s. It was Governor Phillip who used timber directly cut from standing logs and who found to his great cost that the timbers, twisted, warped and split after a short time in the sun. All his early work had to be rebuilt after allowing the sawn timber to naturally dry before nailing into place. It took many years for the colonial building supervisors to understand the dimension and nature of the native timbers and understand how different they were to the English timbers

The third main function of the Timber Yard was to cut the rough sawn timber to preferred sizes and after the drying process to rack them until required for construction purposes. From early records, it appears that there were never sufficient sawn timbers and demand always outstripped supply. So much so that many British ships were still bringing in timber from Britain and the Continent as ballast. Also local supplies were used in growing quantities for transfer back to and sale in Britain. Although an import tax was imposed on timber originating from colonial NSW but was still in great demand for specific uses, especially for naval purposes and as hardwood.

The Timber Yard was the main timber operation in the colony, but as the source of most timbers was in the Castle Hill and Pennant Hills area, a second but smaller timber yard was built adjoining the Pennant Hills Forests.

Ralph Hawkins in a study of the Convict Timber getters of Pennants Hills, for the Hornsby historical Society has detailed the names and occupations of both the convict workers and the non-convict workers, employed at the timber-getting establishment in the Hills area from the 1828 census (the first complete census following the last of the musters.

In all there were 166 active convict workers who were employed as timber-fellers, wood and post splitters, sawyers, shingle makers, carpenters, charcoal burners, sawpit clearers and basket makers. A number of the convicts (10 in total) were working with animals. Bullock drivers, stock keepers and grass cutters, whilst another sub-operation were metal workers – i.e. blacksmiths and wheelwrights. As the finished products or cut timbers were moved by water, there were boatmen, wharf workers, and then as it was a self-contained camp there were men used as hut-keepers, barbers, shoemakers and tailors. Convicts were also used on the administrative side and this included approx 40 men acting in a military capacity, as superintendents, overseers, watchmen, constables, clerks and a school teacher. The commissariat victualled and provided supplies for the grand total of 166 convicts and provisions would be taken by the boatmen returning from the Timber Yard, having delivered a supply of product from the Pennant Hills establishment.

The Timber Yard was an important aspect of the commissariat operations and underpinned the substantial quantity of timber supplies necessary to the colonial building program commencing under Macquarie.

The Female Factory of Parramatta

Convicts arriving in the settlement were both male and female prisoners. As far as balance between the sexes was concerned, the numbers seemed to be of little interest to the authorities in Britain. Upon arrival in the colony, male prisoners were housed in barracks in Sydney, Parramatta, Liverpool or Windsor. Female prisoners were expected to be retained only for a short period before assignment into the private sector as housekeepers or manual workers, and whilst awaiting assignment were temporarily housed in the female barracks in Parramatta. Governor King renamed the facility to 'The Female Factory'

In his report on the Parramatta Gaol, Greenway recommended that the existing female factory be removed and rebuilt on a new site as early as possible, since the *factory had a very bad moral tendency'*.[28]

Governor Macquarie had included a new factory and barracks for female convicts in his 'List of essentially necessary Public Buildings' of January 1817[29]. In March 1817 Macquarie identified to Greenway[30] the 'intended site for the new Factory and Barrack' but it was not until 1818 that he instructed Greenway to 'make a plan and elevation of a factory and barrack sufficient to lodge 300 female convicts, on an area of ground of 4 acres, enclosed by a stone wall, 9 feet high'[31]. The site chosen lay between the old Government millrace and the river, opposite the Governor's domain. Greenway based his plan on a design submitted by Samuel Marsden.

The contract was let in April 1818, for completion within 18 months, and Macquarie laid the foundation stone in July 1818. However, due to numerous delays the building was not completed until 30th January 1821.

Commissioner Bigge described the building, in the following way: [32]

'The design for the building consists of a basement story containing two large rooms (for the females to take their meals), two upper stories with large sleeping rooms. Each sleeping area will contain 20 double beds (containing accommodation for 172 females). The rooms are separated by a staircase and landing places, and in the centre of the roof is a cupola for ornamental purposes and ventilation.

---

[28] Broadbent & Hughes *Francis Greenway Architect*

[29] HRA 1:17:255 *Governor's despatches*
[30] Greenway had been appointed Colonial Architect and had responsibility for building what he had designed
[31] HRA 1:17:255 *Governor's despatches*
[32] Bigge, J. T *Third Report on the Colony of NSW* (1823)

In the outer yard is the principal entrance and the porter's lodge, and rooms for the superintendent and his family. In the inner yard is the hospital, a room for weaving cloth and four very small lodges for constables or overseers. Other buildings include the bakehouse and kitchen, provisions and stores, storing wool, a spinning room, a carding room and a large storeroom for wool and cloth. No washrooms or *privies* had been included in the original design and these were added later with drainage to the river.'

Samuel Marsden, whom Governor Macquarie had appointed a Trustee of the Female Factory, [33] had advised the Governor of a little background to the commencement of the Female Factory.

'Nine looms had been operating since 1804 at the Government factory at Parramatta, where 50 women and 18 men were employed. At that time only a small proportion of the colony's sheep grew wool that was worth shearing, let alone exporting, so the course crossbred-wools, which predominated until the early 1820s, had from the King period been manufactured into slop clothing for the convicts, under the arrangement that the grower received $1/4^{th}$ of the cloth as payment for the wool supplied.'

Marsden sought Wilberforce's support in building a new Female factory in 1815. [34]

'One issue over which Marsden became involved with English lobbyists concerned the female convicts at the Parramatta factory. In July 1815, he reminded Macquarie of the appalling conditions at the Parramatta Factory (in 1814, Marsden had told the Secretary of State in England that the absence of barrack accommodation for the female prisoners had forced many into prostitution, in order to find shelter) but in the absence of a favourable response, he wrote to Wilberforce complaining of Government inaction.

Marsden pointed out in early 1816 that the lack of proper accommodation for the convicts employed by the Government at Parramatta not only subverted morality and law in that district, but also destroyed the most distant hope of reformation. The female convicts who were not assigned to private service were employed by day in the Government clothing factory at Parramatta, but only 30 of the 150 women and 70 children slept there, amongst the litter of wool, grime and machinery, while the remainder were forced to cohabit with wretched men or earn lodging money by prostitution'.

'Marsden's water mill was on his land adjoining the female factory grounds. The female factory was a controversial establishment and was reconstructed to Greenway's design with

---

[33] Yarwood, A.T. *Samuel Marsden*
[34] Yarwood, *ibid*

carding, weaving and looming rooms, three storeys high, including single-storey wings to accommodate 300 female convicts. The four-acre site was enclosed by a high stonewall and moat to conserve the morality of townsmen and impose a long-deferred constraint on the inmates.'

Macquarie's explanation for the delay in building the new factory was demonstrably untrue (he claimed he was waiting for Westminster approval – but many of the Macquarie buildings had been commenced and completed without any approval). Bigge wrote that 'Marsden's lack of criticism of Macquarie's inaction was due to his effort to achieve reform, and not the embarrassment of the Governor.'

g. The Female Factory & Commissary Operations

From the Executive Council Minutes of 15th August 1826, we find that it was Darling who proposed a change in the Female Factory operations. The Female Factory Board, established by Darling to examine the overall Convict operations, especially those of the Female Factory at Parramatta, included Major Ovens and William Lithgow. The Board's recommendations included a change to rations for female prisoners. Instead of rations applied as if the females were in the 3rd or Penitentiary class, they were to have, on a weekly basis:

¾ lb of bread (half wheaten and ½ Indian corn); ½ lb fresh meat; 1 lb green vegetables or ½ lb potatoes; 1 oz corn meal to thicken soup; 8 oz corn meal for breakfast and supper; 1 ½ oz sugar; 1 oz salt: [35]

No milk was authorised and corn meal was the substitute for flour.

Personnel arrangements were revised so that salaries were paid instead of a 'percentage' to the supervisors. Average percentage payments had been added to a salary base in order to set overall salaries at no less than the previous six-monthly average payments. In fact after over three years of no increases, salaries were adjusted by about 20%[36]in 1825.

The Board acknowledged how difficult it had been to replace the Factory Storekeeper (the previous occupant of the dual role of storekeeper and Factory Secretary having resigned).

---

[35] These new rations were a significant reduction on the previous rations for 3rd class prisoners. The 1st and 2nd class prison rations included tea and sugar and slightly more quantities of meats and greens (refer also Appendix for changes to rations from 1788)

[36] Salary table with comparisons HRA 1:14:526 Minute by Darling

Allowances for this position had previously been £180 per annum, but the replacement was only to receive a fixed salary of £100. Since there had been no applicants at that salary, the Board decided to revise the overall salary scale so that the Matron would in future receive £200; the Storekeeper/Secretary £150; and Master Manufacturer £150.

The Board had made this latter appointment in the previous year when the original Operations Report was completed, in order to co-ordinate manufacturing standards and output with the commissariat. The Female Factory had also reported a lot of waste in washing the wool, spinning and carding and then weaving. The Master Manufacturing Supervisor was now responsible for machine maintenance, productivity, materials management and transporting finished product to the Commissariats responsible for convict blankets and clothing.

A Government Notice dated 27th June 1826 encouraged matrimony for Female Factory inhabitants (in order to get them out of the Factory and create room for newcomers, as well as getting more persons 'off the store'.

The Notice encouraged assignment for good behaviour,
i.   To the husbands who were newly arrived in the colony (for women who had married in England)
ii.   To free men who married prisoners, since their arrival
iii.   If both husband and wife were prisoners, they would be assigned to the same master
iv.   No female prisoner being married to a free man or ticket-of-leave male was to be kept in the Factory
v.   All prisoners who sleep out of barracks would be allowed to work for themselves on Fridays and Saturdays.
vi.   All prisoners who sleep out of barracks are to be regularly mustered before proceeding to the gangs to which they belong
vii.   To assist in the *public accounts* it is planned to issue rations, to those who sleep out of barracks in arrears instead of in advance and such rations will be issued at the controlling barracks and not directly from the Commissariat.

Obviously bookkeeping simplification was required to keep records of rations issued and to stop these types of prisoners receiving double rations from different issuing points.

William Lithgow and Alexander McLeay responded to Governor Darling's request for financial information on the 23rd November 1826. Whitehall had enquired as to the actual cost of maintaining convicts in the colony, and Lithgow, being Colonial Auditor-General responded with typical detailed accounting.

For his response, he included the cost:
i.   Of running the office of 'Principal Superintendent of Convicts',

ii.   The prisoner's barracks at Sydney, Parramatta, Liverpool and Newcastle (including Carter's Barracks for Boys)
iii.   The Female Factory at Parramatta
iv.   The penal settlements at Port Macquarie, Moreton Bay, Norfolk Island and King George's Sound
v.   The Agricultural Establishments at Grose farm, Long Bottom, Rooty Hill, Emu Plains, Bathurst and Wellington Valley
vi.   The Medical Departments at all stations, where colonial hospitals had been established
vii.   The Police & Gaol Establishments and the Judicial Department

The actual cost of these 7 operational areas for convicts came to £15,500. These expenses were defrayed from the 'proceeds of bills drawn on H. M. Treasury'.
The individual Cost of the Female Factory at Parramatta was £850.00 per annum, for an average of nearly 500 female prisoners. Food and rations cost was borne by the commissariat so the 'establishment' cost referred to was simply salaries and minor maintenance work. The result was a rather meaningless figure that could not be benchmarked to any other costing or in fact guided as to efficiency by any British Treasury directive.

h. The Origins of the Dockyard

King advised the 'Victualling' Board, in London on 16 May 1803 'the Commanders of Ships are requested to sent Boat Bills (i.e. Bills of Lading) of the articles sent in each boat, since a person belonging to the Commissary Department is constantly on the landing wharf, and he gives receipts for the specific quantities landed. Bills are delivered to the Deputy Commissary, who accounts finally to the Commissary-General, and the masters of the ships' expenses in charge of the provisions produce the receipts, when the whole are landed. On producing those receipts, the numbers of casks stated by the commissary were found to be deficient or rather no receipt was produced by the Purser.'

i. Land- clearing Gangs

Major Ovens arrived in the Colony with Governor Brisbane and, as the new Superintendent of Convicts was set the task of organising convict work gangs to produce more control and better productivity. He reported to Brisbane in 1824. Ovens recommended that 'clearing' gangs (for clearing land before sale) be split into two divisions, each under a Superintendent, who in turn would be responsible to the Chief Inspector and Chief Engineer. The Southward gang would be headquartered in Liverpool, whilst the Northward gang would headquarter in Rooty Hill.

Ovens reported that the food rations, clothing, sugar, tea and tobacco made available to the 1,150 convicts working on the gangs amounted to approx £23,000 whilst the value of the wheat being able to be grown on the 9,000 acres cleared would be £23,000 (at six bushels per acre and 8/6d per bushel). So Ovens was justifying to the end buyers the value of the clearing work, not as an addition to the selling price of the land per acre but to the yield of grain. Ovens recommended that 23 men be included in each gang under one supervisor, with 50 gangs in total making 1,150 convicts in all. The amount of clearing by each gang was to be 15 acres monthly or 180 acres per annum, or 9,000 acres per annum in total. The incentive payments to each supervisor was 3/6 per acre, and to each convict was ½ lb tea, 6 lb of sugar, 10 2/3 oz of tobacco

Ovens noted that a certain amount of the timber being cleared was suitable for milling and would arrange for its transportation to the Lumber Yard.

The significance of the Ovens plan is that he reorganised convict work practices on a cost-benefit basis, but in doing so used invalid assumptions. With the assignment system being current government policy whereby any settler was entitled to as many convicts as he could maintain and employ, there was little demand for 'cleared' land at a higher price when in the master's eyes he could clear his own land and at the same time employ his own labour. However, Ovens' overall analysis and reorganisation of convict labour should have been seen by the British government as a reason for valuing the output of convict labour on government assignment and instead of trying to cut maintenance costs, to offset benefits of public infrastructure programs with the monetary costs of utilising this source of low-cost labour

j. Establishing & Operating the Government Farms

Governor Hunter had set the pattern for later government farming when in June 1797 he wrote to his Lt.-Gov and stated, 'I trust I shall soon have as much ground in cultivation on government account as will prevent the necessity of purchasing to such an extent from individuals, grain of any kind". So Hunter accepted the role and necessity of government farms and passed this same philosophy onto his successor – Governor King.

'Your shortage of public labourers to cultivate the extensive quantity of public land set aside for such purposes (Hunter had previously advised the public land to be cultivated is one-third more that that land in possession of all civil and military officers) will mean that the many buildings you are in need of will not be constructed if you use labour for cultivating rather than building. Your approach calls for such radical reform as may affect a system of real and substantial economy, and confine the issues from the stores such as to eliminate individual production'.[37]

King took a particular interest in agriculture – not as an academic exercise but as a necessity of life in the colony – the regular production of foodstuffs, grain and meat in sufficient quantities to meet projected demand in a growing settlement together with strategic reserves for emergencies when floods and droughts impacted on the settlements. King also took a forward-looking approach to the use of Crown timber. He could envisage the productive use of the enormous quantities of standing timber that was being carelessly axed to open up land for grazing when a better system of timber preservation and a grazing use of naturally open pastures could be adopted.

Early timber of useable quality was not to be found around Sydney Cove, and so Phillip required pine from Norfolk Island, until he found good stands of eucalypts, blue gum, Black-butt, flooded gum and box around the upper reaches of Lane Cove River and Middle Harbour. These logs were so heavy (and unable to float) that they had to be cut to length for moving by boat. However, there was plenty of good stone and clay for bricks, but again shortage of skilled labour made these materials unusable in the early days of the colony. Bricks began to be more usable in 1789 when the early timber constructions were decaying and in need of replacement. Roofing tiles became necessary as well to replace grass or reed thatching previously used for storehouses but which needed other than highly inflammable materials to protect the valuable foodstuffs and other stores. Collins records that the living huts were constructed from pine frames with sides filled with lengths of cabbage palm plastered over with clay to form 'a very good hovel'.

In the colony of New South Wales, close confinement was neither necessary nor practical, and except for hospitalisation, most convicts before 1800 had to find their own shelter. Building huts for convicts had not been part of official building policy, although some huts were built especially for convicts. In Rose Hill for instance, Phillip designed and built huts as part of his town layout. Since the sawn timbers were used for officer or public buildings, convicts building their own huts would use saplings covered with a mesh of twigs and walls plastered with clay. Convicts were not given any special favours of the limited quantity of building supplies such as ironmongery and glass, which had been brought from England so that windows were covered by lattices of twigs. The best buildings in the town were those for Government use, such as the stores, the barracks and

---

[37] Hunter had corresponded frequently with his Secretary of State for the Colonies – The Duke of Portland and in August 1797, the Duke responded to Hunter: -

the hospital, housing for officials. Only when convicts became free or went on ticket-of-leave status was there any call or need for private building and a building industry began to emerge.

k. Early Convict Organisation under successive governors

When Phillip returned home in 1792, his successor as interim Administrator (Major Grose), pending arrival of a new governor reallocated convicts to officers and small farmers and succeeded in depleting the government work gangs and could only complete public works by paying soldiers one shilling a day. 'With the depleted government gangs and with no firm direction', Bridges writes that roads and buildings were neglected and fell into disrepair. For lack of barracks, soldiers built their own homes along the road to the brickfield.

David Collins reflected on the difficulties of the time:

'To provide bricks for the barracks, three gangs, each of 30 convicts with an overseer was constantly at work. To convey materials from the brickfields to the barracks site, a distance of about ¾ ths of a mile, three brick-carts were employed, each drawn by 12 men and an overseer. Each cart held 700 tiles or 350 bricks and each day, the cart made 5 loads with bricks or 4 loads with tiles. To bring the timber to the site, 4 timber carriages were used, each drawn by 24 men. So 228 men were constantly used in heavy labour in the building of a barracks or storehouse, in addition to the sawyers, carpenters, smiths, painters, glaziers and stonemasons'.

Bricks were used mainly for government buildings or official houses, because of the cost, and private housing continued to use timber framing. Private buildings activities increased and slowly improved and in the year following Phillip's departure 160 houses were built in Sydney, with an allowance of 1,400 bricks for the chimney and floor. When Hunter finally arrived, public works had languished and his first action was to plaster soft brick buildings as some protection against wind and rain. Hunter ordered the collection of foreshore shells for lime making and plaster. In a map prepared by the Frenchman Leseur in 1802, some 260 houses are identified but in 1804 an official count listed 673 houses in Sydney, indicating a rapid building program between 1802 and 1804.

King again wrote to the Duke of Portland in July 1801, trying to re-state his position on government farms: -

'Although I have been obliged to rent a large farm to employ the government convicts on, and the rent is to be paid from the produce, I have no doubt of its turning out very advantageously. I have previously described how very circumscribed government cultivated lands are, and the cause of it. I am now beginning another farm for the Crown and shall take care the grants of land are not made so as to exclude government from the ground cleared by the convicts at public labour, which had been the case at Toongabbie and Parramatta, to the great accumulation of expense to the public'.

Later in August 1801, King reminded the Duke 'As the land at Toongabbie and Parramatta (being only 380 acres) had been improperly leased and granted to individuals, perverting Gov. Phillip's plan of concentrating the labour of government servants to one place, which would have greatly facilitated the public work and interest, instead of employing the convicts at public labour in detached situations, and not having people to direct their labour and secure the produce of it without incurring much additional expense.'

King advised that Toongabbie and Parramatta were to be closed because the soil was 'of the most unproductive kind', and he was moving the farm to a location selected by Phillip (Castle Hill), where 'the soil was of the best and most productive kind. 50 men have been clearing the land and much public benefit will be realised in raiding grain and feeding government cattle'.

After King's energetic administration, Bligh's government was not very interested in agriculture.

An earlier report had outlined the minimal cost of guaranteeing food supply by government in the face of regular floods and droughts. Government storage was an important part of the government farms plan, and in economic terms it was cheaper for the government to maintain its own team of convict labourers and produce its own grain, vegetables and meat for commissariat use and even resale when appropriate than rely on the private sector and pay above market prices in a competitive market. But the Colonial Office did not see it that way.

King had set down the facts about government farms some four years before Macquarie's arrival.

Governor King had prepared a comprehensive report on the state of the colony on 12th August 1806, [39] in which he described the status of the government agricultural farms.

'Cultivation on the public account is confined to the agricultural settlement at Castle Hill, where only 177 convicts are employed, the remaining 1,774 full rations victualled being composed of the civil, military, stockmen, artisans, and others employed at necessary public works, with the women, children, invalids and aged (who) do not productive labour in agriculture on the public account; nevertheless that object has continued on the part of the Crown, which goes to prove the disadvantage of any cultivation on the part of the public. By the annual muster, taken August 1806, the land in cultivation for the Crown was 330 acres, and 854 acres being worn out by repeated and

---

[39] HRNSW Vol 6, page 135

constant cultivation, and the want of labourers to till it. The government herds will in time remedy the first evil, but the others will continue to diminish or increase in proportion as the convicts now in the colony sand those sent in future may be appropriated to public labour or assigned to individuals. It seems advisable to encourage the latter, which eases the public of a very considerable expense; but relinquishing public cultivation entirely, and depending on that of individuals, will be far from beneficial to the interests or safety of the colony'.

King reported that land grants and leased land amounted to 84,465 acres of which less than 11,227 were under private cultivation. There was a further 19,768 acres cleared of timber, leaving 15,000 acres fallow and in pastureland and reserves. On the question of livestock, King reported that cattle were from the Cape and small buffalo from Calcutta, with the most valuable cross of the Cape and Bengal cows mated with an English breed sent from St. Helena. King further noted that as of August 1806 there were 552 horses, 5286 cattle, 21457 sheep, 2358 goats and 6988 swine, in the colony. The swine numbers had dropped from 23,000 a year earlier, apparently due the great flood in March 1806. By this time, convicts had ceased being the draught men, and instead, over 100 oxen, belonging to the government, were yoked and did much work in ploughs, timber carriages, wagons etc, which saved much manual labour.

King referred to the levels of grain in storage in the colony.

'For the number necessarily victualled from the public stores, there remains in the government stores, sufficient wheat (and maize being harvested) to last until July 1807 (i.e. less than 12 months supply). Vegetables are also scarce, with turnip-seed and cabbage being in reasonable supply and seeds being provided to individual gardens for additional support to offer food supplies".

Table 6.8   Summary of expenditures in the colony between 1800 and 1806.

'Stores, clothing, provisions for the commissary'	£186,431.02.11
'Bills drawn by commissary on treasury'	£ 87,477.14.09
'Cattle on hand, belonging to the Crown'	£ 36,317.00.00
'Value of inventory in government stores'	£180,246.13.06[40]

---

[40]   This figure includes cattle loaned to private farmers, the value of private buildings, the value of clothing, gra store and growing), and debts due to the commissary for barter and sale items less store receipts issued.

This submission by King was following the precedent of other governors in trying to estimate for the British Treasury the 'wealth' of the colony. In their mind the estimate of wealth needed to match or exceed the 'investment' made by the British Treasury in the colony. However, as Coghlan found some 85 years later[41], the estimation of wealth was a flawed exercise and in essence quite meaningless, since the admonition by Treasury to the governors was to make the colony self-supporting and the British government would only be delivering, at their expense, the convicts into Botany Bay. The Treasury wanted to reach the exalted plateau, where every 'local' expense, other than this 'delivery' cost, would be met by the colonial administration funds. It was King who decided that the only way to meet these goals was to raise 'local' revenues, although he hoped that there would be an element of discretionary expenditure available to the governor.

King advised his Secretary of State for the Colonies, Lord Hobart, of progress in other government operated sidelines – the Crown had sent hops and brewing equipment for a government owned brewery at Parramatta; barley and hops were bartered from a local settlers for the same purpose, while encouragement was given to the local growing of hops and grapes.

King visited the Cow Pastures – 18 miles beyond the Nepean River – and recorded seeing 'streams sufficient for water-mills, and an abundance of feed and water for livestock'. King also saw, in the Cow Pastures, the wild cattle (which had escaped some ten years previously) and now counted about 630 head[42]

The mills operated in the Sydney and Parramatta settlements were both wind and water mills, and could grind sufficient grain to meet the weekly ration requirements of 8 lb of meal to those victualled by the Crown. King observed that 8 lb of flour made 10 lb of bread, which 'had we public ovens built [43], would be a saving of one pound of flour on each full ration, using Hobart's suggestion that an allowance of 9 ½ lb of bread be made each week.

---

[41] T. A. Coghlan *Labour & Industry in Australia*

[42] It took a number of years before Governor Macquarie decided to capture this government owned livestock and two years to round up and pen these 'wild' cattle and the majority were slaughtered for sale as fresh meat. Macquarie estimated their value to the colony as over 17,000 pound. Macarthur had demanded part of the Cow Pastures as his special grant of land and caused long delays in the recapturing of the wild cattle by claiming 'ownership'. His claims were dismissed sand title remained with the government.

[43] This same argument was later used by Commissioner Bigge when he recommended (Report to the House of Commons # 3- 1823) that it would be more efficient use of grain if contracted bakers were substituted for government bakers in making bread for official uses such as the hospitals. King had supported public employment whilst Bigge supported privatisation

King also advised that potatoes and yams had been grown on public land at every opportunity (since 1788). Such plantations were maintained on public lands at Castle Hill. 'The yams being eleven months before they come to perfection, the cultivation of potatoes is preferable, as two crops a year of that root is not uncommon.'

Lord Hobart had suggested to King that public farms should be minimised in favour of private farming. King responded that 'the greater part of improved land should be kept for pasturage and the stock of government cattle should be regarded as the foundation of the stock of individual settlers'. King also adds that 'before I left England, I was directed to promote the public cultivation, and encourage that of individuals. To this end, I hired the Hawkesbury Farm in 1801, and began clearing the public agricultural settlement at Castle Hill in August 1802, where there are now 700 acres of ground cleared and durable stone buildings erected upon it. 350-400 convicts are employed at public cultivation. The result is that at present (1st March 1804) the government has a store of 11,000 bushels of wheat and maize of 7,000 bushels. After deducting 1200 bushels of wheat for seed, this leaves only 4 months reserve of grain'.

The Convicts at Work in 1806

We learn from Governor King's Report to Earl Camden (which due to a change of office holder, should have been addressed to Viscount Castlereagh as Colonial Secretary) dated 15th March 1806 that the Convicts engaged in widely diverse work.

Large-scale employment of convicts by government was not the preserve of Macquarie. Governor King had set a major part of the convict population of 1806 to work on government activities.

A Report on employment of convicts was sent to the Colonial Office, as Enclosure #2 is entitled:[44]

Table 7.6 'Public Labour of Convicts maintained by the Crown at Sydney, Parramatta, Hawkesbury, Toongabbie and Castle Hill, for the year 1805'

---

[44] HRNSW - Vol 1 Part 2 Page 7 Enclosure 2 King to   'Public Labour of Convicts maintained by the Crown at Sydney, Parramatta, Hawkesbury, Toongabbie and Castle Hill, for the year 1805'

Cultivation - Gathering, husking and shelling maize from 200 acres sowed last year - Breaking up ground and planting 1230 acres of wheat, 100 acre of Barley, 250 acres of Maize, 14 acres of Flax, and 3 acres of potatoes - Hoeing the above maize and threshing wheat.

Stock - Taking care of Government stock as herdsmen, watchmen etc

Buildings -

At Sydney: Building and constructing of stone, a citadel, a stone house, a brick dwelling for the Judge Advocate, a commodious brick house for the main guard, a brick printing office

At Parramatta: Alterations at the Brewery, a brick house as clergyman's residence

At Hawkesbury: completing a public school

A Gaol House with offices, at the expense of the Colony

Boat and Ship Builders: refitting vessels and building rowboats

Wheel and Millwrights: making and repairing carts

Manufacturing: sawing, preparing and manufacturing hemp, flax and wool, bricks and tiles

Road Gangs: repairing roads, and building new roads

Other Gangs: loading and unloading boats"[45]

Thus the total benefits from these six (6) items of direct gain to the British comes to well over £174 million, and this is compared to Professor N. G. Butlin's proposal that the British 'invested' £5.6 million.

However, in 1810 Macquarie offered his advice on government agriculture to Viscount Castlereagh.

'Your Lordship entertains doubts as to maintaining government farms or government cattle in the colony, but from what I have seen for myself I conceive it will be highly desirable to

---

[45]   HRNSW -Vol 6 P43

continue a stock of government cattle for several years to come, and also a government farm on a limited economical plan'.

In response the Secretary of State urged Macquarie to see 'that every department of the government farm was managed with the strictest economy'. The scheme was not popular at the Colonial office, and soon, on 18th October 1811, Macquarie advised London that 'he had totally abolished the government agricultural establishments'[38]

Thus Macquarie's decision brought to an end an experience with public agriculture which was appropriate enough for its time but which had obviously run its course in the then climate of vicious cost-cutting for any and all colonial operations. This new policy was short sighted and would come back within a few years to add to the political woes of not only Macquarie but also the Colonial office. Due to food shortages, Macquarie was forced to reinstate government farms and government food production in 1815. The ill-considered policy of relying totally for strategic support in food production on the private sector was not aligned with other government policies. The farmlets approach to grain production and other foodstuffs, initiated by Phillip was suitable only for the population of 1-2,000 in the colony. Macquarie's population was ten-fold that administered by Phillip but even the broad acre approach by Macquarie was presently unsuitable. Macquarie needed a comprehensive plan of market-oriented prices offered by the commissariat, and since farm to market roads were far from reliable or passable at most times, the commissariat would need to find storage in the grain growing areas rather than require the farmers to deliver to Sydney.

The commissariat could do well by providing seed grain for farmers, instead of them withholding portion of their crop from the market. The commissariat could dispose of dirty grain or unmillable grain for planting purposes and purchase the best quality from all farmers at reasonable market prices.

Summary of Chapter 5

The Commissariat was the manufacturing centre for the colony and the Lumber Yard was its hub. Both in terms of physical output and in terms of convicts and supervisors employed, the Lumber Yard was the key to the success or failure of the Commissariat in

---

[38] HRA 1: 7: 339 Bligh to Castlereagh

the Colony. The overall operations of the Commissariat were discussed in Chapter 3 & 4 above, but in this chapter (6) the detailed operations, output and staffing of the key work centre have been discussed especially in the context of the commissariat being an 'economic driver' in the colony.

In addition to the highly influential financial services role played by the commissariat, the government store maintained responsibility for food production planning and supplies, a wide range of manufacturing operations from equipment to tools, to clothing, building materials, and commodities.

The Commissariat was the powerhouse of economic activity in the colony as well as the catalyst and facilitator for large amounts of public investment. Without the commissariat acting so responsibly, the colony could not have grown and matured as it did. The private sector could not have developed as it did, nor the rural sector, mainly by the loan to farmers and pastoralists of breeding stock, which assisted with the upgrade of livestock for the export market. Nowhere was the commissariat more important than its personal encouragement of a manufacturing industry, which became an important source of import replacement and encouraged British industry to invest in or transfer to the colony.

The commissariat assisted private industry, in conjunction with the training program instituted by the adult education program of the government, and the transfer from the public to the private sector of many items of manufacture.

The transition of the store through many phases of colonial economic growth was an important vehicle for the dramatic development of the colony. The commissariat was on hand to assist in the barter system, the store receipts system, the farming of a new range of vegetables, grain and livestock, and the creation of financial systems that allowed future governments access to the London capital markets.

The importance of the Government Store can be seen from the effect any contraction or expansion of commissariat expenditures had on the colonial economy. The commissariat payments by Treasury Bills regularly eased the coin shortage in the colony, but the most telling aspect of the commissariat importance comes from the 1812 *Select Committee on Transportation Report.* ' Settlers had no market but that of the government; government purchased from them what corn they wanted for the feeding of convicts on the hands of the Crown.[29] Robert Campbell estimated government demand for grain as 60% of the total and increasing in relative importance.[46]

---

[29] *Evidence by Governor Hunter to the Select Committee on Transportation* 1812

[46] Steven, Margaret *Merchant Campbell*

None of the historians describing the commissariat in their literature disagree that the commissariat was the first colonial bank. What has been missing in the various texts is the impact of the commissariat as an early financial institution. There were a number of 'pre-Treasury' financial institutions, and each had a specific role to play and contribution to make.

CHAPTER 6

THE GROWTH OF MANUFACTURING
AS A RESULT OF PUBLIC ENTERPRISES

Introduction to Chapter Six

Hainsworth in the prologue to *The Sydney Traders* writes 'To study the 'entrepreneur' is to study the central figure in modern economic history - the central figure in economics'. The years 1788 to 1821 are the seed-time of Australian government'.[27]

Although it is difficult to connect the growth of economic development for any one sector in terms of percentage of contribution, we know that the more important sectors must be;

1. Growth of population
2. Government immigration policy
3. Foreign capital
4. The need for import replacement
5. The need for foreign exchange through exports.

In each of these sectors, the commissariat had a role and there was an important government need. The government had to grow the economy at the lowest practical cost, while also offering official services which would attract growth, trade and population. It achieved this, at least through 1821, by using the commissariat as the quasi-treasury, the manager of government business enterprises, and the employer of government-sponsored convict labour. The point here is that the economic model had to incorporate and reflect each of these 'input' factors. Here in brief is the methodology used.

The influence of the commissariat over foreign exchange, imports and exports, government-sponsored manufacturing and even attracting foreign investment capital is without comparison, but it is measurable. The economic model for the period does not nor cannot parallel Butlin's measurement of post-1861 GDP, but it does use basic ingredients like:

1. Computing the free working population
2. Computing the working convict population

---

[27] Hainsworth *Sydney Traders* prologue page 14

3. Assuming a productivity adjustment for lower than expected convict output

4. Valuing productive labour at Coghlan suggested rates

5. Interpolating labour product to total output.

6. Comparing annual total production per head of population and per head of 'worker'

7. Estimating total output by industry and comparing this to underlying assumptions about labour output.

8. Extending the estimated GDP from 1800 to 1860 to ensure the recessions of 1810-1816, 1828-29 and 1842-45 as shown in the GDP figures were responsive to these downturns.

9. Comparing the growth of local revenues from 1801 and of trade, for the same period reflected changes to estimated GDP.

10. Announcing the adopted GDP figures for the period 1800 -1860 and seeing how they blended in with the Butlin figures.

The results are assembled on a spreadsheet for each year, but a summary has been produced as an extract in order to evidence gains for each ten-year interval, and to show that the Beckett compilations and the Butlin compilations fit in with each other.

Table 7.1: Estimates of GDP between 1800 and 1900

Year	GDP per head of population	GDP per head of workforce
1801	13.61	35.10
1811	28.06	49.95
1821		59.70
1831	35.68	63.51
1841	39.66	70.60
1851	40.13	76.43
1861	46.00	85.00
1871	47.00	118.00
1877	57.00	139.00
1881	63.00	151.00
1889	67.00	158.00
1891	66.00	155.00
1900	57.00	132.00

Source: Beckett *Handbook of Colonial Statistics for period 1800-1860*
Butlin, N.G. *Investment in Australian Economic Development 1861-1900*

Certain conclusions can be reached about this table. GDP in the colony grew in each ten year period because the components of that GDP grew eg population, manufacturing enterprises, convict numbers, exports and immigration. As the colony went through its transition from penal to free, especially a free market-based economy, so government investment in services and infrastructure grew. Personal investment in housing increased and the wealth of individuals grew, as well as the collective wealth of the colony. The downturn in 1900 was due to the recession in the mid-1890s when many banks failed, unemployment increased and the previous land boom of the 1870-80s crashed, leaving many families and businesses in financial difficulty.

However certain questions remain: This model relates to restricted sectors of the colonial economy, but it only touches indirectly on important sectors such as the pastoral, whaling and seal industries. These sectors were indirectly reflective of a growing export market and a more detailed model with declared sub-elements would express the importance of the natural resource and primary production industries including timber, shipping, coal, minerals, wool and wool by-products.

There were some distractions from within the colony to Macquarie's aggressive enterprise policies. In a wave of perversion, William Charles Wentworth led an anti-Macquarie movement against local manufacturing in favour of importations. In January 1819, Macquarie gave permission for a group of clergy, merchants, settlers, and other gentlemen to convene a meeting in the court-room of the new General Hospital, to prepare a petition. The petition was for a redress of grievances and essentially sought expand rather than restrict imports into the colony. Macquarie, by trying to match exports with imports in value terms, was restricting the type of imports authorised. In a despatch to Bathurst of 22 March 1819, Macquarie notates[28] the resolution:

> *1. That a regular demand exists in the colony for British manufactures of nearly all descriptions, greater than the established mercantile houses here have supplied or are likely to supply regularly.*
> *2. Restrictions prevent merchants from employing ships of less three hundred and fifty tons burthen (under the Navigation Acts)*
> *3. That this meeting requests Gov Macquarie to try and expand shipping between Britain and Australia for transporting Manufactures and colonial produce.*

The sentiments were laudable but the request baseless. The commissariat, with its huge buying opportunities, could have achieved the desired result as could merchants collaborating into a buying group. The obvious solution was to encourage the local production of all imported items at a lower cost. Macquarie made no recommendations to Bathurst, which meant that he had strictly fulfilled his role to the petitioners and left

---

[28]   HRA 1:10:52 Macquarie to Bathurst   22nd March, 1819

Bathurst with the opinion that the colonial manufacturers and merchants were ill-prepared to fight British exports.

In over 300 pages of text, John Ritchie[29] reviews the submissions made in the colony to Commissioner Bigge, but does not recite any submission made by merchants or manufacturers. However in the Bigge reports, we find details of evidence submitted by Simeon Lord about his manufacturing activities. At his factory at Botany Bay, he employed between 15 and 20 convicts in the making of:

Blankets	Possum skin hats	Glass tumblers
Wool hats	Boot leather	Kettles
Kangaroo hats	Stockings	Thread
Seal hats	Trousers	Shirts

Between 1810 and 1820 the number of sheep trebled, and many producers were finding it more profitable to sell carcasses rather than fleeces.

Local manufactured items did not entirely replace imports and items were still imported from India and China.

From India	from China	Local exports included
Sugar	Sugar Candy	Sandalwood
Spirits	Silks	Pearl Shells
Soap	Wearing Apparel	Bêche-de-Mer
Cotton goods		Whale Oil and Meat
		Seal Oil

Trade exchange was made on a barter basis, of 'coarse cotton' and ironware for coconut and salt pork was carried on with a number of the Pacific Islands

Among other evidence to the Bigge Enquiry, there were numerous complaints by manufacturers about the limited supply of materials and the high cost of buying from government business enterprises – for instance the cloth produced by workers at the government female factory was 2/9d per yard, whereas at Mr Kenyon's private establishment it was only 11d. The manager of the Robert Campbell merchant business complained to Commissioner Bigge about the duties levied in England on whale and seal oil from the colony. He also criticised the port regulations which required captains to give 10 day's

---

[29] Ritchie, John *Punishment and Profit - The Bigge Commission into NSW'*

notice of intention to sail – he claimed this resulted in high wharfage charges. Ritchie *'Punishment & Profit'* concludes that, although Bigge wanted to encourage trade and certain manufacturing, he was reconciled to the fact that their promotion would not provide an adequate or proper solution to the question of convict employment, punishment and reform.[30]

Observations on Industry and Commerce in NSW

By 1820, Simeon Lord had turned the profits of fishing in the south seas and trade in the Pacific Islands into a manufactory at Botany Bay where he employed convicts and 15 to 20 colonial youths making blankets, stockings and hats of wool, kangaroo, seal and possum skin. All were shoddy but cheaper than similar items imported from England. [31]

The heavy influx of immigrants during the Darling Administration brought its own difficulties, especially when drought and depression descended on the colony at the end of the 1830s. This period led on to the severe economic depression of 1842 which had been fuelled by a reduction of foreign investment, a cessation of British speculation and a further withdrawal of absentee landlords. There were also numerous local factors, partly encouraged by Sir George Gipps, Governor Darling's successor. Between 1831 and 1841, imports had increased by 1257 percent to a total of over £2.5 million.[32] The severe drought of 1825-8 was unfairly blamed on Darling, as were the epidemics of 'hooping cough' and smallpox which afflicted the colony. Darling's own son died in the whooping cough epidemic.

Between December 1831 and December 1832, 325,549 gallons of spirits and 109,406 gallons of wine were imported and at least another 11,000 gallons of gin were distilled locally – all for a population of only 15,000. As for the prices of consumer items, milk was 8 pence per quart, potatoes 15/- a hundredweight, beef had declined to 1 ½ pence[33], mutton 2 ½ pence, veal 5 pence, pork 4 ½ pence. Fowls cost from 1/9d to 2/3d per pair, whilst butter varied from season to season between 1/- and 3/- per pound and cheese sold at 4 pence per pound. Cape wine was 8d to 8½ per pint and port was 1/5 to 2/- per quart. Respectable lodgings were a £1 per week and a horse could be hired for 10/- a day and a gig for 15/- per day. Housing costs had risen to £530 for a six-roomed cottage.

---

[30] Evidence by sundry manufacturers to Commissioner Bigge Enquiry
[31]   An quote extracted from Clark, A History of Australia sourced by Clark from 'An account of Mr Lord's manufactures, submitted to Commissioner Bigge, 1ˢᵗ February 1821
[32]   Barnard, Marjorie   *Story of a City* p.18
[33]   Beef during the Macquarie Administration was bought by the Commissariat at 5 pence per pound

The depression had lasted from the late 1830s to 1842 but it created a slow down in the colony which lasted until gold was discovered in 1852, causing an estimated 1638 bankruptcies. There was a glut of livestock and sheep were selling for 6 pence per head. Land sales ceased and there was an oversupply of labour for the first time in 50 years. Another blow to the struggling economy came with the discovery of gold in California, with estimates of 5757 houses being empty out of the 7100 houses in Sydney town.[34]

In the period up to 1800, the economy was based upon the limited trade monopolised by military men like John Macarthur, as well as a steady expansion of government-financed agriculture to feed the growing number of convicts. This expansion could only continue until the colony became self-sufficient in food; then an alternative product of sufficient value to be exported, would be required to generate the hard currency to pay for the increasing number of imports demanded by the growing economy. Only by developing such a staple export could the colony become economically viable and thereby partially relieve the Treasury of the burden of supporting it. With such a staple export attracting additional population, the colonists would also have some hope of eventually claiming the continent's wide interior.

By 1802, Governor King could report to London that seal skins were the way ahead in terms of exports. More than 100,000 skins were landed in and shipped from Sydney between 1800 and 1806. In 1804, 11 Sydney-based ships were engaged in the Bass Strait sealing trade, in addition to the large number of ships engaged in whaling.

By the early 1800s there were four main types of economic activity in the colony. Agriculture and grazing were making the colony almost self-sufficient in these products, and large landowners were undermining the governor's attempts to encourage yeomen farmers. Many of these large landowners also engaged in mercantile activities but a growing number of emancipated convicts became traders on their own account, with speculation in trade marked by gluts and scarcities. Many merchants also operated their own vessels, engaging in sealing and whaling. The number of whalers operating out of Sydney rose from 5 in 1827 to 76 in 1835. Between 1826 and 1835 the value of fishery

---

[34] Barnard Marjorie *ibid*

products passing through Sydney reached £950,000 and in 1849, there were 37 boats based in Hobart employing 1000 seamen.[35]

Sealing and whaling exports were followed by wool. Although only 29 sheep had arrived with the First Fleet, successive convict fleets added to the flocks and numbers quickly expanded by natural increase. By 1805, there were 20,000 sheep in the colony, in addition to the 4,000 cattle, 5,000 goats, 23,000 pigs and 500 horses. The efforts of these large landowners, including John Macarthur, resulted in a dramatic change in the export statistics with the weight of wool exports rising from just 167 pounds in 1811 to 175,433 pounds in 1821.[36]

By 1835, the supremacy of pastoralism was beyond dispute, with exports of fine wool dominating the trade figures. The success of the pastoral industry defeated the British government's efforts to slow the invasion of the interior. The success was the result of a combination of factors - cheap land taken from the Aborigines, cheap labour in the form of convict workers and even Aboriginal labour from those able to supervise large flocks over extensive unfenced grasslands in the interior.[37]

Not surprisingly the Europeans found the places they wished to settle were those the aborigines had found most desirable – land with water sources and native grasslands. By 1850 over 4,000 pastoralists with their 20 million sheep occupied 400 million hectares (1,000 million acres) of inland Australia.

Population growth contributed greatly to the rise of manufacturing and the general economic growth in the economy. NSW grew from 76,845 Europeans in 1836 to 187,243 in 1851, and growth in Port Phillip and South Australia was even more dramatic. By 1841, more than half the male population of NSW had been born in the colony or was an immigrant rather than convict, while convicts and emancipists comprised just over one-third of the total population. However males still outnumbered females by roughly two to one.

When it comes to identifying special and important exports, one aspect of trade is generally overlooked. Wool exports began to drop in the early 1820s, but most historians

---

[35] Day, David *Claiming a Continent   A new History of Australia.* Pages 49,50,51
[36] Day, David *Ibid pages 52,53*
[37] Day, David *ibid* page 74

claim wool dominated agricultural exports and that opinion clouds the real truth. In fact in the 49 years from 1788 to 1828, if a reliable set of export statistics were compiled, it would be surprising if Australian-owned whaling and sealing vessels were found to be less productive than sheep. Figures do exist for the next six years from 1828 and for Australia as a whole. Whaling narrowly exceeded wool for that period whilst, as late as 1833, it was the main export industry of NSW. However, after that time, 'wool races away, yielding in the last three years of the 1830s almost double the export value of Australia's whale products' [38]

A secondary importance of the whaling industry is that each vessel is estimated to have spent an average of £300 whilst in port. This did not include the sovereigns spent by the crews in the inns and elsewhere.[39] There was also the work for the dockyards and shipbuilding was probably the largest and most dynamic colonial manufacture before 1850. Tasmania alone built 400 vessels, from small cutters to ships of 500 tons, which joined the England-Australia run. Blainey also observes that reluctance to put whaling into an accurate perspective in importance to the colonial economy stems from apathy towards maritime history. He claims that 'except for ship-lovers, the sea and ships are still virtually banished from written history'.[40]

In his third report in 1823[41,] Commissioner Bigge referred to the high level of efficiency amongst the convicts assigned to 'task work' for the government manufactures. He discovered that, at the close of the Macquarie period, the significance of the Government Store as a market for colonial produce and a source of foreign exchange were greater than ever. A heavy increase in the number of convicts transported after the end of the Napoleonic wars had correspondingly increased the government's demand for foodstuffs. Bigge reported that the concentration on producing foodstuffs had retarded the growth of export industries while encouraging the growth of agriculture – farming as opposed to grazing. He added: 'it is possible, given other circumstances the settlers might have turned their attention to the production of other objects than those that solely depended upon the demands of the Government'.[42]

---

[38] Blainey, Geoffrey *The tyranny of Distance* Page 115
[39] Coughlin, T.A. *Labour & Industry in Australia* Volume 1, Page 367
[40] Blainey *ibid* Page 116-7
[41] Commissioner Bigge's Estimate of the value of convict labour in Sydney for 1822
[42] Bigge, J.T. *Report on the Agriculture and Trade of NSW* 1823 Page 22

Bigge also referred to the high level of skills used in the Government Business Centre - the Lumber Yard - and to the benefit derived by the colony from the local public sector manufacturing.

Commissioner Bigge reported on the extent of the trades utilised in the Lumber Yard and it was an impressive list[43]. The trades carried on in this government business enterprise [in this case, the Lumber Yard] were also reported on by Major Ovens, the former Superintendent of Convicts[44]:

> 'In the Lumber Yard are assembled all the indoor tradesmen who work in the shops such as blacksmiths, carpenters, sawyers, shoemakers, tailors etc. The workmen, carrying on their occupations under the immediate eye of the Chief Engineer are probably kept in a better state of discipline than those, who working more remote, are dependent on the good behaviour of an overseer for any work they may perform. Whatever is produced from the labour of these persons[45], which is not applied to any public work or for any supply of authorised requisitions, is placed in a large store and kept to furnish the exigencies of future occasions.'

In the colonial economy, growth came in numerous guises including as technological progress in industry and agriculture, transport and communication, population growth, the accumulation of capital; the discovery of raw materials and the spread of economic freedom.

The rise of a manufacturing sector relied on most of these areas, especially technological gains, supply of capital, immigration of skilled trades and Macquarie's sympathetic encouragement of entrepreneurs. Although not as vital as the agricultural sector, the manufacturing sector provided substantial employment, innovation, skills training, and a basis for potential decentralisation. Most importantly, during the Macquarie Administration, the manufacturing sector supported the colony's transition from a penal to free market economy. As it stabilised, it became attractive for a large number of British-based industries wishing to open branch offices in the colonies and invest in small-scale activities, often transferring skilled labour from Britain to underpin their colonial operations.

---

[43]   Bigge, J.T. *Report on the Agriculture and Trade of NSW* 1823 Page 22
[44]   Report by Major Ovens to Governor Brisbane on reorganisation for the Lumber Yard   HRA 1:11:655-7
[45]   Sawn timber for framing, roof battens, flooring, window frames, doors, nails, bolts, bellows, barrels, furniture - from Beckett *The Operations of the Commissariat of NSW 1788-1856*

Local industry also helped to develop local resources, both human and capital. Both coal and timber became important exports for the colony, whilst the list of other natural resources being developed for both local use and export continued to expand. New industry required new talents and skills, so a number of adjunct industries came into being - engineering design, equipment manufacturing and equipment maintenance. Not all new equipment was imported and, particularly for agricultural equipment suitable for local conditions, local manufacture and assembly was the norm rather than the exception.

Employment in the sector grew to an important level, with the number of factories in NSW increasing from 37 in 1829 to 174 in 1850[46]. Exports increased during the same period from £79,000 p.a. to over £8,000,000[47]. Boatbuilding peaked in 1843 at 46 vessels for the year, although the average size halved between 1841 and 1843. There were 102 vessels registered in the colony in 1841 displacing 12,153 tons; by 1843 this number had declined to 77 and it continued to decline until the 1900s.[48]

Even as late as 1827, the Colonial Office was still very suspicious about the expenses of the convict establishment. Lord Bathurst wrote of '...the difficulty I feel in reconciling the scarcity of assignable convicts...with the enormous and increasing expense with which this country is still charged'.[49]

Every effort to trim convict maintenance expenses or expand the assignment system impacted on commissariat business operations. The Superintendent of Convicts would agree to the training of apprentices only to find them sent off 'on assignment', whilst the best workers in the Lumber Yard were always in demand by private manufacturers and government building workers were constantly in demand by the private contractors.

There are few signs that the colonial governors attached great importance to colonial manufacturing. Bligh dismissed it as trifling and, while Lord's textile and hat ventures were launched whilst he was Governor and there is no evidence Macquarie appreciated the long-term significance of such enterprise; he only saw that Lord employed an average of about 20 convicts. However, the rise of manufacturing did not depend entirely on private enterprise, for there was plenty of government enterprise for instance the Female Factory at Parramatta, which enjoyed the dual role of maintaining about 300 single 'at risk' women

---

[46] ` Butlin, Ginswick & Statham *The Economy before 1850* (Australians: Historical statistics – p.108)
[47] Butlin et al *ibid* - P. 109
[48] Sourced by Beckett from original data in *Australians: Historical Statistics,* Coghlan and Butlin
[49] HRA 1:8:221

and providing the spun yarn for slops. There was also the contribution made by privately-owned industries which became so important to the colony's development. The search for staple basic industries began early; shipping, sealing and whaling were the first industries followed by wool.

Since European settlement, there had always been two frontiers – the interior and the ocean. As noted by Hainsworth, 'between 1800 and 1821, the more enterprising settlers, found the oceanic frontier a more hopeful source of gain than the harsh and alien terrain at their backs'.[50]

Therefore, it was not illogical that the first activity undertaken by convicts and free settlers with the necessary skills was the building of boats. Boat building led on to the second phase of staple activity, the use of those boats for exploiting the ocean's possibilities. Not only was construction a challenge but the task of keeping them seaworthy year after year was even more formidable. As Hainsworth points out[51], to harvest export staples from the Pacific and Australian coastal waters, and to establish a colonial carrying trade with outlying settlements, the traders needed a large number of smaller craft. This rationale even sat comfortably with instructions to successive governors from Phillip to Macquarie, *viz* 'It is our royal will and pleasure that you do not on any account allow craft to be built for the use of private individuals.'[52] Activity was brisk and during the first 25 years of the colony's development, hundreds of vessels of up to 200 tons were built.

Sealing, the first staple export industry, followed because '...the agriculturalists, knowing that exports in grain were altogether impracticable, resorted to the external, though near resources of the colony, viz: in procuring seal-skins about Bass's Straits'[53]. The story of sealing is that of a cruel industry set in a harsh environment. Total numbers were not recorded, but from Macquarie Island alone over 101,000 skins were taken[54] each season. In addition to the skins, which usually brought about 5/- each in the English market,

[50] Hainsworth, D.R *The Sydney Traders* page 115
[51] Hainsworth, D.R *The Sydney Traders* page 117
[52] From HRNSW I (part 2) – Phillip's instructions which became a model for Hunter, King, Bligh and Macquarie)
[53] Collins, David; *An Account of the English Colony in NSW '- 1806. Collin's reference notes also records (page 581) a report from Grose to Dundas of September 1793 (also found HRA 1:1:447) that 'Dusky Bay possessed all the advantages of Norfolk Island, but had a safe harbour and could become the centre of a sealing industry.*
[54] The *Sydney Gazette* in 1815 made this comment, but also noted that the numbers declined rapidly as the trade became more competitive. The muster of July 1804 showed 123 'free men' (emancipists) 'off the store' and in the southern ocean 'sealing'. By 1805, one private firm (Lord, Kable and Underwood) alone reported 206 men sealing –HRA 1:5:371

hundreds of tons of oil were exported to Britain. It usually took about 3,000 seals to produce 100 tons of oil; and from the gross earnings the British Treasury extracted a duty of £24 a ton for oil. Many sealers working for small firms would be paid, not on a piece rate, but as a percentage of the gross value of the catch at Sydney prices.

The Need for Manufacturing

G.P. Walsh, a historian, has already made two significant contributions to the literature on the 'Dawn of Industry'. This writer's purpose is not to retrace the same ground but to examine closely how the traders supplemented or replaced government activity, and how they launched types of manufacturing which had no government involvement. At first, it was only natural that the government should play a dominant role, for it had the responsibility of clothing, housing, feeding and finding employment for its convict charges, both male and female. Thus it became the chief employer of labour, provider of capital and the chief consumer. The local government was also prepared to foster industrial enterprise, though their support was haphazard and random. In fact after they had launched brewing, salt-making, milling and crude textiles, and operated a number of crude industrial processes, needed for their convict charges, the government allowed some of these ventures to pass into private hands.

In Chapter 12 'Dawn of Industry' of 'The Sydney Traders[55.] Hainsworth guides us in a review of the growth of manufactures before 1825. He pointed out that 'Thanks to the initiative of Sydney traders, manufacturing and processing industries emerged very early and helped to transform NSW from penal settlement to colony'.

By 1800, sealing[56] was dominating the trading calendar. The official return for that year showed over 118,000 skins had passed through Sydney with Simeon Lord and his fellow ex-convicts, Kable and Underwood, handling over 72,000 from just one source – Antipodes Island. By 1815, the Sydney Gazette was reporting the sealing industry was in decline as this intense harvesting had lowered their natural numbers. However, the British Government was influenced by the 'whale lobby' to raise discriminatory duties against colonial oil, seal and whale. Spermaceti oil was to bear a duty of 15s 9d per ton for British ships but £24 18s 9d if obtained by colonial ships and £8 8s a ton were imposed on Black Whale oil from the Derwent estuary. Thus, through these discriminatory tariffs, colonial oil was virtually barred from London.

---

55   Hainsworth, D.R. The Sydney Traders
56   Based on Hainsworth 'The Sydney Traders Ch12 'The Dawn of Industry'

Cottage industries were not only the preserve of the small home-based manufacturers. Coghlan[57] points out 'those who had the enterprise and industry to devote land to gardening were amply repaid'. The broad acre crops raised were chiefly wheat and maize, with a little oats and barley, and some potatoes and other vegetables. Excellent opportunities for growing fresh fruit and vegetables were provided by the weather, the climate and the generally good soil around Sydney, but gardening was not generally undertaken except by the few who were conscious of home grown vegetables. They were able, says Coghlan:

> 'To grow almost all ordinary English vegetables, all the English fruits and some fruits, such as grapes, grew in abundance. Macquarie described his garden at Parramatta as 'full of vines and fruit trees and abounding in the most excellent vegetables.'

In 1805, stock-raising was given impetus when the two Blaxland brothers arrived in the colony, bringing a considerable amount of capital and more than a little acquaintance with cattle husbandry. In 1810, horned cattle numbers stood at 12,442. When Macquarie left 10 years later the herds numbered 102,939, an annual increase of 20.5%. Herd numbers were carefully guarded with no undue slaughtering and in 1814 salt beef was still being imported. Even so, the records show that beef was cheap with a herd selling at £8 per head. Horses, says Coghlan, 'throve[58] in the settlement from the beginning although their numbers increased very slowly'. In 1800 there were only 203 horses, but by 1810 numbers had grown to 1134 and they totalled 4564 by 1821.

Coghlan recognises the importance of the timber industry and writes

> '...the export of timber became fairly considerable and in 1803, Governor King spoke of it as 'the only staple of the colony' – the inland forests could not be exploited because of the lack of any means of transport, and as a result 'numerous saw-pits were established on the inlets of Port Jackson, along the banks of the Hawkesbury, and later at Newcastle on the Hunter, where convicts were engaged cutting timber as well as in mining coal.'

Occasionally cargoes were shipped to India; in 1809 timber to the value of £1500 was sent there in part payment for a return shipment of rice.

> 'The presence of so much valuable timber would in ordinary circumstances have led to the establishment of shipbuilding yards. Vessels were built for sealing purposes as early as 1791, but the presence of craft capable of going to sea was considered a menace to the safe-keeping of the convicts and the governor directed no boats were to be built of greater length than 14 feet.'

---

[57] Coghlan, T.A. 'Labour & Industry in Australia' (Page 117 –Vol I)
[58] This is an editor's change – the Coghlan text states 'shrove'

In 1798, Hunter removed this restriction, and encouraged the shipbuilding industry by permitting a vessel of 'thirty tons to be built to procure seal skins and oil in Bass Straits'[59] Campbell then built a vessel of 130 tons which was launched in 1805[60]. There was considerable activity mostly through the Dockyard, attached to the commissariat, in boat-repairs, refurbishing and provisioning, but the stoppage of the fishery in 1810 was a serious blow to the industry.

Between 1821 and 1826, immigration to the colony was mostly by way of assigned servants, but it was difficult to collect the payments due, and this made the whole notion impractical. Coghlan writes:

> 'in the matter of indentured service many employers, principally those in the country districts were willing to advance £8 –10 towards the cost of each immigrant labourer obtained by them and in February 1832 Governor Bourke despatched a list of 803 labourers who might be sent out on these terms. It was on immigration at the cost of land revenue that the colonial authorities placed their confidence. They offered to set aside £10,000 from the land fund for emigration purposes; of this sum they desired that about two-thirds be devoted to promoting the emigration of unmarried women, as the proportion of men in the colony was excessive and that one-third should be used in loans for the emigration of mechanics.'

---

[59]   Coghlan, Labour & Industry Vol 1 Page 121-2
[60]   Steven, Margaret 'Merchant Campbell 1769-1846'

After 1836, it was decided that the rapidly increasing land revenue of NSW should be entirely devoted to immigration[61] and in 1837 over 3090 immigrants were brought to the colony of whom 2688 were sponsored through the Emigration Commissioners in London and 405 were under the bounty scheme by colonial employers.

The need for manufacturing in the colony was created by local demand for tools, materials and supplies, largely for meeting general construction and housing needs. Manufacturing in the colony was carried out by both the private and government sectors. The private sector was sponsored by a handful of entrepreneurs or skilled settlers who sought to create a 'cottage industry' to satisfy local demand for their products, sales of which were affected by limited demand and a constantly changing market.

Through the commissariat, the public/government sector became involved. The aims were to put convicts to productive work, reverse the long lead time for purchasing urgent materials from Britain and more fully utilise the 'free' local resources such as timber and convict labour. Barnard observes[62]:

> 'The colony was never wholly penal, nor was it intended to be. It was, in due course, to be balanced by freed men, their children, and such other settlers, soldiers, seamen and the like who cared to take the reward for their services in land, of which the Crown had a superfluity. Actually, NSW suffered very little from being a penal settlement and was fortunate in that her first unpromising colonizing material was early swamped by infusions of new blood, that wool, land grants and then gold attracted free colonists. There were no foreign elements to arouse Imperial suspicion, no subject race to put what might have been considered a necessary brake on progress.'

This statement by Barnard is a rewriting of history but it would be an ideal policy, if it were true. It was designed to be a penal settlement and every move made centred on the convicts - their work, protecting them from themselves, feeding, clothing and maintaining them and providing them with tools, equipment and supplies. Laissez-faire might have been the vogue in London but during the Phillip Administration the settlement struggled whilst awaiting food and other supplies, and convicts were held tightly accountable for all their activities. Until 1823, the entire responsibility for the settlement rested on the Governor; upon him was bestowed a power to control lawlessness, and he effectively exercised it.

---

[61] Coghlan 'Labour & Industry in Australia –Vol I Page 178
[62] Barnard, Marjorie *A History of Australia* 1962 (Page 304)

By 1821 at the end of the Macquarie Administration, the diversity of manufacturing in the colony was far more impressive than could reasonably be expected from a former penal colony transforming itself into a free market economy. Macquarie's enthusiasm for free enterprise and 'cost saving' led to a great deal of production sponsored by the commissariat. Convict labour was considered to be without 'cost' and therefore without 'value' as were local raw materials, so much of the output of the commissariat business enterprises left without recognition of their value, which well-suited Macquarie's purposes. As early as 1812, he had been sternly warned by Colonial Secretary Liverpool [63] that:

> '...the burden of the colony of NSW upon the Mother Country has been so much increased since the period of your assumption of the government of it, that it becomes necessary that you should transmit a more satisfactory explanation of the grounds upon which the unusual expenditure has been sanctioned by you.'

Liverpool admitted he had misgivings about this attack when he continued his letter to Macquarie in terms of: 'I can't point out what expenses have been unnecessarily incurred, and the only ground I have for forming a judgement is by comparison of the total amount of bills by your predecessors and yourself'.'

Naturally enough, the absolute totals became progressively higher but, in terms of bills drawn on the store per convict head on the store, the comparisons declined. Macquarie was actively creating an investment for the future so that at some point the colony could be self-supporting and outside the need for Treasury appropriations. However, in philosophical terms, why should local revenues be used to support any form of penal colony for Britain? Surely the population of free settlers could grow in conjunction with the transfer of convicts to the colony; whilst Britain supported the convicts and the colony supported its own operations. One of Macquarie's goals in encouraging active government business enterprises was the early achievement of self-sufficiency so that the colony would be out of the clutches of Whitehall. His thinking was only half right. He was so preoccupied with the colony's economic and fiscal arrangements that he lost sight of the overall plan. Local revenues were first raised in 1802, designed for 'discretionary' expenditure by the governor of the day. The reason for this loose arrangement was that the Treasury appropriated funds for specific purposes such as convict maintenance and civil establishment salaries, but did not see the need for maintenance works, repairs, infrastructure development and the like. Thus the money for these essentials had to be sourced locally and reserved for deployment by the government. Whitehall soon discovered this stream of revenue and, although the Treasury officials knew it was

---

[63] HRA 1:7:476 Liverpool to Macquarie 4th May, 1812

illegally-raised, they restricted its use by withholding British funds to the amount of revenue raised within the colony. Thus in Macquarie's administration, private enterprise figured as a means of both import replacement and cost saving and manufacturing filled the joint roles of availability of key/essential merchandise and of putting convicts to productive work.

Barnard records[64] that even:

> '...boys - some as young as eleven- were kept in Sydney at Carter's Barracks near Brickfield Hill and were working as a carpenter, shoemaker, stone-cutter, blacksmith, and other trades to which the boys were apprenticed. The product of their labour went into the public store, and a pool of much needed mechanics was created.'

This observation is rather unique; it is unsourced but it does not have the ring of accuracy about it. Barnard is implying that these trades were carried out at the Barracks, which means that materials and tools were brought there daily. With carts and manpower for hauling purposes being in very short supply, it seems unlikely that large lumps of stone or tree trunks would be hauled from Upper George Street (the Lumber Yard was at the corner of George and Bridge Streets) all the way to Brickfield Hill for young boys to play with. Carter's Barracks were used for confinement and punishment, and there was little space for practicing woodcraft or stone masonry. It is much more likely that the boys were released under supervision on a weekly basis and taken to the source of the raw materials, for instance the stone-yard and the Timber Yard, which were both on George Street North. This is a rare unsourced and apparent contradiction by Barnard. She is probably incorrect when she states the output of the apprentices went to the public store – it is likely that it went to the Lumber Yard store, - where all building materials, supplies and tools were inventoried. The public store kept only for dry goods, fresh foods or grain.

The extent of private sector manufacturing ranged from clothing, castings and carts to soap, silver-smithing, tanneries and tin-smithing. Government manufacturing covered an equally broad range – from nails to timber framing, bricks, tiles and stone blocks, forged items and boot making. Because the small local population would not have supported such a sector by itself, the broad intent was two-fold – to replace imports and negate the timeframe of at least a year between the ordering and receipt of goods, and to create an export market of sorts.

---

[64] Barnard, M *A History of Australia* Page 237

According to Jackson[65], the population in the colony during 1820 was only 34,000, too small to create sufficient demand for private sector output and encourage economic development. The early entrepreneurs and their activities raise numerous questions which have not been studied in the literature to date. Hainsworth records[66]

> '*Simeon Lord cannot be described as a typical emancipist trader for his operations were too large and diverse, but he was a member of numerous local groups. Another was Henry Kable, whose commercial beginnings are still more shadowy - an illiterate man transported in the first fleet, Kable was for several years a constable of Sydney and probably profitably plied with liquor by the drunks he locked up.*'

By implication, Hainsworth is questioning how these two (of many) eventually became such successful traders? What was their source of start up monies? How did these emancipist traders get started? Hainsworth concludes 'the capital they mobilised for shipbuilding and sealing in 1800 must have come from trading'.[67] Other examples of early unexplained success include John Palmer and his close colleagues. Palmer was the third Commissary who began on 5/- per day and became the wealthiest man in the colony during the King Administration. Later his sister Sophia married the largest merchant in the colony, Robert Campbell. Palmer and his trading colleagues prospered in a colony where the commercial life was supposedly monopolised by an officer clique.[68]

Historians usually describe the officer class as having cast a large shadow in the early 1790s under Hunter but the officers could not stop an undertow of small dealers and emerging traders growing up around them. Rather the officers themselves brought this about by allowing the retail trade to fall into the hands of 'ambitious and able (if uneducated) men with no gentility to lose'[69] In many cases, because the wholesale market was officer-controlled and these emancipist retailers wanted to continue to expand and grow, they moved into 'cottage' manufacturing – often working with the commissariat to supply finished goods or raw materials for further processing by the Lumber Yard or Female Factory (such as tanned leather, scoured wool, and crushed grain). For many emerging entrepreneurs, this was the way they commenced their manufacturing activities – trader, marketer and then manufacturer.

---

[65] R.V. Jackson *Australian Economic Development in the 19th Century*
[66] H.R. Hainsworth *Sydney Traders* P.41
[67] Hainsworth refers his readers, on this point, to his inserts in the ADB for Lord, Kable and Underwood Volumes 1 & 2
[68] ADB Volume 2 – John Palmer (Hainsworth)
[69] Hainsworth *The Sydney Traders* Page 42

According to Hainsworth[70], Simeon Lord was typical of the early merchant traders. When a shortage of circulating notes occurred, Lord (amongst others) requested his creditor customers to liquidate their debts to him by any means possible. The result was that Lord accepted grain, most of which he had bartered from his retail customers and then sold into the store on his own account. He also accepted payroll bills from military officers with whom he was dealing on a wholesale basis and individual 'notes or bills' payable which were freely circulating and classed as petty banking. Lord would consolidate these bills and exchange them for one large bill drawn by the commissariat on the Treasury in London. He would then release this bill to his suppliers, usually visiting ships' captains, or transfer them to his Indian or Macao (Hong Kong) suppliers. Obviously the greatest limitation to entrepreneurial activity in the colony was 'the medium of exchange': the lack of a mint, a Treasury or even a private bank of issue. However with all its faults the system worked; it was the only system they had and the traders made the best use of it'[71]. Thus private sector output was limited by government demand for food and materials.

The Jackson theory is that the sale of goods to the government store (commissariat) provided a major source of foreign exchange to the private sector because sale proceeds were made available in the form of Treasury Bills drawn on London.

Summary of Chapter 7

Of the nine economic drivers within the colonial economy, manufacturing had the most far-reaching and desirable results.

The Macquarie Administration decided to centralise and highly regulate the labour and output of the more than 50% of the convicts who were assigned to private or government work after their arrival in the colony. For those assigned to government labour, the broad range of activities required a smarter government store than had hitherto been the case. The store had to have on hand sufficient tools and materials to keep these people fully utilised. Those convicts assigned to land and road clearing needed grubbing tools and axes as well as hauling equipment and food supplies. Those allocated to public building and infrastructure projects required tools, bricks, blocks, tiles and a large array of sawn timbers.

---

[70] Hainsworth *Sydney Traders* Page 83
[71] Abbott & Nairn (*Growth*) Chapters 8 & 9

The Governor ordered the commissariat to create a central facility for assembling and distributing these materials. Most items could have been ordered in from Britain or elsewhere in Europe but the lengthy purchasing and requisition procedures required a lead-time of between 15 months and 2 years. Thus Macquarie's charge to the commissariat, to employ convict labour to manufacture locally as many imported items as possible created an import replacement program which resulted in employment and the rise of private sector entrepreneurs as well as generating the transition of local manufacturing from the public to the private sector.

The story of the rise of manufacturing in the colony of NSW is that of the business enterprises promoted and operated by the commissariat. The 900-page volume of the story of manufacturing in Australia, *'Industrial Awakening'* by G.J.R. Linge, does not officially recognise the link between the growth of manufacturing and the commissariat business enterprises. After a few definitions of business enterprise, manufacturing and secondary industry, Linge claims on page 24 claims:

> '...the importance of government activities during the whole of this first period can hardly be overstressed. To a considerable extent the administration controlled the factors of production: it regulated, restricted, and occasionally encouraged the private sector: it ran its own farms, herds and workshops and above all it was the main consumer of goods produced'.

In fact, there was no manufacturing prior to the introduction of the Lumber Yard. Although Linge and others refer to this merely as a workshop to keep convicts busy, the Lumber Yard was strategically located, well supervised and enjoyed a sophisticated production-planning regime that would still be admired in industry today. Just to place the Lumber Yard in perspective, it was not only as a means of 'working' convicts but a source of making locally many items needed within the settlement. You cannot have 2,000 convicts in a facility without producing some items of value and necessity. So the Lumber Yard commenced with the goal of using local resources and local labour to produce a wide range of products for local consumption and use.

Linge makes the comment on page 30-1 that 'at first most of the convicts worked for the government, but from late 1792 some were assigned to officers as agricultural labourers'. He refers extensively to the shortage of skilled labour as well as a general shortage of labour. What he does not recognise is that the forced labour of the Lumber Yard and its associated enterprises enabled this important, if not essential, business enterprise to get off the ground and created an opportunity for 'cluster' industries to be established, the starting point of the real secondary industries.

As was stated in the introduction to this chapter, 'out of necessity the demand for timber products, bricks, tiles, stones, rude furnishings and hand carts needed to be and could be supplied locally'. Wheelwrights forged simple iron rims, while coopers steamed woods for barrel making. Local timbers were cleared from suitable timbered hills on the north shore, clay was extracted from location at Brickfield Hill and on the south side of the Parramatta River, government buildings were being erected in Sydney and the new outlying towns, land was being cleared to the north, south, east and west of the settlement roads were under construction, and the commissariat was responsible for its coordination and planning. It was a massive planning exercise as well as a major exercise in saving government funds. Although no-one in the Colonial Office thought in terms of opportunity cost, there is sufficient evidence to suggest that import replacements were saving hundreds of thousands of pounds each year, and underpinning the desire for the colony to be self-sufficient.

The commissariat business enterprises drove the growth of the colony for over 30 years but most importantly, they created a manufacturing base for the colony and that, in turn, provided some balance to and support of the agricultural industry that was producing much needed foreign exchange and exports.

CHAPTER 7

OPERATING AND MANAGING THE GOVERNMENT FARMS AND THE PUBLIC ENTERPRISES

Introduction to Chapter Seven

The operations of the commissariat managed enterprises revolved around the very specific needs given to those enterprises – for instance to feed the colony and to support the colony's building program by making locally those items usually imported from Britain.

Already by 1791 a government yard had been established on the western side of the Tank Stream to collect and prepare timber for building and was the recognised meeting place where the gangs picked up their tools and materials and were assigned to work. Here also, building materials were collected, prepared for use and distributed to the various work-sites, tools were issued and gangs allocated and checked. This system became the core of the government's labour scheme [Peter Cunningham *Two years in NSW* (1827) p.360] Subsequently, under Macquarie's rapidly expanding work's program, developed to cope with the growing number of transportees arriving in Sydney,. The Lumber Yard became the centre of the largest single industrial enterprise in the colony. The first 'manager' was Captain Gill, who as Inspector of Public Works, generally exercised the general direction of the facility whilst William Hutchison as Superintendent of Convicts, distributed convicts to the work gangs. Gill was replaced in 1817 by Major Druitt. Druitt extended the size of the yard by taking over the adjacent property of the debt-ridden Garnham Blaxcell, who had fled the colony. Druitt built 'new covered saw pits, furnaces for iron and brass founders and workshops for blacksmiths, nailers, painters and glaziers and harness makers. He raised the surrounding walls and built a solid gate to discourage truancy and pilfering; he also built moveable rain-sheds for remote jobs and provided two drags with draft animals to replace the 90-100 men previously employed on the task of rolling logs from the dock to the yard [*ADB- Druitt*]

So a look at the output, for example of the public farming program, provided by the *Sydney Gazette*, shows a variety of vegetables (carrots, turnips, beans, onions and potatoes were grown, and these were grown in locations such as Emu Plains, because of the additional convict labour located there, its proximity to the river and the soil quality. Other locations where grain production was coupled with livestock management included Castle Hill, Rooty Hill, Field of Mars, *Green Hills* (Hawkesbury), Wellington Valley and Grose Farm, where the intelligent use of livestock wastes for field fertilising was practiced. The first fencing or enclosure practices were utilised by these government farms, initially to separate livestock from new plantings of grain. Fruit was still being grown on Garden Island into the 1820s even though the first plantings were in 1788 in that location. Oranges and lemons were the main fruit grown. Grain harvesting was followed by grinding at government-owned water, wind or mechanical mills around the Sydney area. This processed flour was supplied to a series of bakeries around Sydney town and these bakeries, also under government direction as to weights and measures baked the bread for all convicts living in government barracks.

Supervision at this level was work related and for security purposes, since remote convict barracks, for instance, at Castle Hill and Emu Plains was essentially on a low security system and any absconding could be easily accomplished. Planning for cropping and livestock management (breeding and transfers) was centralised.

Management of the timber sites was more localised, with the exception that site managers were required to meet harvesting targets on a weekly and monthly basis.

Unlike timber processing where the harvesting was remote to the drying, cutting and storing, brick-making clay deposits had been located next to the moulding and kiln-burning process, thus allowing one site manager to make about 30,000 bricks weekly. The first two locations were Brickfield Hill in Sydney and Rosehill. For a short-time before these products were surrendered to the private sector, the lumber yard was responsible for making candles, and soap.

Just about every product required in a building was available from the lumber yard. For example, hand-forged mails, bolts, hinges, window dashes, door hardware and locks, and the full range of wooden framing for floor, walls ceiling and roofing were all made in the yard, stored and distributed from the commissariat dry store building in George Street and fully accounted for, at each step. A clerically-intense process was involved in recording the manufacture of each item, then its transfer into inventory at the main store, then its order from the building site, then its usage in the building. Great use could have been made of all this information, but it was not to be and so the detailed requisition, and despatch paperwork was lost and not retained. The thought process was apparently that with convict labour and output having no value, any record of their manufacture, or inventorying was of no concern. In fact, only the bills drawn by the commissariat or the appropriations to the commissariat was of any interest to the British Treasury.

The management of the enterprise was really split into three. Firstly, there was the centralised production planning carried out by the commissariat; secondly, there was the overall convict management carried out by the Superintendent of Convicts; and thirdly there was the on-site works management, which ensured that the commissariat program and instructions were carried out. The two most forward thinking Superintendents were Major s Druitt and Ovens Druitt was promoted within the 58[th]Regiment in 14813 to rank of Major. He transferred to the 48[th]Regiment in 1816 and accompanied it to NSW. He assumed the duties of civil engineer and became responsible for many important roads and bridges, including those to South Head and Parramatta. He also controlled the Dockyard, the government stables, St. James Church, and Hyde Park Barracks. His successor in n1824 was John Ovens, appointed in general charge of public works and then acting chief engineer under Governor Brisbane to whom he was also Captain Aide-de-camp. Ovens had general supervision of convict gangs, improved the efficiency of the convicts employed on public works, supervised 'land-clearing' gangs until he had 50 gangs preparing 'extensive tracts of land into a state for cultivation by the settler'. Brisbane secured his promotion to Major in 1824 in the 57[th]Regiment. It was Druitt in conjunction with Greenway, whilst both were engaged in construction of the Government Stables who developed an incentive scheme for working convicts. Ellis describes the plan on p.106 of *Francis Greenway*. 'To a certain set of men, including ten masons, a certain portion of work, sixteen feet of ashlar, twelve feet of base work was allotted per man, per day. If they did this portion of work soundly and well, sooner than the end of their normal hours, they were allowed a period during that day or week, fixed at the direction of the Engineer, to go out and work for themselves'.

According to Ellis (p.108) Greenway also tried an incentive program. He allowed ten men to build the stonework of one tower of the stables in a week [which would normally take 30 men ten weeks to complete]. The ten men finished the assigned task in three and a half days. Macquarie, however, was opposed to 'task work'. It afforded, he claimed, too much leisure time to the felon who desired to spend this extra time in plunder and highway robbery As well it was a cause, argued Macquarie, of great discontent among workmen whose occupations were such that they could not be tasked.

The Age of Macquarie, edited by Broadbent and Hughes offer some insight into the early lumber yard. (p.130) 'A great amount of furniture was made for government offices, military barracks and hospitals and produced by convict labour in the government workshops (lumber yards) in Sydney, Parramatta, Newcastle and /Hobart Town. Major Druitt described the operation in 1819 to Commissioner John Thomas Bigge 'those occupations relating to furniture-making included carpenters, joiners, cabinet-makers, wood turners and sawyers. He noted that convicts employed in government service were allowed to work in their free time on their own account or to obtain casual employment with those willing to hire their services'. *The Age of Macquarie* also notes 'while the Sydney lumber yard was the largest, employing 78 men in 1814, the one in Parramatta was also the same size but employing only 53 men (p.130). The returns of labour at the Parramatta lumber yard confirms that between 1813 and 1821, furniture-making there was confined to convicts who provided tables, a dresser and two drawers for several military barracks and bedsteads for the hospital.

As efficient and large as both Druitt and Ovens considered the Sydney lumber yard to be, it was unacceptable to Macquarie and he commissioned Greenway to carry out substantial design work for 'alterations and additions, for completion in 1820'.Kitchen later submitted to Commissioner Bigge that if contract workers had undertaken the project works the coat would have been £2,000 instead of the 'nil' cost recorded. Kitchen as the public antagonist of Greenway also submitted to Bigge that the total cost of the Macquarie public works would have been nearly one million pound if costed, but in fact there was again nil cost recorded. In the same vein, Greenway, in an unsolicited submission to the Bigge enquiry informed the commissioner that the 21 public works and buildings completed to that time would have cost, Greenway estimated, £112,580 if the system of contracting had been followed.

Broadbent writes (p.25) of *Francis Greenway- Architect* Major John Ovens succeeded Major Druitt as chief engineer and a Board of Works was created'. Peter Bridges in *Foundations of Identity –Building early Sydney 1788-1822* writes (p.123) 'Along with Hyde Park Barracks, Macquarie built other barracks to accommodate the ever increasing numbers of convicts. In 1819 the Carters' Barracks were built on a smaller scale near the Brickfields to plans prepared by the overseer of bricklayers Francis Lawless; it housed 180 men with outbuildings for boy convicts, horses, bullocks and carts, together with workshops for carpenters, smiths and wheelwrights. The gangs working on boats were given a house near the dockyard and other barracks were built in Parramatta and Windsor. In the Emu Plains government farm, convicts were encouraged to build themselves little wooden cottages which housed between two and ten men. They made beds with wooden

.

trellises on which they spread large sheets of bark and the mattresses they brought from ships, and every man could have his own little garden'.

Bridges concludes (p.57) 'successive governors followed an *ad hoc* system of delegating responsibility for buildings, roads, bridges and other public works [e.g. Lt Barrallier built Fort Phillip for King; Foveaux designed the first commissariat store and a military barracks] by appointing an officer to direct each project; the Superintendent organised the working gangs and the Colonial Engineer distributed the materials and tools they used'.

When Druitt succeeded Gill in 14817, one of his new tasks was to board each arriving ship to select skilled men and apprentices for government service. Within the lumber yard, they were set to work according to their trades or capabilities. Some went to the workshops, others to building sites or to the Brickfields. Unskilled labour was allocated according to their physical condition; the fittest went to felling trees, or moving heavy stone, or dragging brick carts to building sites. The weak and ailing went to gardening and grass cutting duties; an armless man could tend the livestock; whilst a legless man could be a watchman.

Bridges records (p.59) 'Under Macquarie the lumber yard had become the centre of the government's engineering and building activities. It had become a first step towards the creation of an organisation which evolved into the NSW Public Works Department which has played a continuing major role in the development of the state down to the present day'.

CHAPTER 8

ACCOUNTING AND FINANCE FOR THE PUBLIC ENTERPRISES.

Introduction to this Chapter 8

As mentioned in previous chapters, there were many clerks employed in the commissariat [mostly convicts] together with some limiting accounting policies in vogue at the time. An example of a restrictive bookkeeping policy was the failure to account for convict output. The British Treasury was always busy harassing governors about their spending within the colony by using bills drawn on the Treasury for payment of goods supplied to or bought on behalf of the government. Bills were used for purchasing food stuffs from local farmers and from visiting ships. Private bills were used by military officers who were trading in the colony and who purchased shiploads of goods or imported goods from India, China, Batavia or the Cape. The official policies necessitated these payments. Public farming using convict labour was discouraged in favour of land grant (farmlets) production by military officers or emancipists. Naturally the commissariat had to pay these free enterprise farmers for their supplies. Another policy to come about was the direction from Whitehall that contractors for building needs in the colony were to be preferred over using convict labour. As Greenway made known to Commissioner Bigge, the public works that would have cost £112,000 through a contractor, had 'nil' cost in the books under the convict scheme. In neither the private bookkeeping maintained by Samuel Marsden or Darcy Wentworth, nor in the public bookkeeping scheme set up for the *Blue Books* program, was any value ever assigned to convict labour, natural resources extracted or cut, nor to finished materials prepared by the lumber yard, the stone yard, the dockyard, or the public farms, which produced livestock, grain and vegetables. So the rather strange situation arose that the British Treasury was comparing between governors the absolute costs for maintaining the convicts, even though the number was growing annually, rather than comparing governor's performance in managing the convicts by allocating a per head cost of maintenance. An obvious offset to the governor's cost of maintaining convicts would be the value of output produced by the convicts during their daily work allocation. Even to Treasury officials, what ids the difference in the net revenue stream between convicts assigned to 'masters' who in turn picked up all the cost of feeding, clothing and housing that convict, and the value of a convict in government service, producing important, import replacement items such as tools or building components?

In 1788, one goal of the Governor was to achieve self-sufficiency even though it was a penal colony. By 1823, the British Government had decided to limit its direct expenditure on relocating prisoners from Britain to the colony to the costs of transportation of the convicts, their victualling during the voyage and supplies. The colonial administrators would be responsible for the security and accommodation of the convicts upon arrival, whilst the commissariat would be responsible for food and clothing in the colony[22]. The proceeds from the sale of Crown land were to be the exclusive reserve of the British authorities, and not that of the colonists. In fact, Governor Brisbane was instructed that the newly formed NSW Legislative Council, a body appointed to advise the governor, was not to have any authority over or become involved with any aspect of Crown lands. Each of the governors (from Phillip though to Macquarie) had employed the convicts for growing food, extracting minerals (e.g. coal production), clearing land, developing roads, and building housing and public buildings. They paid their own way but no British government saw it in those terms. By 1796, government convicts were being assigned to landowners on a fully-maintained basis, thus saving the British Treasury a great deal of money. The whole purpose of such transfers was to move as many convicts as practical off the government work rolls into the private sector, where they were fully maintained by their masters.

This policy of Government maintenance of convicts created the need for the colony to set up accounting procedures to keep the British Parliament informed. This would require the appointment of a Treasurer acting as a Financial Controller, who could prepare monthly and annual reports to the British Colonial Secretary. Following responsible government in 1856, these procedures changed as the colony became fully responsible for their own economic planning and fiscal management.

Colonial Accounting in NSW

The colony went through two stages before adopting the standards recommended for the 1822 'Blue Book', which replaced the privatised colonial accounting through the 'Gaol/Police' and' Orphan' funds. These two phases were the Gaol and Orphan Funds before 1810, and the Macquarie-promoted Police and Orphan Funds of 1811-1821. The

---

[2] Although this was a charge on the British Treasury, it was spread between a number of budget items and responsibility areas

financial statements of the latter were published quarterly in the *Sydney Gazette*, after a cursory glance, officially an 'audit', by the Lt-Governor. The Gaol fund was a record of funds raised by a surcharge on the citizens of Sydney town, as a means of completing the construction of the Sydney gaol, which had burnt down in 1798. The voluntary collections fell far short of the funds needed, and the partly completed gaol required official support, by Governor King misappropriating funds from the General Account for a short period until they were replenished by locally raised revenues. From 1802 customs duties were imposed on imports (especially spirits) and, since the gaol had been completed with government monies, these local revenues were reported in the 'Goal fund', but the fund was later renamed the Police fund. In 1802 the Orphan Fund started; it had as its source of funds a share of the customs duties on spirits and tobacco. In 1810 it was re-named the Orphan School Fund with the intention of creating a fund to erect the first school building in Sydney town. The advisory Legislative Council was appointed in 1823, and the first Appropriation Act was passed in 1832 under the guidance of Governor Bourke. In the interim, the governors passed annual 'messages' of the financial condition of the colony to the members of the Council.

The colony adopted the standards recommended in the 1823 *'Blue Book'*, which replaced the 'gaol' and 'orphan' funds. The 'gaol' fund was a record of funds raised by a surcharge on the citizens of Sydney town, as a means of completing the construction of the Sydney 'gaol'. Once customs duties had been imposed on imports and the gaol had been completed with government monies, the fund was renamed the 'police' fund. The orphan fund recorded the customs duties on spirits and tobacco and was later named the Orphan School Fund with the intention of creating a fund to erect the first school building in Sydney town for the education of the large number of orphans roaming the streets.

Upon self-government in 1851, government accounting procedures were again revised, since the colony was now fully responsible for all its fiscal policy. At this time, gold was discovered and license fees, duties on exports of gold and duties on the domestic conversion of gold were applied, helping to fill the Treasury coffers. The first Appropriation Bills and 'Ways and Means' were introduced by Governor Bourke in 1832 and passed through the NSW Legislative Assembly. This was a major step forward in Government economic planning, as was the limited deficit budgeting that commenced at this time. Deficits were short term and recovered usually within five years, although the colonial debt, mainly to overseas bondholders was kept very much in check after the surge of investment in railways and telegraph services.

The first written instructions [6] required appropriate record-keeping in conformance with information being received from other colonies:

'It is highly necessary that a yearly return should be made and signed by the governor of the settlement, or the person administering the government thereof, of all births and deaths within the settlement. A like return should be transmitted of all provisions, clothing and stores annually received for the use of the settlement; and you will, therefore, not fail to regularly transmit such return to the secretary of state for this department, and to the Lords of H.M Treasury, with the commissary's returns of their distribution, under separate heads of clothing, stores and provisions. The distribution of the provisions should appear in a victualling book, which should be kept by the commissary, in like manner as is usual with pursers in the navy, bearing the persons on separate lists, where their rations differ, the title of each list expressing the ration; and the ready-made clothing should be distributed in the manner above mentioned; and a regular account, both as to the time and the numbers, mentioning their names to whom it is distributed, should appear in a yearly return of clothing' [7]

By the 1820s, this simple system had been entirely overturned and Governor Darling was able to advise Earl Bathurst that the commissariat was now so complex that it had responsibility for many departments within the public service of the colony.

Table 6.1: Commissariat Responsibilities Transferred to the Military in 1813[8]

Public Works and Engineering
Dockyards
Civil and Medical
Clothing, bedding and utensils for the convicts
Observatory and Trigonometrical survey
Ordnance
Surveyor-General
Horticulture
Mineralogical
Clothing for Mounted Police and Orderlies

Darling also suggested that theft could account for a proportion of the growing cost of commissariat operations:

---

[6]   Commissary-Generals Instructions to Colonial Officer 1808

[7]   Further discussion of the Governor King instructions, the Treasury instructions and Colonial Office Instructions are to be found in the next Chapter of this study.

[8] A discussion of the military role and the rise of the public service in the colony, which included the establishment of numerous Government Departments, are to be found elsewhere in this study.

'The loss by theft has been very great, particularly in nails and other articles of iron. When articles are purchased on the spot, the expense is enormous; every argument is therefore in articles of stores being sent out from England, rather than depend on our means of making them or on the supplies of merchants who require large profits.'

Darling was turning the clock back before the Macquarie era. Governor Macquarie had observed the growth in import replacement products and free enterprise in the colonial economy, as well as the growth of the merchant class.

The Cost of Keeping the Convicts

The commissariat provided of all material items required in the colony, from food supplies to tools, and the British Treasury was continually seeking ways of controlling and cutting colonial operating costs. The largest portion of colonial expenditures was the cost of maintaining convicts. The challenge of computing the cost to Treasury of keeping the convicts in the settlement is a complex one.

A first step would be to estimate the number of persons on rations, estimate the cost of rations and compute a total cost per head. However there was not one single ration but a number of different categories.[30] Hard-working men in the service of the government received the full ration without tea or sugar, men of age or infirmity who were incapable of work received less, and the ration for men returned from settlers because they would not work was to:

'Be limited both in quantity and quality to the smallest ration consistent with the support of such individuals. In fixing the ration, it is important that it operates as a punishment to the men without permanently endangering their health'[31]

On the other hand, convicts designated as working in a harsh occupation were given 1½ or even double rations. There were also civilian rations for government employees, military rations for officers, military rations for other ranks, rations for Female Factory workers and rations for the children of the convicts. Substitutions and changes were authorised. The Under Secretary of the Treasury advised the State Department 'the substitution of corn, for Indian Maize, or wheat, would give stimulus to the cultivation of land, and create a demand for the labour of convicts'. This had originally been recommended in Commissioner Bigge's report. The next suggestion was the elimination of tea and sugar from the rations but this decision created a black market in these two precious commodities.

---

[30] HRA 1:11:135 Bathurst to Brisbane
[31] HRA 1:11:140

In fact, if what would be considered an average ration for each category of person victualled could be determined, as well as an estimate of the average number of persons victualled, the remaining obstacle would be to discover the prevailing price of provisions. Grain purchased in the colony was a very different price from imported grain, whilst provisions might be fresh or imported (salted meats etc), and some self-provisioning occurred when the convicts were encouraged to grow their own vegetables. Certain convicts were encouraged to find board and lodging in private houses, rather than the convict barracks, while were given monetary allowances instead of actual rations and could buy what they liked.

According to a Return of Convicts employed in government establishments, on 2 April 1830 there were 358 mechanics and 1169 labourers, making a total of 1527 convict men working for the government. They were employed in various remote convict settlements including Port Macquarie, Moreton Bay, Norfolk Island, Port Raffles as well as road and bridge gangs. They were working in irons and on the Tread Mill at Carter's barracks in Sydney. A number were described as invalids, cripples and idiots and there were boys at Carter's Barracks who worked and were housed in separate accommodation. On 1 January 1830, a total of 4879 convicts were provisioned by the Government.

Location made it difficult to provide equal rations. The road gangs were often provided with one set of rations in the field and, because of poor record keeping and inadequate supervision, they would receive a further ration when they returned to their huts or barracks. Numbers were continually changing: the return of convicts for 1828 showed 1,918 convicts working, even though there were only 4,877 convicts in the full count.[32] In addition to food rations, convicts in each location received issues of clothing and bedding once each year.

In determining the cost of keeping the convicts it is necessary to track total costs through the '*Blue Books*'. However, what should be treated as a cost for keeping convicts? It must be remembered that there was an 'opportunity' cost of keeping them in British prisons and it was actually found that the cost of maintaining prisoners in the colony was significantly cheaper per head than in England.

---

[3]   [2] HRA 1:11:145

In the *Blue Books,* expenditure was listed under headings such as Public Works (including costs of tools and convict work clothing), Police Establishment (including the apprehension of 148 escaped convicts; fuel for the gaol cells and food for prisoners), Commissariat (including rent for store houses), the Parramatta establishment (including superintendents), the Windsor establishment (including cost of carrying convict baggage)and Crown livestock (including three bulls, and the costs of the castrator and stockyard). In other words, the early goal of maintaining the convicts for less than 4 pence per day was affected by and complicated through many innovations, such as food production within the colony, import replacing supplies and provisions made in the colony and regular changes of rations. In addition there was the question of fluctuating commodity prices and changing numbers being victualled.

Further complications arise from the distribution of costs between the accounting of H.M. Treasury and the Colonial Fund. Naturally, the benefits of the work carried out by the convicts must have offset the cost of maintaining them. These benefits included the public building and infrastructure program and the land improvements (the clearing gangs) from which higher land sale prices were achieved. The benefit of exports to Britain from the colony was a further gain but it cannot easily be measured, since the value of colonial trade lay partly in the security of supply it afforded Britain, especially in war time. Britain also imposed duties on imports from the colony, increasing the cost of doing business in the colony, as well as revenues for the British Treasury.

Valuing Convict Labour

As has been noted earlier in this chapter, colonial record-keeping and financial statements allocated no value to convict labour. Initially this may have been an oversight on the part of the British Treasury, but it is more likely that the exercise of 'valuing' convict labour was just too difficult to compute and it was not regarded as a cost benefit exercise of any worth. For instance, how was the commissariat to value coal, extracted from the coalfields of Newcastle? 'Mining' convicts had been assigned to the AAC (Australian Agricultural Company) and their only cost was maintenance paid by AAC. Coal production was significant; the AAC colliery in Newcastle increased output from 5,000 tons in 1831 to 12,000 tons in 1835 and 30,500 tons in 1840. It was only in 1840 that convict labour was found not to be as productive or as suitable for mining work as private contractors. Coal was shipped to Sydney and sold through the commissariat. Initially, zero 'cost' was recognised, although revenues were identified and recorded.

A similar situation occurred with bricks, tiles and timber. Convict work gangs dug clay for the three brickfields around Sydney and Rosehill, making over 30,000 bricks each week. However, apart from the commercial sale of bricks, tiles and timber framing, no 'value' or cost was attributed to those materials used in public buildings.

Even the products of the commissariat's own manufacturing centres, such as government farms, livestock areas, stone quarries or the Lumber Yard never had a value assigned to them. Products from the Lumber Yard, the farms and the female factory are identified above, but had no value other than in the market place when excess or surplus product was available for retail. In line with no convict output having any value, convict labour itself also had no value. Convicts were sometimes hired out to settlers for specific work; a daily rate was charged for this labour and the money collected was allocated to general revenue.

The Accounts Branch of the Colonial Commissariat

It has been established that the colonial commissariat was a huge operation, employing directly and indirectly nearly 500 people (refer table 8.2) and creating work for nearly 5,000 convicts. Operationally, this huge task was managed well, but what about the accounting for the establishment. Accounting fell into three areas of requirement: accounting for government revenues to keep the commissariat operating efficiently; accounting for all expenditures and revealing where all the government funds had gone; and accounting for the output and assets of the commissariat. These accounting activities revolved largely around the future planning for work and the future planning for purchases to keep all foodstuffs, tools and equipment in stock sufficient to keep every part of the colony operating. Not every aspect of the commissariat's accounting services was carried out efficiently.

As a way of introducing the commissary accounts for the period 1788 to 1835, an outline of the working of the commissariat's Accounts Branch is to be identified in this chapter. It can be seen from the various instructions on commissariat procedures that the British government (as well as the British Treasury) imposed huge burden on the colonial governors and their officials by insisting that they sign each requisition and authorise the weekly distributions of stores.

It was not until after the arrival of Governor Brisbane in 1821 that 'public' attention was drawn to the fact that the signing of treasury bills and other commissariat accounts was taking up a high proportion of the Governor's time. In a despatch to the Secretary of State[1], Brisbane requested that a 'Public Accountant' be appointed to assist with the fiscal control of the commissariat. In response, Secretary Harrison wrote to William Lithgow, the Commissary of Accounts at Mauritius, directing him to proceed as soon as possible to NSW, where he was to be appointed as the head of the Accounts Branch of the New South Wales Commissariat[2]. It was mentioned that the accounts branch would be established 'or the examination of the military expenditure within that command and for all other expenditures defrayed by the commissariat'. Lithgow was advised he would have three deputy assistants in the establishment of the new branch. Duplicate accounts would be sent to his office from Van Diemen's Land and NSW departmental locations and he was instructed to examine these thoroughly before he sent them to London.

The *Sydney Gazette* reported Lithgow's arrival in Sydney in early May 1824 and then on 27 May it reported that Lithgow had taken up his new office[3]. However, a government notice dated 25 June 1824 stated that the new office had just been established,[4] a month after Lithgow had taken up his position. The notice also set out instructions that quarterly accounts and estimates were to be drawn up after the 24th day of March, June, September and December each year. In October, Brisbane wrote expressing gratification that the new Branch had been established[5]. He wrote:

> *'I am happy to bear testimony to the value I attach to Mr Lithgow's services, since his arrival in the colony; as I am sure his appointment will be productive of incalculable benefit to me in regard to the reduction in the amount of the expenditure, as in the systematically arrangements and simplification of the disbursements connected with the whole commissariat department'[6].*

---

[1] HRA 1:11:58 Brisbane to Secretary Lushington 20th March 1823: Brisbane submitted a contradictory argument to support his contention of wasting his time. He referred to the charge of theft and fraud against D.C. Drennan and his subsequent dismissal; he referred to a decreased quarterly expenditure by the Commissary; but then pointed out he wished to be relieved of the unpleasant responsibility' of countersigning bills, as well as the protracted suspense attendant on these measures'
2 SRO - copy in Colonial Secretary letter file 1824 (from PRO records and AJCP)
[3] *Sydney Gazette* 27 May 1824
[4] The *Australian* 14th October includes the government notice dated 25th June 1824
[5] HRA 1:11:379 Brisbane to Bathurst - Governor's despatch #8. In the same despatch, Brisbane begged Bathurst to allow Lithgow to be made responsible for all colonial revenue, in order 'that he may have the entire financial state of the colony under his eye'. Brisbane wanted to pay Lithgow an additional £100 per annum from local revenue
[6] HRA 1:11:380 Brisbane to Bathurst

Lithgow was officially appointed as the colony's first Auditor General on 8 November 1824[7]. When Bathurst would not approve Brisbane's request for an additional £50 per annum for Lithgow to attend upon the general accounts of the VDL commissary branch, Brisbane separated the two commissariats and the Hobart store was no longer responsible to Sydney[8]. DAC Boyes was transferred from Sydney to Hobart to head the new independent VDL accounts branch and commenced his new duties in November 1826. The office of Auditor of Colonial Accounts was also instituted in Van Diemen's Land so that the administrative separation of the two colonies was complete. Darling also brought to the colony instructions on the keeping of the colonial accounts which had been issued to all colonies. This approach was intended to make colonial expenditures comparable and, in an overly simplistic plan, attempted to classify expenditures into two categories, ordinary and extraordinary. Two subcategories were required, contingency charges and fixed expenses (rent, stationery etc) and variable (construction and repair of public buildings etc – although such expenditure was uncertain in occurrence and amount). No expenditure over £200 could be incurred under the latter category unless specifically authorised by Treasury. Darling protested strongly on this latter point and argued that, by the time approval was received, any cost estimate might have doubled. Having disagreed with the notion of approval for every small expenditure, Darling put this loophole to very good use in future years.

A similar lack of understanding of local conditions was demonstrated following the Bigge Commission of Inquiry. Treasury recommended that all public works should be carried out by private contractors instead of by convict labour - this would enable more convicts to be assigned to settlers and 'taken off the stores'[9]. The fallacy of this argument was that contractors charged much more than the cost of convict support by the store; there was also a shortage of free labourers and mechanics. In fact, where contractors were used, it was necessary for the governor to provide a number of convicts as labourers.

The instructions to the new Governor (The Darling Commission) ran to 20 pages[10] and mostly refer to the establishment of a Lands Board, the sale of public lands and the use of revenues there from as well as changes to be made to accounting and recording of

---

[7] Blue Book for 1826
[8] HRA 1:12:124 These changes were incorporated into Brisbane's successor - Governor Darling - and the commission dated 16th July 1825
[9] Bigge Report # 3 p69
[10] HRA 1:12:107-126

transactions in the colony. Lithgow raised a concern about the inefficiency of commissariat record keeping and recommended additional records are maintained.[11]

In 1826, Lithgow's successor as Commissary of Accounts, George Maddox (like Lithgow, transferred from Mauritius Commissariat), was charged with keeping a set of 'nominal ledgers' for the several convict, gaol, hospital establishments and the female factory, in which the name of every person ascertained by muster (on the 25th of each month) as actually entitled to receive rations was to be recorded. These records were maintained from 1828 to 1831 when Governor Bourke found them to be 'totally useless'.[12] Bourke found that the keeping of such records required a great many efficient clerks, although McMartin in *Public Servants & Patronage* appears to justify the increasing numbers of support staff (total establishment) involved[13]. McMartin relates clerical assistance in the commissariat to total population numbers and finds that in ratio terms the clerical numbers had to increase annually and this is exactly what happened in practice. After 1840, the accounts branch in NSW became of little importance after 1840 and it was reduced from 11 to only four persons. It was expected the Department would be abolished and this eventually took place in 1846. Commissary accounts summaries are found in a variety of sources. The SRO maintains the detailed transactions directed by Governor King, and the AJCP details the records available from the PRO; but most records are intertwined in the Military Chest records in the '*Blue Books*' from 1822. Prior to this, the Commissary sent summaries to England and the Treasury assembled parliamentary reports and requested appropriations.

As a percentage to total white population, the number of convicts in the colony reduced from 100% in 1788, to 54% in 1793, and to a low of 38% in 1804, before rising again to 61% and stabilising at about 35-40%. These statistics are important because they reflect the numbers 'on the store' and, as long as there were many convicts victualled by the store, commissariat expenses were going to be heavy. Treasury issued constant instructions Treasury to minimise the numbers 'on the store' so, even though many convicts were arriving in the colony, the governors found ways of assigning them into private hands and

---

[11] Lithgow letter to Darling June 1826

[12] HRA 1:16:399 since none of the ledgers have survived; the SRO considers that their apparent uselessness resulted in their destruction.

[13] McMartin: '*Public Servants and Patronage*' incorporates a table (P129) reflecting that each commissary employee served more and more population and therefore were increasingly efficient in their operation.

taking them off public 'support', which in effect represented a cost transfer from government to private employers.

It is of interest to compare various statistics relating to NSW colonial revenue and NSW commissariat revenue. Such an analysis has been undertaken in the statistical synopsis of this study (Chapter 8) and some initial observations are set out below:

Both revenue and expenditure rise at a similar rate and move through the same fluctuations, which are reflective of economic conditions in the colony and in Britain. Further analysis using the commissariat expenditure and comparing it against the convict population, which for the first 40 years of the colony averaged 77% of the population 'on the store', shows an average cost of 1/3d per head per day to maintain a convict in the colony[14,] the cost of food, clothing, bedding and a rooming allowance, paid by the commissariat. This cost of 1/3d per head per day should be compared against the average pay rate of a labourer of 5/- per head per day. If we accept Coghlan's[15] assertion that a convict was only 60% as productive as a free worker, the cost of convict labour compared with free labour was approximately 2:1 or 5/- versus 2/6d. This raises the question of why the British Treasury wished to use contractors for public building construction instead of convict labour, as they would have known that the cost would double. By following this policy, convicts were restricted to work gangs on road making and repair and land clearing as by this time the British Government had also abolished government farms. This annual maintenance charge of £4.15.0 per head per annum for convicts in the colony compares favourably with the cost to the British Treasury of prisoner maintenance in England at the same period , approximately £24 per annum[16]

The colonial population was subjected to a taxation impost averaging £5.15.4 per head per annum, within a range of £6.2.6 in 1822 to £2.15.0 in 1848[17]. This was a significant charge against the colony's settlers and added an average 10% to their cost of living. Such

---

[14] W. C. Wentworth in *Statistical, Historical & Political Account of the Colony* uses this figure and supports its computation by referring to then current costs referred to the House of Commons Committee on Transportation.

[15] T.A. Coghlan 'Labour & Industry in Australia' - Vol 1 Coghlan makes this reference in a comparison of building costs using contract labour in lieu of convict or government labour.

[16] E.A. Wrigley & R.S. Schofield 'The Population History of England 1541-1871'. An excellent work about trends in British population movements and discourses on the prison populations and the cost of their maintenance between 1775 and 1855.

[17] These calculations have been made by the writer from an analysis of colonial revenues raised from import duties and reflect an added cost to the consumer of government charges. Obviously the charges declined per head of population as the colony grew and the internal demographics changed

an impost was higher in the colony than it was for the people of Britain who suffered taxation of an average of 4%[18] for the same period. The point being made here is that the colonial free settlers were more heavily taxed than taxpayers in Britain. Although this is a social economics and quality of life issue, it is relevant that taxation rates between the colony and the mother country be comparable. The colony had been set on the path to becoming self-sustaining and self-supporting, but it had to endure tax on exports into Britain with no preferential advantages. Settlers also had to pay taxation by way of government duties on every item imported. Indirectly the government was promoting 'home' manufacturing.

The final statistical observation that should be made relates to the cost of operating the colony and the benefits that flowed to Britain there from. The total cost between 1788 and 1827 was in excess of £4.7 million[19], but the minimum direct savings to Britain can be assessed at over £50 million[20]. In addition to the direct savings to Britain, English industry gained a new source of raw materials for its wool, oil and timber manufacturers, and the efficiency of the shipping industry increased by full loads being carried to the colony and ships returning with full loads from India, China or Batavia.[21]

The commissariat fed and clothed the convicts, the military and the civil officers. It also victualled all those settlers, mainly emancipists, who were supported by the government for at least the first two years of their freedom and provided them with tools and clothing. It was the principal market for colonial produce, buying grain and other products from the settlers, who relied on it for a secure, stable income. Commissariat bills and store receipts were the first currency of NSW. The commissariat dominated colonial finance, acting as a bank, controlling and administering the flow of foreign exchange in the shape of treasury bills issued to pay for the cost of the colony, providing loans and credit and encouraging the establishment of enterprises that could meet its demands. These activities were the basis for the story of the economic role of the commissariat and an analysis of its operations in the colony of NSW.

---

[18] Biggs & Jordan 'An Economic History of England'

[19] N.G. Butlin *'What a way to run an Empire, fiscally'*

[20] Beckett 'British Colonial Investment in the Colony 1788-1851' SLNSW & NLA

[21] The statistics have been assembled from the following sources: Butlin, Forster and Schedvin, and are to be found as an attachment to this paper.

Fiscal Policy Before 1820

The governors' need for a 'discretionary' fund from which they could draw funds for 'special' purposes prompted revision of the fiscal management in the pre-Macquarie era and set the standard for 'local revenue raising'. The governors wanted to do something other than perform the minimalist functions allowed by the British Treasury. Every official pound sterling had to be begged, and the governors needed just a little extra for the people of the settlement, especially to carry out public works of a slightly better quality than that officially authorised for this minimalist public bureaucracy

From the earliest records (as recorded in HRNSW), certain conclusions can be drawn on colonial public finance and these can summarised. These revenue-raising measures impacted on the commissariat because all locally raised revenues affected the cost of goods in the colony and the cost of doing business. Although the commissariat was not a public department store, its role included the purchase of provisions from visiting ships and import duties on the major portion of those cargoes affected the pricing of all goods in the colony.

There was a wide range of duties and taxes imposed on the early settlers, ranging from duties on imported alcoholic beverages, such as spirits, beer and wine, to license fees, tolls and a general duty on all imports. The general rate of duty was 10/4 per gallon on spirits and 9d per gallon on wine. On tobacco the rate was 6d per pound, while timber attracted a rate of 1/- per lineal foot. General Cargo attracted an ad valorem duty at a flat 5% rate. There were also a variety of licenses and tolls. Hawker's licenses sold for £20, and it cost a settler 2d (tuppence) to go from Sydney town to the settlement of Parramatta. A country settler in the Hawkesbury district paid 1d to cross the Nepean River at Windsor. The rationale behind the tolls on public roads built by convict labour was that tolls collected would and should offset not only the cost of construction but also the cost of maintenance. Between 1789 and 1850, a substantial amount of land was granted to settlers and the British Treasury reached the conclusion that the revenue sourced from 'rents' on Crown land grants could accumulate into a considerable future windfall for the Crown.

The total of Civil List salaries in 1792 was only £4,726.0.0 (of which the governor's salary was £1,000 per annum), but by 1812 the total had increased to £9,828.15.0, due to both individual salary increases as well as more names being placed on the Civil List. By 1815, the governors' establishment budget was now over £15,000 per annum.

Fiscal Policy post-1820

Crown land sales were first recorded in the 1825 '*Blue Book*'. A proclamation of 25 March 1825 by George III imposed a new charge on crown lands at the rate of 1/- for every 50 acres, to commence five years after the date of the original grant. To that date all crown lands had been disposed of by grants, and this 'quit' rent was a form of back-door compensation to the crown. In the official grant documents, the receiver of the land grant was given notice that further costs may attach at some future time to the land, and this gave the Crown the opportunity raise this 'rent' charge on the land. There was to be a landholder's fee of 15/- per 100 acres of crown land reserved for each three years for free settlers, followed by a 2/- fee per 100 hundred acres redeemable after 20 years from purchase. On 18 May 1825, the Governor Sir Thomas Brisbane ordered that the 'rent' be changed to a flat rate of 5% of the estimated value of the grants, without purchase (as opposed to purchased land), to commence 7 years from the date of grant. 'Rents' on any second and subsequent grants were payable immediately, without the benefit of the 7 year grace period. By Proclamation, also dated 18 May 1825, George III authorised the sale of crown lands at the rate of 10/- per acre, to a maximum of 4,000 acres per individual or a maximum of 5,000 acres per family. Payment was by way of a 10% deposit and four equal quarterly instalments.

The 1822 '*Blue Book*' are titled 'Abstract of the Net Revenue and Expenditure of the Colony of New South Wales for the Year 1822', which indicates that all colonial revenue and expenses were consolidated in the '*Blue Book*'. The detailed records confirm this.

'*Observations upon revenue for the Colony in 1828*' by James Thomson, a consultant to the Colonial Treasurer of NSW [23] observes that the 'net colonial income' for the year 1828, as actually collected, was exclusive of sums *in aid of revenue* which could not be viewed in the character of income. This item is further defined as 'the proceeds of the labour of convicts, and establishments connected with them, being applied to the reduction of the amount of parliamentary grants for their maintenance'. In subsequent reports, the item 'receipts in aid of revenue' appeared in the '*Blue Books*', and included revenues such as - 'sale of Crown livestock; sale of government farms produce; sale of clothing and cloth made at the Female Factory at Parramatta; sale of wheat, sugar, molasses and tobacco

---

[2] [3] The piece by Thomson is an Appendix in *Financial Statements of the Colonial Treasurers of NSW 1855-1881 - already cited*

produced by the convicts at new settlements such as Port Macquarie'. Such revenues were reluctantly included in official financial statements on the grounds that livestock had originally been included as an 'expense', whilst convict production was produced by 'prisoners' whose cost of maintenance was not recorded if self-produced. This is a significant point and has been made previously. There was no recorded value attached to the output of convicts and, even though their production was sold through the commissariat store and the revenue was recorded, there was no 'cost of sale' attached to this revenue. This practice defied logic, common sense and all accounting conventions.

James Thomson's note show the total quantity of alcohol imported into, and thus consumed in, the colony, in 1828 when the population was only 37,000, of which adults would have numbered less than 25,000. 162,167 gallons of spirits and 15,000 gallons of wine were imported, a total of 177,167 gallons or the equivalent of $3/4^{ths}$ of a pint per week of Colonial alcohol beverage for each person –men, women and children. Local distillation from sugar was prohibited in 1828 and the high price of grain and the higher taxing of locally-manufactured spirits also became a natural deterrent to local production. A final observation was made in the '*Blue Book*' compilation of 1829 that the only duties imposed on spirits that year was upon those imported directly from H.M. Plantations in the West Indies. So the British authorities received the double financial benefit from the trading in spirits and charging duties on them at their destination. Local duties were collected in the colony but used to offset British Treasury expenditures, so in effect the British government reaped the benefit.

In 1828 the quantity of dutiable tobacco was 136,748 pounds weight, compared with 91,893 pounds in 1825. The government experimented with locally-grown tobacco at establishments in Emu Plains and Port Macquarie with 51,306 pounds being produced. In 1828, total consumption of tobacco was 5 lb. per head of adult population per annum or 3 oz per head per day.

Shipping companies paid lighthouse charges, along with wharfage. The growth of shipping into the Port of Sydney was so great that, by 1828 revenue from lighthouse dues, harbour dues and wharfage was over £4,000.

In 1828, the postage of letters attracted fees for the first time and the official Postmaster collected £598 for general revenue. This grew rapidly so that by 1832 the amount of postage collected was £2,000. Each colony imposed its own postage and printed its own stamps until Federation.

The commencement of sales of both crown lands and crown timbers increased general revenues to the extent that in 1828, the amounts realised were as follows:

Table 6.2: Crown Revenue Earnings for the Treasury in 1828

Sales of Crown Land	£5,004.19.02
Sales of Cedar on Crown Land	744.15.11
Sales of Other Timber	9,365.11.04

The British Treasury had reserved for itself all revenues from crown lands, and from standing timber on crown lands. The Governor had also imposed a fee of one halfpenny per foot for all cedar cut on crown lands. The *Blue Book* makes the further observation that this charge 'has checked bushrangers and other lawless depredators by depriving them of ready means of subsistence by the absence of all restraint from cutting Cedar upon unallocated lands'.[24]

Historical financial data is relevant to understanding the social conditions in the colony. The application of duties, tariffs, tolls and fees made up the essential revenue of a colony that was designed to be self-sufficient. It was being given minimal economic support by the British Government, even though the opportunity cost of housing 'prisoners' in the colony was a fraction of the cost of housing them in England.

Stores to the Colony

In June 1801, the Duke of Portland advised the Treasury Commissioners of new arrangements for regular transportation of stores to Sydney:

> '*I transmit to your Lordships a list of articles necessary to be sent out yearly to New South Wales, consigned to the Governor and to be used by settlers, and convict labour, or exchanged for grain or animal food supplied His Majesty's stores (exclusive of stores, implements, sent for the use of convicts at public labour), 30% to be charged on all such items to indemnify government for freight, losses and issuing in small quantities. These items are to be sent out annually in the South Sea Whalers, or other vessels destined to the colony. The advantages which government, as well as settlers, will derive from this proceeding are very considerable. At present the charges made by individuals on such items of necessity are calculated on a profit of from 100% to 500%*'.[25]

---

2 [24] 1824 *Blue Book* p.6
2 [25] HRA 1:3:167 Portland to King

It was the intention of the British Government, in a belated response to Governor Hunter's suggestion of a government retail monopoly store to combat the price hiking by local traders, to purchase consumption items in Britain and ship them to the colony and make a limited profit from such trade.'

The pre-1800 years brought the desire to expand commissariat operations into retailing goods at reasonable prices, which in turn would inhibit military officers from charging exorbitant prices for similar goods through the military monopoly. The expansion of the commissariat into retailing, together with the arrival of 'resident merchants from Madras and London, marked the end of their monopoly'.[26] In February 1805 some of the officers successfully applied for an advance of special 'commissary notes' equivalent to sterling with which to buy stock and other articles from the captain of the *Lady Barlow*. Others found kangaroo products a lucrative source of business, bringing more profitable returns from the commissariat than agriculture.[27]

The Blue Books

Whatever happened in the colony was reflected in the '*Blue Books*' one way or another. They commenced in 1822 and provide a fascinating glimpse into the early colony. Although they will be seen as financial statements, because they reflect the financial condition of the settlement, they are, in fact, much more. They included details of births, deaths and marriages, they showed the substantial number of shipping movements into and out of Port Jackson, they listed all imports and exports, and they recorded the values of all production in the colony. As statements of accounts, they are reproduced in great detail and are valuable sources for the economic historian. Prior to 1822 and the introduction of the '*Blue Books',* the financial records of the colony were privatised in their preparation. Two non-salaried, non-government individuals were appointed to keep the records for an annual fee. Both were well-known and probably well-intentioned, but they both became very wealthy as a result of being in charge of the colonial 'treasury'. Their remunerations as treasurers was supplementary to the already generous civil salary they earned in other capacities

In 1800, Governor King began to raise local private revenue; he was acting illegally because it was not authorised by the British Parliament. When the wooden gaol in Sydney was sabotaged and burnt down, it had to be replaced and Governor King promised the

---

2   6   Oxford History of Australia Vol 2 'Possessions 1770-1860'

2   7 Oxford History *ibid* p98

Secretary of State the building would be replaced by public subscription, because the British Treasury balked at paying for another gaol. King's attempts to find public labour and contributed materials failed, and he was left with a shortage of funds if the building was to be completed. However, the work was finished using government funds, which he agreed to 'make good'.[28 and, to achieve this, h]e instituted a basic form of duty on spirits entering the colony. Like any form of 'taxation' it was easily manipulated, both as to the rate and the application. The revenue grew and King looked for to apply the revenue locally, rather than allow it to be appropriated by the H.M. Treasury. King and his successors were well aware of the British Government's wish to place a limit on growing colonial expenditure and they wanted to see local revenue used to 'top' up limited funds coming from London, not to replace them. The biggest appeal of this local revenue was its use on a 'discretionary' basis, rather than having to conform to prior appropriations by the Parliament. The Gaol Fund was established to rebuild the Town gaol and was administered by Darcy Wentworth, an official assistant Surgeon. Its successor by name change was the Police Fund, also administered by Wentworth. The second fund was the Orphan Fund, officially known as the Female Orphan Fund, which was administered by the Reverend Samuel Marsden. The starting point of the Orphan Fund was when Governor King purchased, on behalf of the colony, the residence of Lieutenant Kent who was returning to London and had no further need of one of the finest houses in the colony. The house was located on the northeast corner of 'High' street (now George) and Bridge Streets, so named because of the wooden bridge erected for the public to cross the Tank Stream. It also led to the second Governor's Residence, the so-called 'Governor's Mansion', located further down Bridge Street.

Initially the revenues raised from duties on spirits, and later all imports, grew rapidly along with the economy as immigrants, convicts, emancipists and free settlers swelled the population. Almost everything had to be imported from Britain and so, with import duties, harbour and wharfage charges, and even charges for fresh water taken on by visiting ships, the colonial coffers overflowed. A primary collection agent, the Naval Officer for the Port of Sydney, was installed in 1803, sharing his net collections between the two funds[29]. Essentially, the problem of formalising collections and recording and reporting local revenues was not brought under any form of control until the arrival of Macquarie. The colony had no treasury, other than the commissariat, but Macquarie manipulated a novel

---

[28] HRA 1:3:167 King to Portland

[29] The Naval Officer was John Piper, who was remunerated on a percentage of his collections. His annual emoluments grew to over £5,000 until William Lithgow, the Colonial Auditor, uncovered a 'deficiency' of £6,000 in his monies, and Piper was dismissed from office. At that time the position was converted to a salaried remuneration.

means of exchange in common practice. Store receipts issued by the commissary sufficed in lieu of coinage until Britain finally agreed to transfer basic coinage to the colonial commissary[30]. This marked the beginning of the increasingly important role for the commissariat, the provision of financial services, including banking activities, to and within the colony.

The '*Blue Books*' replaced this antiquated mode of record-keeping. Governor Brisbane was selected to implement the Commissioner Bigge's proposal that the financial recording in the colony be broadened, and the '*Blue Books*'[31] were thus born. The Books were assembled annually from subsidiary hand-kept records, so they were not original documents as such but were rewritten once each year from other assembled documents. This system, and indeed duplication of many records, made additional work for the commissary clerical staff, the colonial treasurer, the centralised government accounting staff and especially the newly-appointed Colonial Auditor, William Lithgow. For all years between 1822 and 1844, the fiscal year for the *Blue Books* ended on 30 December, the calendar year. In 1843, the Lord Treasurers in London directed that the new fiscal year would end on 30 September. Lord John Russell instructed Sir George Gipps to have a Governor's Report on the State of the Colony accompany the '*Blue Books*' to London each year which he would lay on the table of both houses of parliament. In general, the '*Blue Books*' gave no hint of the policies being pursued in the colony; they were the bookkeeping records of today, a tedious list of past historical past facts, rather than forward-looking road map of economic and fiscal planning.

In 1832, Sir Richard Bourke introduced Estimates and Appropriation Bills for local expenditures before the NSW Legislative Council. The Legislative Council's realisation that the Governor had acquired additional fiscal responsibilities on behalf of the colony compromised planning opportunities when estimates were presented, along with the actual statements of revenue and expense. This caused some members to become quite vocal in opposition to the governor's plans; for instance, in 1843 Blaxland and Wentworth were adamant and vociferous when they learnt from the estimates that the British Government did not intend to subsidise colonial expenditure on police and gaols. This practice began in 1834, and the cost to the colony over the eight years after it commenced was in excess of £700,000. Members of the Legislative Council thought this sum could have been better

---

[30] Beckett, Gordon 'The Public Finance of the Colony' and 'The Development of the Public Accounts', -a full description of the early record-keeping and revenue raising in the colony.

[31] The name came from the blue coloured covers in which these extensive reports are contained

used by the colony for education, public works, and the reduction of unemployment or even to replace the British investor funds, the withdrawal of which had largely caused the 1841-1843 recession in the colony. This 'political storm' was the result of a misunderstanding, for the British Treasury had written to Bourke's predecessor stating quite clearly that the cost of policing was to be a charge against local revenues. The governor had not advised to the NSW LC of the amended policy and, in any case, the 'principle' was quite out of step with the protection of local revenues, which the members considered should be used for developing the local economy, not controlled by the British Treasury.

The estimates were of great advantage to the members of the Council and provided an opportunity for Treasury to quickly compare what had been planned with what had actually been achieved. By this time, local revenues were a significant portion of total colonial revenues and they had largely replaced transfers of funds from Britain. The 1843 Gipps Report to the Colonial Office shows that, whilst in 1838 local revenues had reached £211,988; by 1842 they had doubled to £414,156. These figures excluded crown land sales revenue, which Britain had reserved for its exclusive accounting and appropriation. Annual revenues and expenses may be related to the growth in population which was growing in excess of 5,000 people per annum and this rate kept the 'per head' figure of revenue expenses, imports and exports, very much in line. By 1843 exports were running at £1,579,000 per annum of which wool was 50%, and growing. In line with economic thinking of the day, and government planning generally, the colonial colony was running at a small surplus each year between 1838 and 1842.[32]

The next year's report by Gipps highlighted the dramatic effect of natural elements on the agricultural sector. Even though production of wheat and maize grew from 1,335,000 bushels in 1842 to 1,719,000 bushels in 1844, the importation of these grains grew from 178,000 in 1842 to 265,000 bushels in 1844. Most imports were from Tasmania by private traders and speculators.

A solid indicator of the growth in the colonial economy may be found in the 1844 'Blue Book' reference to banking statistics, which included commissary advances and deposits. Discounted paper held by the banks fell from £2,562,000 in 1842 to £1,583,000 in 1844,

---

[32] Elsewhere in this study is a statistical analysis of local revenues per head of population, which indicates the colony was highly taxed compared with other British subjects

this being the central period of a very bad recession. These figures are in contrast to those of deposits held in the same banks which rose from £988,000 in 1842 to £1,028,000 in 1844.

Military Rations Cost Offset by Deduction

In November 1802, King informed Palmer, his Commissary-in-chief that,

> '...in accordance with His Majesty's warrant of February 1799, each non-commissioned officer, and private, shall have deducted from their full pay the amount of three pence halfpenny (3 1/2d per quarter) – this was applied to each corporal, sergeant, trumpeter, drummer and fifer when stationed in Jamaica, New South Wales or Gibraltar.'

The commissariat, at this stage was also the paymaster within the colony and handled both civilian and military pay vouchers or bills and assisted in crediting these bills to the official's account at the commissariat for purchasing purposes or exchanging for goods, since no cash was available in the colony. The purpose of the deduction was to contribute to the military costs of rations from the commissariat.

Valuing the Commissariat Inventory

In August 1804, King advised Hobart that the value of inventory and stores held by the commissariat amounted to £243,519.10.00. These stores consisted of: [38]

Table 6.3: The Value of Store Stocks and Inventory in Sydney - 1804

Livestock	£75,628
Grain and flour	£14,833
Salt meat	£41,134
Clothing	£20,562
Spirits	£2,047
Debts to the crown	£10,396
Public buildings	£54,100
Vessels and boats	£2,250
Land in cultivation	£6,375

At the same time King advised Hobart that livestock and stores items belonging to private individuals in the colony amounted to £245,543. A large part of the private stores would have been held by the trader, Robert Campbell, who was in the process of transferring large quantities of stores and other inventory from his head office in India, by way of back-loading after delivering quantities of sandalwood to Indian merchants. It is difficult to imagine why King bothered to value the livestock and stores in private hands, other than that he was trying to impress the Colonial Office with the colony's progress. It was a part of each muster that the numbers of livestock were collected, but their value was artificial at best and of little interest to any party.

Store Receipts as an alternative to Specie

In March 1815, Macquarie issued a general order stating:

> *'In order to obviate the inconveniences that are likely to result to the public from the want of a sufficient quantity of Specie belonging to the government, the Governor deems it advisable to return to issuing 'store receipts' for all purchases made on account of the crown, at all commissary locations. The store receipts are to be declared every two months and 'be redeemed' or be forfeited. In order to avoid fraud each receipt is to be matched against the original 'cheque book' before being despatched to London.'[39]*

Setting Prices for Grain to be sold to the Commissariat Store

David Allen, who succeeded John Palmer as Commissary-General, wrote to his superior (the Commissary-in-Chief) about problems with setting fixed prices to purchase grain and provisions from settlers:

> *'The mode of supplying His Majesty's stores in the colony has to-date been by the governor fixing by general orders, the price at which grain and fresh provisions were to be paid for by the crown. Notice would be given that the stores were open to receive goods at set prices and when the desired quantity was attained, the notice was withdrawn. The order of 10th December 1812, directs 8 shillings per bushel to be paid for all wheat, and 7p per pound for all meat supplied. In years of plenty this system works fine, but when supplies are in short supply, then the price is generally well below that available on the open market and the stores remain empty.*
> *It would be most beneficial to the Crown if all purchases were to be made by public tender or contract, as no individual could be expected to supply wheat at 8s, when the market is paying 9s, 10s, or even 15s for each bushel'[40]*

Circulating Currency and the Recession of 1827

Governor Darling released the colony's first coinage August 1826. Prior to the administration of Sir Thomas Brisbane, drafts, drawn on the English Treasury for government services and sold in the colony, had formed a convenient and practical medium of paying for imports in London and had eliminated the necessity of developing an export trade. By utilising a local currency and setting exchange rates, an export industry became necessary. During the Macquarie era, the annual total of these drafts increased disproportionately to the population; however, in reality there was a great deal of deferred maintenance work which needed completing. However, in any case Macquarie

---

[39] Governor's despatches 1814-1816
[40] HRA 1:4:387 David Allan to Lords of the Treasury (including the Commissary-in –Chief)

did increase government spending– but the real question was not what was expended, but whether it had real value to the colony and the British Treasury. In 1806-1809, the annual average was £29,415; by 1821 it was £166,315. During this time the population had trebled, but the value of bills drawn had risen even faster. Under Macquarie, the colony's prosperity was largely based on the 'money' circulating in the colonial economy. Successive governors discovered that this was contrary to London's expectations, but also Macquarie's successors did not have the stamina to continue in this frenetic pace of activity. Darling complained directly to Bathurst that he had 'never worked so hard in his life'.

In proposing the release of a 'circulating currency', Darling commented to Bathurst: 'as a result of the speculation of individuals and the excessive discounts on the part of the Bank of New South Wales, the present distresses in the colony have taken place' when referring to the 1827 Recession. During the period 1827-1834 (the duration of the recession and its aftermath) the amount of circulating and usable currency in the colony was not less than £200,000 sterling. For the most part, this large sum consisted of drafts on the British Treasury.

The following information, in pounds sterling is extracted from the 1826 'Blue Book':

Table 6.4: The Amount of Circulating Currency in the Colonial Economy 1827-1834

Drafts estimated at	140,000
Store receipts for grain and beef	20,000
Notes of the commissary due on demand	15,000
Notes of the Bank of NSW	15,000
Notes of respectable individuals	10,000
Total (in Sterling)	£210,000

Macquarie had left a legacy of over £150,000 in Treasury drafts and Darling accused building speculators of using this circulating currency as the basis for their activities. Brisbane had been directed by the British Treasury to reduce the amount of Treasury bills, as they were considered inflationary, and it was not until his arrival in 1821 that their value was reduced to about £80,000.

Darling wrote to Bathurst:

> 'The introduction of a sum of £400,000 at this period, and the commencement of the Dollar System, while it made a very serious alteration in the property and profits of the bulk of the people, still afforded a sufficient circulating

medium for all the purposes of an increasing trade; and, including the value of our exportable produce, there was still a floating capital of nearly 200,000. The alleged over speculation of individuals and the apparent excess of discounts on the back of the bank, therefore, had the amount of our circulating available and usable capital remained unaltered; but, such speculations and discounts, supposing the customary average circulation to be afloat, must have reached considerably higher, and the present difficulties of our money market may fairly be attributable, as much as the cessation of the ordinary and expected expenditure of government, as to the mentioned causes'

Darling correctly anticipated the coming financial crisis and, with the help of the NSW Chamber of Commerce, persuaded the Legislative Council to enact such measures as controlling discount rates and interest rates so as to minimise the impact of the recession. This measure of public relations was pursued by William Lithgow on Darling's behalf, since

Darling was not the most favoured official in the colony. However, Lithgow's measure enhanced Darling's reputation amongst the settlers, traders and investors.

Darling reported to Bathurst:

'Anxious to promote the commercial prosperity of the colony, at all times by every lawful means, the Committee of the NSW Chamber of Commerce feel themselves more especially called upon at the present moment to endeavour to prevent by timely measures the otherwise approaching crisis and, satisfied that His Excellency desires nothing so much as the permanent association of his name with the wealth and happiness of the community, they are more confident in laying before him their suggestions for effecting the purposed relief.'[42]

How far the internal consumption and the consequent energies of the industrious settler may be curtailed, and all other channels of our colonial wealth obstructed, it is painful for the committee (of the Chamber of Commerce) to contemplate: this hitherto prosperous colony with its large tracts of the finest soil, and a climate with natural resources, inferior to no country on the Globe, to see its active and intelligent population plunged into difficulties of a pecuniary nature, unless some immediate aid be given to the commercial body. Already large failures have been announced among one class of traders, and a closure of that important branch of commerce, the Whale fishery.'

The day before his appeal to Bathurst, Darling prepared a Memorandum [43] on measures that could be taken to relieve the money market. He proposed that:

'Treasury bills were to be issued in the amount equivalent to the Commissariat debt to the Colonial Fund and the money thus paid out will enable merchants

---

[42] HRA I: 12:512 (July 1827) Darling to Bathurst on the subject of the anticipated financial crisis
[43] HRA 1:12:398 Memorandums from Darling to Bathurst in Governor's Despatches dated 30th August 1826.

to obtain bills on demand, which bills would assist the banks promoting circulation of their own notes, and therefore add to the circulating medium'.

Darling felt the 'depression' was a commercial one, caused by British investors withdrawing their funds from the colony, banks speculating on highly discounted bills resulting in borrowers becoming insolvent and commercial lenders 'loaning on mortgages' but using short term depositor funds[44]. All these components made for a severe and desperate shortage of ready cash in the colony and Darling's answer was to inject new monetary capacity into the economy and use the multiplier effect to generate more circulation of funds. The commissariat was a most useful tool in all of this. Darling wanted to use the funds borrowed by the commissariat from the colonial treasury to put circulating currency in the hands of the banks.

Darling's solution would not occur in today's economic thinking. The result would be a commercial recession which would spread very quickly through the consumer ranks. Inventories would decline, imports would slow, exports would decline and a full-scale recession would be at hand, together with spiralling inflation. In the colonial economy, the commissariat played such a large and controlling role; its action or lack thereof would determine the length and extent of any recession.

In 1826 the commissariat was preparing for large intakes of convicts and anticipating a great deal of activity in the Lumber Yard and the Female Factory. Exports were growing but were in line with the growth of imports. However, British investors had reacted to the decline in the British economy, and the resultant build-up of manufacturing raw materials in the hands of British industry and the decline of prices, and they chose the cautious alternative of withholding investment and speculation abroad whilst they waited for the British economy to recover.

In these circumstances, Darling's response was reasoned and valid, even if it did pass the major responsibility to the banks and their shareholders. The banks in fact had to bear some responsibility as they had been discounting the commissariat notes at high rates, before they were finally shut out of that market by a restoration of the store receipts program. Their response was to withdraw funds from the money market and, move into mortgages and fixed term securities, which decreased the amount of currency circulating in

---

[44] From the 'Memorandum' from Darling to Bathurst – August 1826

the economy. This, in turn, slowed the whole economy and created a 'commercial recession'.[45]

Accounting for the Commissariat

As recorded by both N.G. and S.J. Butlin, details of commissariat financial statements before 1832 have been lost. Analysis of total expenditures has been prepared from other PRO records, such as summaries of bills paid between 1788 and 1830. Parliamentary appropriations for the Colonial Office have also been prepared and the results of both these sources are incorporated into the tables below.

The other analysis prepared and also set down below relates to the accounting classifications. We know from other records of the same period[57] that accountants and auditors used ledger systems not unlike those manual systems still used today including a chart of accounts. Government ledgers between 1810 and 1822, like private company ledgers, were all prepared on a strictly cash basis; there were no accruals, depreciation or provisions. All appropriations were accounted for by a funds statement for annual presentation to parliament.[58] Thus the internal (revised) accounting system introduced by William Lithgow, the first Deputy-Commissary General (Accounts), in 1824 would have been moulded on Lithgow's experience of the commissariat accounting systems he had installed in Heligoland in 1807, and Mauritius in 1812. Lithgow was an experienced commissariat accountant and would have established a set of accounting records showing the accumulation of revenue and expenditures, not unlike the classifications set down in the table below:

Table 6.5: Probable Financial Reporting Structure within the Colonial Commissariat

Consolidated Commissariat Statement of Revenues and Expenditures

Revenues
Appropriations from British Treasury, for:
Convict maintenance – clothing, bedding, general supplies
Purchase of commissariat inventory
Purchase of convict, civil and military foodstuffs
Purchase of building materials for public works – lot prepared by convict labour from commissariat resources

---

[45] This concept is referred to by S.J. Butlin *Foundations*
[57] Beckett, G. W. ' An Economic History of the Van Diemen's Land Company 1824-1900'
[58] Appropriation statements and 'Appropriation Bills' were introduced to the NSW Legislative Council in 1832 by Governor Richard Bourke

Proceeds of sale of minerals, government livestock, produce and grain to the general population
Proceeds of 'renting' out part-time convict labour

Expenditures
Purchases from U.K. paid by bills drawn on the British Treasury
Purchases of local colonial supplies, initially paid by store receipts and then consolidated into bills drawn on the Treasury
Purchases of merchandise from visiting ships arriving in Sydney Harbour and paid by bills drawn on the Treasury

Raw materials purchased for reworking by convict labour in commissariat manufacturing centres

Payment to independent contractors for providing services to the commissariat e.g.
grinding and milling of grain, contract transportation and shipping services

Purchases of meat, livestock, grain and vegetables and commodities for use as rations for persons 'on the store'

Categories/classifications of expenditures
Convict Maintenance
Military and Civil personnel maintenance
Government public works – construction & maintenance

Inventory Classifications
Purchased supplies, produce and provisions
Stocks of building parts and products, including timber
Stocks of manufactured items by convict labour
Stocks of minerals and other extracted products by convict labour
Stocks of livestock and other farm supplies

What the commissariat accounting system could not, and did not report, was a new classification designed specifically to account for output by convict labour. Convict production of coal, timber, lime, tiles and bricks was important; these commodities were used extensively for government public works and they were also sold onto the public. Revenue from these sales was usually credited to the commissariat, apart from in 1823, when it was recognised in the *Blue Books* (refer Table 8.1). In all other years the substantial value of convict output used in the commissariat escaped unrecorded and unreported. In just one year the estimated value of manufacturing output from the various government instrumentalities which relied on convict labour has been computed at nearly £500,000 [59] per annum. In addition, the value of public works during the Macquarie administration has been estimated at £2,000,000[60]. What has not been estimated as yet is a breakdown of convict output identifying the value of the natural resources used, which is timber, clay, seashell, and coal were significant raw materials used for local manufacturing and export.

What Does This Mean?

From this brief analysis, the conclusion can be drawn that any accounting system would identify purchases made for convict maintenance, civil and military support costs and the costs of supporting other settlers placed 'on the store' as part of their inducement to

---

[59] This writer's estimated of production from the Lumber Yard, Timber Yard, Brick & Tile Yard, Female Factory and mineral extraction

[60] This writer's estimate of construction costs including valuing labour for the 76 buildings listed as being completed by Macquarie – refer Table 4.5 herein

relocate in the colony. The commissariat accounting system should also have identified, but did not, was the value of local resources and convict labour used on the public works program, acting like a simple job cost system, and then the value of natural resources produced for use both within and outside the colony and developed by convict labour. An example of the first analysis would give an understanding of the true costs attributed to the major public buildings and other significant public works (such as the four main roads within the colony), whilst the second analysis would identify the value of local timber used and the value of coal extracted.

It is of interest to note that William Lithgow, as Colonial Auditor-General, joined in Governor Darling's strategy to cover up the true costs of public works. He urged Darling to react to the request from the Secretary of State that London pre-approve any public works costing over £200 by declaring that no public works cost that much because the convict labour and native resources had 'no value'. Thus the British Treasury had no opportunity of reviewing let alone controlling, expenditures on public works. Of course, despatches from the Secretary's office made it plain to the governors that public works was a low expenditure priority but, as responsible government developed and members of the NSW Legislative Council pursued natural justice and better living conditions, no governor could resist the minor beautification projects or slightly wasteful government services over and above the officially authorised basic amenities. Even if all development work, standing timber and minerals belonged to the Crown under the *Terra Nullius* concept as ratified by British laws, their usage had value and a fairer and more rational accounting system would have given credit to the development of these and other Crown resources

In summary, convict maintenance as required under the transportation program cost the British Government nearly £150,000 each year, but use of convict labour and Crown natural resources benefited the colony to the extent of nearly £500,000 per annum. Most of this benefit came via commissariat operations, achieved by effectively using convict labour in the various manufacturing operations, on government farms and other commissariat-sponsored work centres. In addition to these non-recorded entitlements, the Crown received the benefits of the revenues from the sale or lease of all land in the colony. This summary does not fit with the N.G. Butlin conclusion that the British government spent over £5 million in the colony without seeing any return. What Butlin and others[61]

---

[61] Brian Fitzpatrick in The *British Empire in Australia* took a similar position regarding Britain's one-sided generosity.

with a similar pro-Mother country disposition should have concluded was that 'The British involvement in the colony of NSW necessitated funding from the British Treasury for a variety of expenditures associated with the transportation program and the use of the colony as a penal settlement'. The development of colonial natural resources, together with its public investment program, increased the pace of growth and the promotion of two-way trade. In return the British economy received raw materials for its manufacturing industries, benefits which relieved it of dependence on European suppliers and allowed greater utilisation of its shipping interests and the emigration of a substantial number of its prison population, together with a good sampling of its poor and social outcasts. The British Treasury saved the cost of housing nearly 16,000 medium term convicted criminals and benefited also from the accompanying reduction in crime. British manufacturers exported nearly £400,000 of goods to the colony each year between 1810 and 1820.

Table 6.6: NSW Commissariat Financial Operations 1788-1820

Year	Expenses £'000	Year	Expenses £'000
1787	211	1801	10,786
1788	4,346	1802	16,468
1789	831	1803	16,975
1790	1,309	1804	10,192
1791	1,075	1805	17,442
1792	5,127	1806	9,083
1793	15,807	1807	10,483
1794	3,572	1808	13,800
1795	32,103	1809	25,199
1796	41,736	1810-1815	259,972
1797	19,465	1816	12,0673
1798	27,035	1817	112,691
1799	41,588	1818-19	188,700
1800	50,910	1820-21	428,986

Table 6.7: NSW Commissariat Revenues and Expenditures 1822-1836

Year	Revenues £'000			Expenditures £'000	
	Treasury Bills	Sale of Goods	Total Revenues	Supplies	Total Expenditures
1822	230.1	4.4	253.5	175.9	212.2
1823	119.0	4.7	134.1	110.7	149.7
1824	n.a.	n.a.	n.a.	n.a.	n.a.
1825	193.9	4.4	198.3	13.8	155.0
1826	59.3	3.9	63.2	68.8	103.3
1827	164.6	1.6	166.2	81.6	130.7
1828	98.5	n.a.	98.5	69.0	238.0
1829	154.4	n.a.	158.9	71.4	243.2
1830	138.7	n.a.	139.6	46.0	196.8
1831	117.8	5.8	182.6	46.9	203.6
1832	114.8	9.3	165.7	n.a.	194.3
1833	81.0	15.0	146.5	42.2	165.5
1834	141.9	20.8	174.2	64.6	187.0
1835	176.9	40.0	250.2	79.1	230.2
1836	223.4	60.0	354.4	100.8	344.4
1837	173.9	n.a.	254.8	92.6	234.8
1838	292.5	n.a.	383.7	97.9	363.7
1839	248.0	n.a.	474.7	132.6	474.7
1840	205.6	n.a.	389.5	126.5	389.5

It has been recorded previously that commissariat records do not exist for the post-Governor King periods but summaries are produced in Table 6.10 of commissariat fiscal operations found in Chapter 5. It should be understood that such summaries as recorded here are essentially unreliable because they are based on bills drawn on the British Treasury by officers of the commissariat and the NSW governor. Many expenditures are based on the consolidating of store receipts into bills, and a number of store receipts which were held firstly by individuals and then by banks and were probably not returned to the commissariat within a reasonable time. Likewise bills drawn in the colony and handed to captains of visiting ships may have taken years to be returned to merchant banks representing the bill's 'payee', before being sent to the Treasury. Thus it is unlikely that the periods of the expenditures, as reported above, are any more than 60-70% accurate but there is no way of adjusting the summaries because the underlying records no longer exist. These figures are extracted from an unpublished manuscript by Julius Ginswick who did not record his sources for these figures. We do know he took them from PRO records in London, and he himself made the observation that they are of questionable accuracy, especially since the allocation of expenditures was taken from a notation on the bottom of each bill and the accuracy of allocations was notoriously biased toward understating expenses in certain areas so as to avoid further examination. Ginswick reported that the figures which are not available are zero in most cases, although one must ask why this could or would be the case.

Another observation which cannot be explained, other than by reporting delays in the return of bills to the Treasury, is why the annual totals of revenues and expenditures do not matching, even though the balance of funds on hand was recorded by the Treasury accounting system. As Colonial Auditor-General, William Lithgow, found in the early 1830s, the old fashioned accounting system of open-ended transactions meant huge delays in reporting, cumbersome ledger-keeping and a mountain of paperwork. The commissariat would have found the same problem with bills issued in one fiscal period but not 'presented' until a later period.

The main components of expenditure were 'convict services', followed by maintenance of various sections of the civil administration such as 'police, clergy charities, the military and pensioners'. The commissariat was a 'banking' institution long before the commercial banks were operating and this is reflected in the loans made to the colonial treasury and loans made by the colonial treasury to the commissariat. This meant that often one or both funds ran short of money and they had to pool their cash resources and help each other over a difficult period. Another interesting method of accounting was the recording of transfers to the colony of 'specie', or notes and coinage from the British Treasury, as 'revenue' to the commissariat. This had the effect of the revenues of the colonial commissariat being overstated quite significantly. For instance, specie transfers in the 1830s were as follows:

Table 6.8: Specie Transfers 1831-1836

	£'000
1831	20.5
1832	5.0
1833	15.0
1834	20.8
1835	40.0
1836	60.0

Thus in a period of five years, commissariat revenues were inflated by over £160,000. The figures above also reflect the cyclical nature of the colonial economy. They were affected by population inflows, the demand for public infrastructure in a developing colony, economic cycles in Britain, the growth of the pastoral industries and the large increase in exports and imports. The advent of the Legislative Council in 1823 and the development of the public service, government departments and a bureaucracy from 1826 also had an impact.

What should be apparent from these tables is the inadequacy of the accounting records provided by the colony which were used by various Parliamentary committees and policy makers to impose governance. The main thrust of Bathurst's administration of the Colonial Office was that Macquarie was overspending and this led to the invaluable Bigge Enquiry. In fact, in economic terms, the Macquarie administration spent less per head of population in commissariat areas of responsibility than any of his predecessors starting from Governor Phillip and certainly less than Governors King and Bligh with whom Macquarie was most often compared. In absolute terms Bathurst was correct but, in a fast growing economy with an exploding convict population who required government maintenance, higher absolute expenditures were to be expected. The underlying problem is that the value of convict output was not measured and therefore it did not offset or benefit commissariat revenues in any way.

Reconstructing the Funds

There is still much to learn about the Military Fund, and neither S.J. nor N.G. Butlin has examined its operation in any detail. In 1830 the Commissariat Department dispersed expenses of £162,717 for the colony out of a total Treasury appropriation of £243,891. By what right, audit or direction, were these transactions made?

At the end of 1830, the balance in the Military Chest stood at £34,123 and the Colonial Treasury had £21,799. Such balances were high in relation to the value of transactions going through the accounts and raised the question as to who in London controlled such bank balances, especially as by this time the City of London had commenced a short term money market, earning interest on short term deposits by matching them with short term credit loans.

In 1825 the Military Chest reported that the 'receipts in aid of revenue' and included a statement that a 'deposit' was made into the Military Chest for 'the amount of the Parliamentary Grant issued for the charge of defraying the Civil Establishment'. This was the first time payment on account of the civil salaries made through channels other than the Colonial Fund or the British Treasury on account of the Colony.

In 1826 'Receipts in Aid of Revenue' included a consignment of specie for the first time as well as the parliamentary grant for regular payments.

The revenue figures appearing in the Colonial Fund reflects loans sometimes drawn against the Military Chest, obviously for funding. What right or direction authorised these transactions? Was any security offered, or should any interest have been paid? In the 1828 revenue statements for the Military Chest, there was an item marked 'receipts in aid of revenue' which included transactions relating to sales of:

> Crown livestock
> Coals ex Newcastle
> Wheat at Bathurst
> Sugar & molasses grown at Port Macquarie
> Cloth manufactured at Parramatta
> Surplus and condemned stores
> Articles of colonial produce delivered to the commissariat from the several
> Convict agricultural farm establishments and coal mines

A special note is included that 'the stores received from England for the service of the colony since 1825, not having been accompanied by Priced Invoices, no appropriation of the value of the issues thereof can be made.'[72]

It is interesting to note that nowhere in the accounts of transactions in the commissariat, Colonial Fund or Military Chest is the value of the convict contribution noted.

In 1829, the Receipts In Aid of Revenue contain a note that 'the total is exclusive of the value of articles of colonial produce delivered to the commissariat from the convict agricultural establishment'. This is the very first reference to the fact that convicts contributed goods and services which obviously had 'value' to the colony and that they should have been recognised and accounted for in the Books of Account (the Blue Books).

In 1830, the 'receipts in aid of revenue' are shown as having been 'paid into the Military Chest'. This is another first since traditionally, and by instruction from the Lords of the Treasury, receipts in aid of revenue were included in the Colonial Fund. That year, the disbursements on account of miscellaneous civil services are recorded as 'total disbursements, out of the military chest, in aid of the civil establishment of the colony'.

Each year the revenues recorded an amount, usually less than 500 pounds, for supplying water to visiting ships. This had originally been a 'Police Fund' transaction but obviously

---

[72] Found in the 1828 Blue Book Statement relating to the Military Chest.

the British Government considered it had the rights in water as a condition of Terra Nullius and wanted their ownership of fresh water recognised in the accounts.

Each year pensions were paid, not only to retirees who remained in the colony, but also former government officials who had returned to England. Retirees in the colony received their pensions through the Colonial Fund. From 1835, school expenses were paid to The Church of England (Episcopalian) school and to Presbyterian and Roman Catholic schools all of which were recognised in the Colonial Fund under the Religious Establishment costs, clerical costs and salaries were also recorded by denomination of church in the Religious Establishment.

In 1837, 'Revenue of the Crown' became a separate heading within the *Blue Books* Revenue and included:

Movement of specie into the colony, first shown in 1826 under the heading 'Receipts in aid of Revenue (in Sterling) - 'consignment of specie' appeared regularly in the Military Chest accounts.

Arrears in payments on account	Proceeds of imported goods
Land sales	Land sales at Port Phillip (1838)
Quit rents	Licenses to depasture cattle
Fees on the delivery of title deeds	Proceeds of the sale of charts of Port Phillip
Leasehold sales	Rent on land

The total amount of fixed revenue was recorded in the accounts in sterling, according to the current rate of exchange (1826). Rates of exchange between sterling and the local currency were originally set by Macquarie and this was retained by his successors. One notation recorded [73] 'of the above total (£216,562.16.2 in Sterling) there is cash expenditure of £196,562.16.2 of which the amount for stores expended is £21,662.16.2.' As can be seen there is still much to learn about the accounting practices and fiscal symbolism shown in the *'Blue Books'*.

The development of the colonial financial institutions reflected the needs of the day, but it took Macquarie's anticipation of a growing economy. and the refinement and reform of the monetary system as the catalyst for foreign investment and economic development, to encourage facilities such as export bills, export financing, auctioning in the colony before export and securing loans over livestock and chattels instead of only fixed assets.

---

[73]   On Page 7 of the 1826 Blue Books

It is now appropriate to develop in more detail the study of the commissariat by identifying its importance within the colonial economy. For instance, what was the impact of commissariat expenditures on the local economy? What areas of the colonial economy were dependent on commissariat expenditures? What direct and indirect benefits did commissariat operations and expenditures bring to the local economy? Did the commissariat grow with the demand for its services, or was it always lagging behind demand and dragging the economy back with it? The commissariat did grow with demand and reflect colonial needs by being true economic driver and acting as a catalyst for foreign investment, immigration and new economic activities.

Summary of Chapter 8

All items produced at the work centres were recorded and reported but not valued. The underlying concept of accounting for official (government) output was that anything produced by convicts had no official value although coal from Newcastle, clothing and materials from the Female Factory and produce and grain from the government farms were all sold publicly. The Commissariat accounted for that revenue, but there was no 'cost' of goods sold, as it would be termed today. No value was ever recorded in the books of the Orphan Fund, Police/Gaol Fund, Commissariat Accounts or '*Blue Books*' for convict output, only the revenue from the sale the items produced. So materials produced in the Lumber Yard, the Timber Yard, the Brick Yard or the Stone Yard had no value even when they comprised 80% or more of the component of public building construction in the colony and the Earl of Bathurst complained regularly of the cost and wastage of such construction. The cost of maintaining convicts was calculated as being officially about £13.10.0, even though their clothing was made locally, their food was grown locally and they were housed in public buildings built by convicts using publicly supplied materials.

Accounting for the commissariat must have been a nightmare and' in 1815, 20 clerical assistants were employed on this work. However because they were convicts, they were not 'expensed' to the commissariat and this high clerical cost was never revealed in the accounting records. Darling's contribution to the post-Macquarie commissariat was significant as the rise of the public service was aligned with a personnel restructure of convict management and maintenance and the role of the commissariat was further integrated into the public service. Darling's management style left many wondering whether progress was being made, as he had surrounded himself with a Board of General Purposes, composed of the colony's intelligencia, and ordered an impressive array of committees and boards which reported on 29 occasions on such important matters as the Crown land management, school and church land management, immigration and a wide range of financial policies in addition to a rational development of the colonial public service.

Before 1820, three governors[46] attempted to improve the operations of the commissariat but it had been in operation for 12 years before the British Treasury released the first set of written instructions on how it should be run.

One aspect of commissariat operations which grew, mainly because it did not fit into any other section of the government was the importation and control of 'specie'. Coinage was a monopoly controlled closely by the commissariat. A total of £60,000 of British coinage imported by the commissariat, of which no less than £50,000 was said to be in the commissariat at one time in September 1827 in payment for bills.[47] This meant that the commercial banks had to cease making advances before ships sailed to limit the outflow, but in fact the outflow continued - £30,000 left for London on the *Elizabeth* in November 1827, £20,000 to Mauritius in March 1828 and £30,000 to London on the *Boddington* in September 1828.[48] This 'run' on the banks seriously reduced coinage and liquidity in the colony and for a third time in four years the Bank of NSW applied for a government loan (this time for £15,000). One reason that this application was for a lower amount than previously was that the Treasury bill rate had been reduced from 3% to 1.5 %, and this somewhat discouraged the amount of coinage exported from the colony.

In its control of the importation of coinage, the commissariat played the role of fiscal and monetary comptroller, principally because the colony still had no 'official' treasury and had subrogated this important role to the commissariat and the banks. On three occasions the Bank of NSW had been granted a short-term loan by the government on condition it increased its capital base but, on each occasion, the nominal capital increased, the subscribed capital increased, but the 'paid-up' capital increased only very marginally, not enough to improve the liquidity or debt-equity ratio of the bank.[49] The dramatically 'illiquid' position of the bank was partly due to advances made by buying up commissariat 'loans', and the high discount rates imposed on Treasury bills for overseas purchases, a policy encouraged by the Executive Council and Governor Darling. The bank had taken

---

[46] Phillip, King & Macquarie
[47] *Australian newspaper* 21 September 1827
[48] *Australian* 7th March 1828   *Sydney Gazette* 3 September 1828
[49] HRA 1:14:549-60 *Darling to Murray*

no action against a large accumulation of overdue loans but part of the governor's support for it was on condition that overdue bills and loans, 'should be retired immediately', with the threat that action (foreclosure and seizure, under the new Insolvent Debtors Act-*NSW LC V &P-1830)* would be taken against all parties 'whether they be drawers, payers, acceptors or endorsers'[50]. This threat could not legally be carried out, but it accomplished its goal. The bank collected over £12,000 in cash or valid security and restored its balance sheet to 'good standing' before the Executive Council's review of the Bank of NSW licence and the threat of closure by Darling.

There was a basic conflict of interest situation in the fact that large shareholders of the Bank of Australia included Colonial Auditor-General and Comptroller of Banking (William Lithgow) as well as various members of the Governor Darling's family.

Apart from the Comptroller of the Currency, the commissariat became the major source of capital imported into the colony through British expenditure on maintenance of the penal establishments. Bills drawn by the commissariat were averaging nearly £150,000 per annum. N.G. Butlin estimates that the commissariat contributed up to 75% of private capital in the colony between 1800 and 1820.

Table 6.9: Bills drawn by NSW Commissariat[51]

1819	129,499
1820	181,376
1821	166,315
1822	229,826
1823	95,828
1824	199,112
1825	170,899

The third type of financial transaction controlled by the Commissariat was that of inter-departmental, government-sponsored loans. The Colonial Treasurer arranged loans to and from the commissariat as a means of strengthening the reserves of the local banks (the Bank of NSW and the Bank of Australia). Both banks were holding large government deposits and Darling, through William Lithgow, his Comptroller of Banking, was concerned about their financial stability. The banks lodged monthly returns with

---

[50] *Sydney Gazette* 29 January 1829
[51] HRA 1:14:130 Darling *to Huskisson*

Lithgow's office, which in turn reported on the 'state' of the banks to Darling and the Executive Council.

In August 1826, Lithgow drafted a memorandum for Darling to send to the Earl of Bathurst[52] proposing that the commissariat issue notes of £100 denomination to a total of £60,000 [53], to be held by the two banks as a reserve. In an endeavour not to interfere with the amount of coinage circulating within the colony, the commissariat was encouraged to make all future payments in British coin. This plan became operative on 1 September 1826[54]. The store was also encouraged to issue £5 and £10 notes.

The use of the commissariat as a 'financier' and comptroller of currency was logical when the flow of imports by the commissary is taken into account. With food short supply from June 1828, and the commissariat stores empty, the governor waived duty collections on wheat imports and the commissariat imported record quantities of wheat in 1828 (85,716 bushels) and 1829 (107,929 bushels) This food relief brought with it an aggravation of the balance of payments problem,[55] and affected cash reserves generally. The *Sydney Gazette* of 27 January 1829 commented:

> '*Such things as ready-money transactions are nowadays never heard of; credit is the only hinge on which business turns; credit in town, credit in country, credit with the wholesale merchant, credit with the retail dealer. Credit with the farmer, the grazier, the butcher, the cabinetmaker, the blacksmith, the mason – everywhere, credit, credit, credit.'*

The *Gazette* brought home to its readers where this credit balloon was leading" 'One in every 4.25 persons was served with a writ of one kind or another...one in every 10.3 persons either had an execution that was held to bail... and one in every 14.3 persons had an execution against his person or his property'.[56]

The commissariat had assumed its most influential role under Macquarie, Brisbane and Darling, and it was becoming the major regulator of the colony's fiscal matters. Although this role was immediately outside the commissariat's terms of instructions, there was

---

5   [2] HRA 1:12:511-12 Darling *to Bathurst*
[53] This was the amount of a loan from the colonial treasury to the commissariat and intended to be repaid by the selling of commissariat notes. This method would obviate the need to export dollars and retain the coins for cash purposes
5   [4] *Sydney Gazette* 2 September 1826
5   [5] S.J. Butlin *Foundations* p.209
5   [6] *Sydney Gazette* 12 July 1831

historical precedent for it to use this opportunity since in reality there was no alternative administrator for this fiscal control elsewhere in the government structure.

CHAPTER 9

MEASURING THE ECONOMIC IMPACT OF THE
ENTERPRISES ON THE COLONIAL ECONOMY+

Purpose
The intent of this chapter is to demonstrate, statistically, the importance to economic
growth of the enterprise system in the colony between 1800 and 1850.

Method
Valuing the convict output is an extremely subjective exercise. One reason being that5 an
assumption has to be made that most internal lumber yard gangs are carrying out their
assigned task. For example, one has to assume that the various gangs such as the
shoemaker, tailor, sawyers, and plasterer carried out their respective role. In the event this
is an incorrect assumption, then the output is the intended or theoretical outcome which
may be slightly higher than the actual outcome.

Let me assume for a moment, that at a specific point in time, we can establish the number
of convicts working in the lumber yard. This in itself is a challenge, because we know that
any number of convicts being marched from the Hyde Park barracks to the lumber yard
would slip away for a day absconding from work in the lumber yard. So once again the
number of workers is a close approximation. Genuine sickness is another reason for
absenteeism, but overall the number would not be significant enough to change the
methodology of the exercise.

Having established the number of convicts in each section of the lumber yard, a double
check can be made of valuing output.

On one hand we know from the Druitt and Ovens' reports in the HRA that each 'gang' or
section had output targets. So the first method of valuing convict output would be to
assign an actual value to expected output. As a cross check on this figure which is
probably higher than the real actual, we know from figures submitted to Commissioner
Bigge and other data prepared by Francis Greenway, that labour represented about one-
third of the total value of production. The other two thirds were represented by [as to
£one-third for materials and a further one-third as to labour and material overheads and
profit]. Thus as set down in the following table, in 1816 there were 4747 convicts
employed in government service. Nearly 1200 were employed in construction of public
works; 550 were employed on government farms, whilst 360 were employed on road-

making gangs, which left 2638 employed in the various government business enterprises. This means that there were 13,823,264 annual labour hours available to the enterprises and gangs. On a labour cost equivalent basis, at a 5/- per week pay-rate, the annual labour cost is 246,844 weeks of work at 5/-per week or £61,711.Assuming the labour content is 1/3rd then the value of annual output is approximately £205,703.

construction gangs	1197
field gangs	550
road gangs	362
enterprise workers	2638
	4747

If we assume that this output could be classified as secondary industry or manufacturing output, then Butlin N.G. Butlin *Forming a Colonial Economy*] determines the value of manufacturing, commerce, services and rent GDP [or output] at 35.36% of £450,000 or £159,120. What this means is that Butlin used private GDP instead of including the public production and output component. So that the Butlin estimate of £159,120 should be added to the public estimated output of £205,703, giving a total GDP for secondary components of £364,823, a figure very close to, or only about 25% greater than the Butlin computed GDP agricultural component of 65.1% of £450,000 or £292,950

Thus a new theorem can be proposed. That between 1810 and 1820, at least, the value of the colonial manufacturing industry was greater than the agricultural or primary industry. The main theory on this subject has been for all economic historians including Shann, Fitzpatrick, Fletcher, Abbott & Nairn and the two Butlins, was that the agricultural component of the economy was absolutely supreme. That this is not the real case, is going to shatter the texts by Shann *'John Bull's Greater Woolsack'* or Fletcher's *'Pastoral Australia in Imperial Economy'*, and *'Pastoral Extension'* or S.J. Butlin's *'The Pastoral Expansion of the 1830s'* or Abbott's claim in *Economic Growth of Australia 1788-1821* that the pastoral sector was the main component of economic growth in the NSW colony This expose is much akin to the Blainey claim that whaling and fisheries was a re important export industry than wool until the 1832 period.

If the theory is correct [and I have no doubt the data supports this conclusion] then what does it all means? Ever since Coghlan led the fight to have labour economics recognised as an important aspect of Australian economic history in 1917 [T.A. Coghlan – *Labour & Industry in Australia*] and thereby demanded more recognition of the growth of the secondary industry and rise of manufacturing in the colonies, economic historians have generally decided that the rise of manufacturing was subservient to the rise of the pastoral industry. No-one, Linge included [G.J.R. Linge *Industrial Awakening*] has doubted this. Walsh in *Manufacturing* concludes 'although there was considerable activity in manufacturing the degree of industrial progress was small in absolute terms and not nearly commensurate with the agricultural progress of the period. [G.P. Walsh *Manufacturing* in Abbott & Nairn *Economic Growth of Australia 1788-1821*]

The theory that the industrial component of Colonial NSW GDP 1810-1820 is greater than the agricultural component for at least the same period is a most important finding.

	GDP Mfgr Industry	adj mfgr Industry	GDP Agri industry		
1810	260.4	458.8	26040	19835.4	2543
1811	234.0	442.1	23400	20810.4	2668
1812	242.8	488.4	24280	24562.2	3149
1813	235.6	582.1	23560	34652.8	3332
1814	225.2	661.9	22520	43669.6	4199
1815	259.7	703.0	25965	44335.2	4263
1816	226.8	843.9	22680	61711	4747
1817	238.5	911.5	23850	67314	5178
1818	243.0	932.1	24300	68913	5301
1819	260.6	962.4	26055	70187	5399
1820	402.1	1,272.3	40209.5	87016.8	5578

Carpenters' Gang	50	Builders, cabinet makers		3510
Blacksmiths' Gang	45	Working in iron, copper or tin		3159
Bricklayers' Gang	10	4,500 bricks per week		702
Sawyers' Gang	25	750 feet of plank per week		1755
Brickmakers' Gang	15	Gang lays 24,000 bricks per week		1053
Plasterers' Gang	8	Lathing, undering, flanking = 20 yds p/week		561
Quarrymen	15	14 Ashlar stones per man per day		1053
Quarry labour	14	25 ft flagging per man per day		983
Wheelwrights' Gang	23	Construct carts, drays, trucks, wheelbarrows		1614
Coopers' Gang	6	1 barrel per man per day		421
Shoemakers Gang	8	1 pair shoes perf man per day		562
Tailors' Gang	8	2 suits of slop clothing per man per day		562
Dockyard	70	Mechanics assisted by labourers		4914
Dockyard Town Gang	22	Loading/unloading vessels or boats		1544
Stone-cutters & Setters	13	Cut 15 ft of fine ashlar stone		913
Brass Founders' Gang	9	Cast iron for wheels and millwork		632
Lumber Yard	319	building products		22394
Construction	1197			84029
Roadmaking	362			25412
Land Clearing	1150	9,000 acres cleared per annum		80730
Cart Operators	268			18813
Brick/tile Makers	124			8704
Boat Navigators	12			842
Grass Cutters	304			21340
Boat Crews - Official	120			8434
Gross Farm	160	Vegetables		11234
Canterbury	11	Cattle		772
*Long Bottom	110	Timber, hay and charcoal		7722
Emu Plains	269	Wheat and maize		18884
	4747			**333248**

If I convert the GDP table to a ration scale, using 1810 as base year at 100, then we can identify two different trends in both primary and secondary industry growth between 1810 and 1820 which reflects the facts of the time and which can be supported by further analysis

Year	Agri Industry	Secondary Industry
1810	100	100
1811	.9	.96
1812	.93	1.06
1813	.90	1.27
1814	.86	1.44
1815	1.00	1.53
1816	.87	1.84
1817	.92	1.99
1818	.93	2.03
1819	1.00	2.10
1820	1.54	2.77

What this table means is that the secondary industry sector incurred substantial fluctuations whilst growing at an annual rate of over 10%. This hypothesis is supported by the growth of public works arising under and sponsored by Macquarie.

The agricultural sector was more unstable especially during the transition from public farming to private farming. One of the limitations of the time was the physical barriers of the Blue Mountains which hindered expansion of grazing. Farm produce prices provided by the commissariat fluctuated due to seasons, the inability of the government store to carry over holdings from year to year, and only the larger officer farmers could afford to forward contract with the commissary. The small 30-acre peasant farmers tried to rotate crops each year but preferred to stay with the one crop, which made the sale of their harvest often quite difficult because the commissariat changed its buying patterns from year to year. Livestock management was still very much in its infancy since most livestock were held for breeding purposes, rather than being slaughtered as fresh meat. This situation impacted on both supplies and on prices

It can be seen that the agricultural sector in1815 saw the return to the base year output, but then followed by further declines until the base year was found again in 1819.

An Economic Model of the Colonial Economy GDP

The pre-1861 period has long been considered[74] too risky for the assembly of data and creating an economic model. However certain elements of such a model can be identified

---

[74] N.G. Butlin and T.A. Coghlan write of the inaccurate statistics and other data for this period.

and used for at least a good indicative assessment of the economic growth between 1788 and 1860. A practical example of an economic model which could be adapted for this period was found in McTaggart, Findlay and Parkin *Macroeconomics*. The basis for the model is that 'aggregate expenditure equals aggregate income i.e. $Y - C + I$, where aggregate income (Y) equals aggregate expenditure $(C + I)$'. A corollary will be that aggregate production or GDP = aggregate expenditure= aggregate income'. There is a circular flow which equates *inputs* and *outputs*. A detailed development of such a model is to be found in Appendix A to this study, together with a valuable outcome of GDP between 1800 and 1860. The rise of manufacturing was a significant part of the economic growth in the early colony. Of all the sectors, agriculture (including whaling, sealing and wool) gave the most significant results in terms of manpower used, capital invested, export returns, and GDP. In second place would have been the development of local natural resources, followed closely by manufacturing outcomes. These observations can be made from individual statistics of employment, exports, convict work organisation and data about immigrants and their assets. However, the more reliable statistics will come from the assembly of a model using either the production approach, or the aggregate income/expenditure approach. Both methods will be attempted and compared but, as can be seen, an understanding and assessment of manufacturing is essential to either methodology

Butlin adopts a difficult stance in determining public sector performance. In his study *forming a colonial economy* [p 148-9] he writes 'clearly the commissariat was a key institution in the early years of the settlement. Its initial importance meant a progressive loss of prominence as the settlements became more complex, dispersed and free. To a very considerable degree, its expansion and decline, was a counterpart of the experience with public infrastructure because the numbers of convicts retained by government and the scale of building, construction, exploration and survey activity were all directly linked to goods, materials and equipment flowing into and out of the store. As convict numbers rose rapidly after 1812 and many were retained by government, so the scale of the public outlet of the commissariat increased. Following assignment, the expansion of the commissariat braked strongly'.

CHAPTER 10

SUMMARY & CONCLUSIONS

The original goal of this study was to establish the credentials of the government business enterprises as essential economic drivers. This was to involve a description of their operations, their output and manpower. This done, it was intended to outline the role of these public enterprises as part of the transportation program, convict management and an essential instrument of utilising convict labour(chapter 1).

The enterprises performed numerous roles – from food production to supplement the production under the 30-acre farmlets system of Phillip, Hunter and King, to a manufacturing unit, to provide items on a timely basis. This was followed by the use of the main enterprises as import replacement mechanisms. On the other hand, there was always the role of certain public enterprises to provide building items that could not be imported. And because they were readily available locally, they became an essential service of the enterprises e.g. bricks, tiles, timber framing etc. Upon the transfer of certain production from the public to the private sector, the catalyst was created for creating the role of entrepreneur for the growing secondary industry (chapter 2)

Thus public enterprises became an important mainstay of the colonial and filled the role as an economic driver by employing over 4,000 convicts in a variety of productive jobs. These ranged from clerical work for the government to road making gangs. However the biggest concentration of workers were in the lumber yard and the associated enterprises of public farming and the timber yard (chapter 3)

Obviously understanding the mechanism and vagaries of the colonial economy, at least before 1830 is a relevant task (chapter 4). The economic policies and highlights of the Phillip, Hunter and King administrations were provided, before turning to the details of convict management in the colony (chapter 5).

The commissariat operations were a constant theme through this study and its role in underpinning, supporting and encouraging the growth of a manufacturing industry in the colony was pursued in chapter 6. The detailed examination of the government farms became necessary when research in the NSW State Records failed to provided information relating to the size, location, or output of the various farms. From the traditional understanding of their being 5 or 6 locations producing grain vegetables and livestock management, the current list sets at 23 the number of active sites, which includes a shell collection depot for the making of lime and mortar (chapter 7).

How did the commissariat account for all this production and labour is the subject of chapter 8? The bottom line is moot because the British Treasury gave no value to convict labour or convict production, even though the revenue from the resale of their labour or output was recorded in the correct way,

A novel approach is taken in attempting to measure the economic impact of the enterprises on the colonial economy. In previous attempts to establish a GDP for the period, no assessment was made [by N.G.Butlin *Forming a Colonial Economy*] of the output of the enterprises, thus perpetuating the falsity of giving no value to the convict output. By including the convict output into the manufacturing sector, another long-term myth has been exploded – the manufacturing sector between 1810 and 1820 far outperformed the primary industry or agricultural sector. This revelation contradicts the traditional views of all economic historians and certainly the thinking of traditional, mainstream historians, who all decided that the agricultural economy drove the way forward.

Thus, this story finishes on an upbeat note. The economic impact of the government business enterprises can be measured and the results demonstrate a new understanding of the colonial economy.